Yuri Nakata

From Press to People
Collecting and Using
U.S. Government Publications

AMERICAN LIBRARY ASSOCIATION
Chicago 1979

Library of Congress Cataloging in Publication Data

Nakata, Yuri.
From press to people.

Includes bibliographical references and
index.
1. Libraries—Special collections—Government
publications. 2. United States—Government
publications. I. Title.
Z688.G6N34   025.17'3   78-26306
ISBN 0-8389-0264-2

Printed in the United States of America

CONTENTS

APPENDIXES

INDEX

ILLUSTRATIONS

PREFACE

In the last decade, a revolution has taken place in the whole field of government publications. At no time in the history of American libraries has there been such a groundswell of support and concern for government publications by as large a group of librarians and publishers as at the present time. And at no time in the history of American libraries has there been the same cooperative spirit between the generators of government information and librarians in an effort to solve mutual problems and to disseminate information more widely.

Other developments include changes in the appearance of government publications, from drab-looking to colorful, eye-appealing publications. There is also some effort to simplify the language in government publications so that it may be understood by all readers.

All of these movements point to a public orientation of government publications and to an attitude and effort on the part of government agencies to respond to the public need for information. To transfer this information to the public is the challenge for all librarians.

INTRODUCTION

For over a century the federal government and librarians have engaged in the dissemination of "government information" to the citizens of the United States. The process by which this information is generated in government agencies and is transferred to the library's public is becoming increasingly complex. The volume of government publications is ever increasing, and a variety of specialized tools to provide access to government information is now available.

Several excellent works on government publications have appeared in recent years as aids to organizing and administering government publications in libraries. The intent of this book is not to tread the same ground covered by others but to present a different emphasis—reference service and documents delivery to the patron—based on my experience as a practicing reference and documents librarian for the past decade. With the change in format of the *Monthly Catalog of United States Government Publications,* the major bibliographic tool for government publications, an update at this juncture appears justified.

This work is designed as a handbook for the beginning documents librarian and for others interested in promoting the use of government publications.

"Documents librarian" is defined very broadly to include any librarian who handles government publications. The librarian who specializes in government publications plays a crucial role in the information transfer process. It is to facilitate this process that I have included chapters that deal with collection development, organization, and use of government publications.

The early chapters provide background information and are concerned with the history of government publications, legislation, and the federal depository program. The section on regional depository libraries by LeRoy Schwarzkopf is a comprehensive treatment, not found in other works. A chapter is devoted to technical reports and data bases as their importance increases with the advent of computer access to data bases in libraries. While not suggesting specific search strategies, I have included a list of selected sources to government publications and a number of aids to assist in reference service. The list is necessarily selective since it is not possible to be comprehensive in a work of this nature. The appendixes bring together information consulted often by documents librarians.

My record of acknowledgments begins with a salute to the documents librarians of earlier years whose persistent efforts to improve the distribution and use of government publications are a matter of record. The deliberations of the Public Documents Round Table of the American Library Association are well documented in the annual reports and proceedings. Its work has been the basis of many achievements.

A work of this nature could not have been written alone. I have depended heavily on contributions to library literature and have credited the individual contributors in the various footnotes and additional references. I have had the assistance of numerous individuals who gave generously of their time with critical comments on various chapters and drafts: Salvatore Attinello, Joyce Ball, Marian Carroll, Barbara Ford, Janet Lyons, Lois Mills, Judith Rowe, and Susan Smith. Marjorie Bengtson and Michele Strange gave me major assistance on parts of two chapters. I also thank Aline Fairbanks, Giles Robertson, and William B. Ernst, without whose support I could not have embarked upon this project. A very special acknowledgment goes to LeRoy Schwarzkopf, who commented critically on some early drafts and who contributed the excellent section on regional depository libraries. He was very generous in sharing many ideas and publications. I also owe a debt of gratitude to Charles Perkins, who offered critical comments, suggestions, and most of all encouragement. Herbert Bloom, Senior Editor of ALA, with much patience and wisdom guided me through many drafts. To Lynn Schied, Helen Li, and Norma Michalski, who assisted me in many ways, I likewise express my gratitude.

GOVERNMENT PRINTING AND LIBRARIES

1

The printing and distribution practices of the United States government have had a major effect on the handling of federal documents in libraries. Ever since its beginnings, the federal government has been concerned with the printing and distribution of government publications.[1] The early publications were oriented only toward printing the deliberations of Congress, but as agencies of government multiplied and assumed various functions, the types of government publications and their purposes also proliferated. This evolution is reflected in the various definitions of government publications that have appeared in print over the years.

The first legal definition of government publications appeared in the laws of the 29th Congress (9 *Stat.* 202, sec. 13, approved March 3, 1847):

> Such publications or books as have been or may be published, procured, or purchased by order of either House of Congress or a joint resolution of the two Houses, shall be considered as public documents.[2]

By 1909, the definition of government publications that appeared in the *Checklist* reflected a considerable broadening of the first definition:

> . . . any publication printed at government expense or published by authority of Congress *or any government publishing office,* or of which an edition has been bought by Congress *or any government office* for division among members of Congress *or distribution to government officials or the public*, shall be considered a public document [emphasis mine].[3]

1. The terms "government publications" and "government documents" are used interchangeably in this book.
2. Ann Morris Boyd, *United States Government Publications*, 3d ed. rev. by Rae Elizabeth Rips (New York: Wilson, 1949), p. 20.
3. U.S. Superintendent of Documents, *Checklist of United States Public Documents, 1789–1909*, 3d ed. (Washington, D.C.: Govt. Print. Off., 1911), p. vii.

For depository libraries, the Depository Library Act of 1962 defines government publications as "informational matter which is published as an individual document at government expense, or as required by law."

The most recent definition of government publications appears in Public Law 94–553 (90 *Stat.* 2541), which revises the copyright law. In section 101 is the definition: "A 'work of the United States Government' is a work prepared by an officer or employee of the United States government as part of that person's official duties."

The significance of these definitions is the interpretation given to them by the Assistant Public Printer (Superintendent of Documents) who is responsible for the major distribution of government publications, and by the librarians who organize and service them. For many years the Superintendent of Documents interpreted government publications to include primarily materials printed by the Government Printing Office (GPO). Individual libraries must further define government publications to include or exclude publications which are printed and distributed by federal agencies, as well as those reprinted by commercial publishers. It is common practice in libraries to regard all publications which originate in governmental bodies as government publications, regardless of who printed them.

Types of Government Publications

The functions of government have some bearing on types of government publications produced. In his study of government publications, Merritt identified six major functions, as follows (in some instances examples have been updated):

1. *Legislative.* Publications of Congress published in the interests of furthering the legislative process. Examples: congressional bills, reports, hearings, public laws
2. *Administrative.* Publications which serve as material aids in the process of public administration. Examples: *Federal Register* and the *Code of Federal Regulations, Calendars of the United States House of Representatives and History of Legislation*
3. *Reportorial.* Reports of activities to the people; documents published after action has been completed. Examples: annual reports of departments and agencies, reports of decisions of the courts, briefs and opinions of the Attorney General
4. *Service.* Documents which in one way or another are concerned with the lives, activities, and welfare of the people. Examples: *Farmers Bulletin,* and statistical and financial data published by the Census Bureau
5. *Research.* Differs from "Service" only in that its production involves research by governmental agency before publication is possible. Example: *Miscellaneous Collections* of the Smithsonian Institution, reports of the Tariff Commission, technical reports, reports of the Bureau of Mines and the Environmental Protection Agency

6. *Informational.* Documents issued in the interest of informing public about nature of activities of government. Examples: information on Social Security and Medicare, infant care, food preservation, menus, gardening, consumer credit[4]

In fulfillment of these functions, government publications appear in a variety of shapes, sizes, and forms, complicating their organization by libraries and access by the public. In addition, the ever-changing organizational patterns necessary to facilitate these functions create unique problems in handling government publications. Knowledge of the organization of the federal government is useful to an understanding of the internal workings of its various parts.

Two publications which are indispensable to librarians are *United States Government Manual* and *Official Congressional Directory.*[5] The former contains information on the creation, formation, and organization of government bodies, including organization charts. The *Official Congressional Directory* is the source for information relating to the organization of Congress.

Government Printing Office

The primary source for the distribution and sale of government publications is the Government Printing Office. Attempts to correct political abuses in the private printing and distribution of government publications resulted in enactment of several pieces of legislation affecting printing in the nineteenth century and led finally to the establishment of the Government Printing Office in 1860. The GPO provided the first printing facility to handle the printing needs of Congress and governmental agencies.[6] It should be pointed out that the GPO is a printing facility and not a publisher, as it is often called. Except for internal publications, all publications are prepared by its clients.[7] The present organizational structure appears in figure 1.

The most significant printing legislation, as far as libraries are concerned, was the Printing Act of 1895, which established the Office of the Superintendent of Documents. This act consolidated all laws relating to public printing into Title 44, *United States Code,* "Public Printing and Documents," under which the Government Printing Office still operates. (See appendix 1.) The activities of the Government Printing Office are outlined and defined in Title 44. In 1973 the position of Superintendent of Documents, formerly separate, was included in a new position, Assistant Public Printer, which also retained the title Superintendent of Documents. Therefore, the titles "Assistant Public Printer" and "Superintendent of Documents" are used interchangeably in this book.

4. LeRoy Charles Merritt, *The United States Government as Publisher* (Chicago: University of Chicago Press, 1943), pp. 5–9.
5. For full citations of titles, see pp. 141–42.
6. Robert E. Kling, Jr., *The Government Printing Office* (New York: Praeger, 1970), p. 17.
7. Ibid., p. 162.

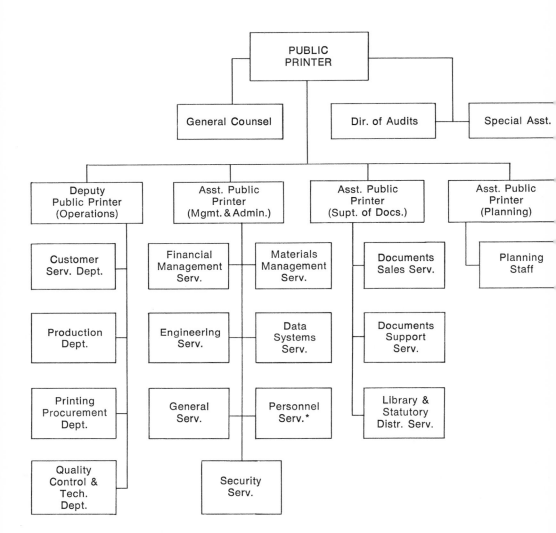

*The Director of Personnel also serves as Director of Equal Opportunity
and in this capacity reports directly to the Public Printer.

Figure 1. United States Government Printing Office, Organization Chart.
Source: *1977/78 United States Government Manual*, p. 58.

Reorganization of the Government Printing Office in 1974 established three major services under the direction of one of the Assistant Public Printers who also serves as the Superintendent of Documents: the Documents Sales Service, Library and Statutory Distribution Service, and Documents Support Service (see figure 2).

The Public Documents functions of the GPO are carried out through four programs:

1. Distribution of government publications to designated depository libraries[8]
2. Compilation of catalogs and indexes to government publications
3. Sale of government publications produced by or through the Government Printing Office
4. Mailing, for members of Congress and government agencies, those government publications authorized by law

The operations of the GPO are influenced by a number of groups, among them the Joint Committee on Printing, the Depository Library Council to the Public Printer, and professional library groups.

Joint Committee on Printing

Congress regulates public printing through enactment of laws and also through the power it invests in the Joint Committee on Printing, created August 3, 1846, and made a permanent committee by the Printing Act of 1895. The committee consists of the chairperson and two members of the Committee on Rules and Administration of the Senate and the chairperson and two members of the Committee on House Administration of the House of Representatives. An influential committee, the Joint Committee has the "power to adopt and employ such measures as, in its discretion, may be deemed necessary to remedy any neglect, delay, duplication, or waste in the public printing and binding and the distribution of government publications."[9]

The committee's authority encompasses the printing, binding, and distribution programs of all three branches of the federal government. It is concerned with governmental publishing, pricing policies of the GPO and other agencies, and distribution of materials through the depository library program.

This committee acts as the board of directors for the Government Printing Office and serves as a monitoring agency. In 1975 Bernadine Hoduski was ap-

8. A significant responsibility is the relationship of GPO to other government printing programs. According to the Depository Library Act of 1962, GPO became the agent to acquire and distribute non-GPO publications—titles which are produced by agencies in printing plants other than GPO. GPO is therefore viewed by librarians as bearing responsibility for the acquisition and dissemination of an increasing amount of documents that do not bear the GPO imprint.

9. 44 *U.S.C.* 103.

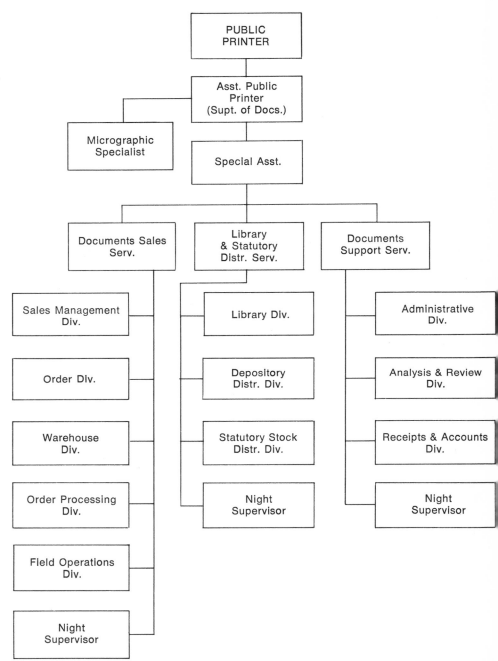

Figure 2. Office of the Assistant Public Printer (Superintendent of Documents), Organization Chart.

Source: *Public Documents Highlights*, no. 3, April 1974.

pointed as the first librarian to serve as a staff member to this committee. The increase in depository items, formerly in the nondepository category, is one evidence of library interests now being represented and heard by this committee.

Depository Library Council to the Public Printer

The Depository Library Council to the Public Printer,[10] composed of 15 highly qualified members of the library profession, was established in 1973 to assist the Public Printer and the Superintendent of Documents in the administration of the Federal Depository Library Program. Appointments are made by the United States Public Printer upon the recommendation of leading professional associations. The council meets twice a year to discuss problems and propose solutions. A major project has been the development of standards and guidelines which could be useful in establishing, evaluating, and improving depository library collections. The final draft of the guidelines was adopted by the council in October 1977 (see appendix 4). Other topics of council discussion are bibliographic control and establishment of a national depository system.

The meetings of the council are announced in the *Federal Register* and are open to the public. The work of the council is reported regularly in *Documents to the People,* the publication of the Government Documents Round Table of the American Library Association.

Professional Associations

Also influencing the work of the Government Printing Office are professional associations like the American Library Association, Special Libraries Association, and the Association of American Law Libraries, which have groups that work on problems faced by librarians who handle government publications. Notable is the ALA Government Documents Round Table (GODORT), established by the ALA Council in February 1972. The purposes of the Round Table are (1) to provide a forum for discussion of problems and concerns, and for exchange of ideas by librarians working with government documents; (2) to provide a force for initiating and supporting programs to increase availability, use, and bibliographic control of documents; (3) to increase communication between documents librarians and other librarians; and (4) to contribute to the extension and improvement of education and training of documents librarians. Through a number of working task forces on various aspects of documents librarianship, the Round Table is an effective forum in providing "Documents to the People."

10. Until 1975 called Advisory Council to the Public Printer on Depository Libraries.

In addition, state and regional library associations sponsor workshops and conferences to assist documents librarians. Individual librarians in local areas have also joined together to discuss problems and to suggest solutions. One such group is the very effective Committee on Information Hangups of the Greater Washington, D.C., area, composed of special and federal government librarians. These groups have been responsible for in-depth studies dealing with various problem areas. Their deliberations are reported regularly in library literature.

During the 1970s a new awareness by librarians of government publications as an information resource has generated grass-roots discussions to improve government publications collections and services in libraries all over this country. Their concerns have been brought to the attention of those in the federal government involved with the printing and distribution of these materials, resulting in a new high level of communication to the mutual benefit of both groups and confirming the notion that government publications have unique characteristics that require special treatment by libraries and librarians.

Additional References

McCamy, James L. *Government Publications for the Citizen: A Report of the Public Library Inquiry.* New York: Columbia University Press, 1949.

Morehead, Joe. *Introduction to United States Public Documents.* Littleton, Colo.: Libraries Unlimited, 1975. 2d ed., 1978.

Powell, John H. *The Books of a New Nation: United States Government Publications, 1774–1814.* Philadelphia: University of Pennsylvania Press, 1957.

Reynolds, Catherine J. "Standards for Depository Libraries, Goals and Roadblocks," *Documents to the People* 4 (March 1976):45–46.

Schmeckebier, Laurence F., and Roy B. Eastin. *Government Publications and Their Use.* 2d rev. ed. Washington, D.C.: Brookings Institution, 1969.

Smith, Ruth S. "About GPO and the Depository Library Council," *Special Libraries* 67 (July 1976):322–26.

THE FEDERAL DEPOSITORY LIBRARY PROGRAM

2

LEGISLATION

The federal depository library program has its roots in a long history of legislative changes that affect both the designation of depository libraries and the distribution of government publications. The concept of distributing government publications through depository libraries, in order to preserve and to make these materials available to the public, was evident in early legislation. Before 1813 Congress authorized the printing of additional copies of the journals of the Senate and House for distribution to "the executives of the several States and each branch of the State and territorial legislatures." Thereafter special acts of Congress extended the types of documents distributed to include acts, documents, and reports to each "university and college incorporated in each State, as well as to the incorporated historical societies."[1]

A resolution passed December 27, 1813, not only committed every future Congress to continue the distribution of the publications of Congress, but authorized the librarian of the Library of the United States to distribute these publications.[2] The first depository of public documents was the American Antiquarian Society of Worcester, Massachusetts, designated by Congress in 1814.[3]

Two important features of the present depository library program can be traced to a resolution passed by Congress on January 28, 1857, as amended by the resolution of March 20, 1858. First, the practice of designated depository libraries was formalized and, second, the practice of congressional selections was instituted.

---

1. U.S. Congress, Joint Committee on Printing, *Government Depository Libraries: The Present Law Governing Depository Libraries* (rev. April 1977), 95th Cong., 1st sess., 1977, p. 4. (Cited hereafter as *Government Depository Libraries*.)
2. U.S. Congress, *Annals of Congress*, 13th Cong., 1st and 2d sess., 1813–14, p. 2855.
3. Ibid., 3d sess., 1814–15, p. 110.

Through this resolution the Secretary of the Interior distributed journals and other documents, formerly distributed by the Library of Congress and the Department of State, to "such colleges, public libraries, atheneums, literary and scientific institutions, and boards of trade or public associations as may be designated by him by the Representative in Congress from each Congressional district and by the Delegate from each Territory in the United States."[4] The Printing Law of February 5, 1859 (11 *Stat.* 379), added senators as designators. Until this time, the distribution of publications by the designated officials was made on personal judgment, with each official having the power to select depository libraries. Congressional designation changed the basis of distribution of depository libraries to one of population, a principle which has far-reaching implications for libraries that seek depository status.

The General Printing Act of January 12, 1895, codified into one law the several unrelated acts and resolutions concerned with the printing and distribution of government publications since 1859 and continued the selection of depositories by members of Congress. The function of distribution of government publications was transferred from the Secretary of the Interior to the Superintendent of Documents within the Government Printing Office, an appointment authorized by the Printing Act.[5] Responsibility for the depository library system was thus centralized in the Government Printing Office, where it remains today.

Between 1895 and 1962, several attempts to revise the Printing Act regarding the printing, binding, and distribution of government publications were made by various committees of Congress at the urging of units of the American Library Association concerned with public documents. Changes sought by librarians in early years varied from minor procedural matters, such as the daily distribution of publications to depository libraries and the establishment of charge accounts for libraries, to rather major requests, such as the establishment of a central source from which all government publications could be obtained, the circulation of government publications (public documents were not allowed to circulate), the issuance of a compendium showing the status of legislation of Congress, the distribution of hearings and committee reports on private bills to depository libraries, and the privilege of selecting government publications.[6] Except for an important provision changing the method of selection of publications in 1922, no other major changes in the depository program were recorded until 1962.

The growing dissatisfaction expressed by many librarians, that they were receiving more government publications through the depository system than could be handled by them, coupled with the high percentage of unwanted documents returned to the Superintendent of Documents by depository libraries (libraries were

---

4. *Government Depository Libraries*, p. 4.

5. U.S. Congress, Senate Committee on Rules and Administration, *Revising the Laws Relating to Depository Libraries*, 87th Cong., 2d sess., 1962. *Senate Report 1587*, pp. 3–4. (Cited hereafter as *Senate Report 1587*.)

6. American Library Association, *Papers and Proceedings of the Forty-fourth Annual Meeting . . . Held at Detroit, Mich., June 26 to July 1, 1922* (New York: Johnson Reprint Corp., 1963), pp. 310–11.

allowed to do this until 1922), led to a change in the policy. Public Act 171 (67th Congress, approved March 20, 1922) permitted libraries to select in advance those publications they wanted. This act provided that no part of the sum appropriated to the Office of the Superintendent of Documents was to be used to supply to depository libraries any documents, books, or other printed matter not required by such libraries. Although, at the time, the Public Documents Round Table of the American Library Association approved this change in law, it realized the danger implicit in it, namely the possibility that a complete set of public documents may not be collected by any library in a particular state. It was hoped that all state libraries or state university libraries would elect to receive all publications, ensuring that at least one library in each state would have a complete set of public documents.[7] The establishment of regional depository libraries in 1962 did not entirely solve this problem (discussed later). The first selective list, titled "Classified List of United States Public Documents for Selection by Depository Libraries, July 1, 1922," was issued soon after the passage of the 1922 act.

Depository Library Act of 1962

The first major revision of the law governing depository libraries was the Depository Library Act of 1962,[8] approved August 9, 1962, and now the law in force governing depository libraries. (See appendix 1.) The 1962 revision was designed to correct three inadequacies, namely, the need for additional depositories, limitation of publications available, and permanent retention of government publications.

ADDITIONAL DEPOSITORIES

Population growth, shifts of population, and establishment of new colleges and universities and research centers during the 100 years since the beginning of the depository system created the demand for additional depositories in areas where there were none. The original principle of one depository library for each district no longer met the needs of some of the libraries in the congressional districts. The 1962 act sought to correct this situation by increasing the number of congressional designations from one to two. This provision did not add depository libraries where desired. Because of redistricting after each decennial census, there is more than the maximum number of depository libraries per district in some congressional areas, all designated by representatives, while in other areas there are unused designations. This is because, once designated, a depository library remains one until the library wishes to discontinue its status or until the designation is removed by the Superintendent of Documents.

7. Ibid., p. 308.
8. P.L. 87–579; 76 *Stat.* 352; codified as Chapter 19, Title 44, *U.S.C.*

The quest to increase designations continues. Bills have been introduced in recent Congresses for special designations on an individual or group basis. The highest state appellate court libraries achieved special designation in 1972.[9] The libraries of accredited law schools have sought such legislation and received depository status on April 17, 1978.[10]

DISTRIBUTION OF NON-GPO PUBLICATIONS

One of the most significant requirements of the 1962 Depository Act, and the most difficult to accomplish, is that the Superintendent of Documents assume responsibility for distributing publications other than those printed by the Government Printing Office. As noted earlier, the GPO, which began as a printer for Congress, later expanded to meet the printing needs of all branches of government. As long as GPO was the sole printing and distribution facility for government publications, the distribution of materials to the depository libraries was fairly clear cut. In time, however, the establishment of subsidiary or departmental printing plants to handle the growing activities of government agencies created a division in the publications produced by government—GPO and non-GPO publications. Since the depository libraries received only those publications printed by GPO, libraries felt this division placed severe limits on public access to an important portion of government publications.

By 1962 there were 352 government presses outside the control of the GPO.[11] Therefore, as pointed out earlier, the 1962 legislation was designed to remedy this problem by requiring components or units of the U.S. government to provide the Superintendent of Documents with copies of publications for distribution to depository libraries and for listing in the *Monthly Catalog*. Since 1962 the implementation of this provision has been the subject of much discussion between librarians and the Superintendent of Documents, as reflected in the literature.

A major breakthrough in the distribution of non-GPO documents came on March 25, 1977, when the Joint Committee on Printing gave approval to GPO to provide on microfiche non-GPO documents for distribution to depository libraries. These titles will be offered to depository libraries in microfiche format only; they will not be offered for sale. Two categories of documents will be distributed: non-GPO material and documents already in the depository program. GPO will request two copies of non-GPO publications from the various agencies, one of which will be added to the GPO collection. The other will be used to produce a microfiche master. The second category consists of documents already in the depository program. Titles will be converted to microfiche, based on a cost analysis of hard copy versus microfiche by GPO and the needs expressed by depository librarians.

This area is still in a state of flux. The distribution procedures remain the same for microfiche as for hard-copy documents. Depository libraries will have an op-

9. P.L. 92–368; 82 *Stat.* 1283.
10. P.L. 95–261.
11. *Senate Report 1587*, pp. 7–8.

portunity to select titles in microfiche or hard copy (not both). At the present time (1978), GPO is not authorized to sell microfiche copies in its sales program.[12]

The authority given the GPO to distribute microfiche copies of non-GPO documents should result in increased availability of nondepository titles to depository libraries, but the number will still be dependent upon the agencies' willingness to comply with the 1962 legislation. Since agencies have to supply only two copies (rather than multiple copies for all depository libraries), they should be more amenable to having their publications listed and distributed to depository libraries in microfiche form.

PERMANENT RETENTION

The third major problem covered by the 1962 legislation was the permanent retention of government publications by depository libraries. The fact that depository libraries were not allowed to discard titles placed a burden upon libraries with limited space. Many libraries became very selective in their choice of depository materials, negating their obligation to provide information for citizens. The 1962 act established regional depository libraries which were charged with the responsibility of maintaining a permanent collection of all materials sent to depository libraries. This provision was to assure permanent collections around the country for use by the public. In addition, other depository libraries within an area served by a regional depository could dispose of unwanted materials after retaining them for five years. (Detailed discussion appears in this chapter under "Regional Libraries.")

The possibility of establishing regional depository libraries did not lead to the desired number of regional depositories in each state, since no financial support was provided for these libraries. Not all states are represented by regionals. Many research libraries, capable of serving as regionals, are reluctant to assume the financial burdens of maintaining a regional collection without some outside support. Documents librarians are pushing for federal funding to assist regional depository libraries.

REVISION OF THE 1962 LEGISLATION

Revision of the 1962 legislation is now being sought by documents librarians. In January 1973, the Council of the American Library Association created an Ad Hoc Committee on the Depository Library System and charged it to prepare a report considering the possibility of proposing a revision of the Depository Act of 1962, incorporating such criteria as adequate financial support, provision of more non-GPO materials, consulting services to the depository libraries, and other changes necessary to implement the basic provision of the 1962 act. The committee

---

12. Letter from C. A. LaBarre, Assistant Public Printer, to Ann Shaw, chairperson, Government Documents Round Table Microforms Task Force, January 18, 1978.

did not touch on these issues in the final report, which was accepted by the ALA Council on July 12, 1974 (subject to the added recommendations of the ALA Legislative Committee). Its chief recommendation was "to strengthen and expand the present depository library system into a comprehensive network of local and regional depositories, with a national federal depository library at the head of the system."[13]

While agreeing with the need for reform in the federal depository system, the ALA Legislative Committee recommended that a detailed study of the existing depository system be made to substantiate a need for change before recommending specific changes in the existing statutes.[14] In 1976 the ALA Ad Hoc Committee on the Depository Library System was replaced by the Ad Hoc Committee on Federal Depository Legislation, which is working on revisions to the 1962 Depository Library Act.

Designated Depository Libraries

The law governing depository libraries, and the regulations and procedures for administration of the depository program by the Office of the Superintendent of Documents, are contained in several sources:

1. Depository Library Act of 1962.
2. Title 44 of *United States Code*, authority for operation of the depository program (appendix 1).
3. U.S. Congress Joint Committee on Printing, *Government Depository Libraries: The Present Law Governing Depository Libraries.* Joint Committee Print (Y 4.P93/1:D44/yr.), issued each session of Congress; includes list of depository libraries by state and district, gives date of designation and type of designation, lists vacancies.
4. U.S. Superintendent of Documents, *Instructions to Depository Libraries.* Frequently revised (appendix 3), the *Instructions* includes several sections of procedures: general information concerning depository status, regional depositories, correspondence with Superintendent of Documents, periodic reports, termination as a depository library, selection of publications by depository libraries, survey for new items, amendment of selections, daily depository shipping list, claims for copies of publications selected but not received and duplicate shipments, disposition of depository publications, and substitution of microcopies for depository publications.[15]

13. "Report of the ALA Ad Hoc Committee on the Depository Library System," *Documents to the People* 3 (January 1975):44–45. See also LeRoy C. Schwarzkopf, "Reaction to the Report of the ALA Ad Hoc Committee on the Depository Library System," pp. 46–48.
    14. "Report of the ALA Ad Hoc Committee on the Depository Library System," p. 45.
    15. Nondepository libraries seeking depository status should see *Instructions*, reproduced in appendix 3.

These documents should be read thoroughly by librarians who work with depository collections. Since these publications are updated frequently, the most recent editions should be consulted.

DISTRIBUTION

The current list of depository libraries appears annually in the September issue of *Monthly Catalog*, and in *Government Depository Libraries* cited above. Special depositories established by individual government agencies (i.e., Census Libraries, HUD 701 libraries, map libraries [Army and Geological Survey]) are outside the scope of the Superintendent of Documents. They have been established by their agencies for one or more of the following reasons: (1) to supplement the GPO depository library system; (2) to ensure that unusual storage and handling requirements will be met; (3) to ensure that special collections are available where heavy use is anticipated, or (4) to ensure that collections are in relatively convenient locations for public use.[16]

The authority for operation of the depository library program is Title 44 of the *United States Code*. A depository library is designated to receive, without charge on a deposit basis, government publications issued by governmental agencies, except those determined by the issuing agencies to be required for official use only or for strictly administrative or operational purposes which have no public interest or educational value, and publications classified for reasons of national security. The automatic distribution of government publications through the depository program is an important factor in the handling of government publications by libraries, reducing substantially the cost of acquisitions. In addition to the stipulation that depository libraries must make government publications available to the public, the publications remain the property of the United States government and cannot be disposed of except as authorized by law.

Depository libraries may be designated under a variety of categories: highest state appellate court libraries; state libraries; libraries of land-grant colleges; libraries of accredited law schools; two libraries for each congressional district, to be designated by the representative from that district (or "at large" in undistricted states); two libraries to be designated in any part of the state by each senator; two libraries to be designated by the resident commissioner from Puerto Rico; two libraries to be designated by the commissioner of the District of Columbia; one library to be designated by the governor of Guam; one library to be designated by the governor of American Samoa; two libraries to be designated by the governor of the Virgin Islands (one on the island of St. Thomas and one on the island of St. Croix); the libraries of the executive department in Washington; libraries of independent agencies and major bureaus and divisions of departments and agencies; and the libraries of the U.S. Air Force, Coast Guard, Merchant Marine, Military, and Naval academies. The American Antiquarian Society Library, Worcester,

16. Beth A. Hamilton, "Selected Special Depository Libraries in HEW Region V," *Illinois Libraries* 56 (April 1975):285.

Massachusetts, and the Public Library of the District of Columbia were designated by special legislation.[17]

Until 1913, a senator or representative had the right to change designations at the beginning of a Congress, often leaving the "discarded" institution with only a partial supply of government publications. The Sundry Civil Act, approved June 23, 1913 (38 *Stat.* 75), as amended, corrected this situation by providing that a designated depository remains a depository until it ceases to exist or voluntarily vacates its privilege. The Superintendent of Documents can also remove depository status from a library which fails to abide by the laws governing depository libraries.

STATUS

The law states that "only a library able to provide custody and service for depository materials and located in an area where it can best serve the public need, and within an area not already adequately served by existing depository libraries may be designated . . . as a depository of Government publications."[18]

A committee of the Depository Library Council to the Public Printer has developed minimum standards and guidelines[19] for depository libraries. The final guidelines were approved by the council in October 1977. (See appendix 4.) Although the Government Printing Office supports these guidelines, they are not legally binding as far as GPO is concerned. The guidelines serve as a useful aid to depository libraries and to those seeking depository status.

The first consideration for a library seeking depository status is to determine whether a vacancy exists in one of the categories of depository libraries (see list in *Government Depository Libraries*, cited above). One might question the theoretical maximum number of designated libraries in each category, since some libraries designated in one category may in reality be eligible for designation under another category. Application for depository status should be sent to the Superintendent of Documents, naming the library and setting forth the justification for such designation. Upon receipt of an application by the Superintendent of Documents, the latter will send the library a questionnaire requesting pertinent information about the library. If the library qualifies, it will be notified by the Superintendent that it has been formally designated and will be sent the "Classified List of U.S. Government Publications Available to Depository Libraries," in card form, from which selections can be made.

The mayor of the District of Columbia and the governors of Guam, American Samoa, and the Virgin Islands may apply directly to the Superintendent of Documents.

Before an additional library within a state, congressional district, or the Commonwealth of Puerto Rico is designated as a depository library, the head of that

17. *Government Depository Libraries*, p. 1.
18. 44 *U.S.C.* 1909.
19. "Proposed Minimum Standards for the Depository Library System," *Public Documents Highlights* (special supplement) (December 1975), p. 1. *Guidelines for the Depository Library System*, as adopted by the Depository Library Council, October 18, 1977 (Washington, D.C.: Govt. Print. Off., 1978).

library must furnish his or her senator, representative, or the resident commissioner of Puerto Rico the justification of the necessity for the additional designation. The justification must include certification of the need for the additional depository library designation, signed by the head of every depository library within the congressional district, or the Commonwealth of Puerto Rico, *or* by the head of the library authority of the state (or Commonwealth of Puerto Rico) within which the additional depository library is located. The justification must be transmitted to the Superintendent of Documents by the senator, representative, or resident commissioner of Puerto Rico.

State libraries, state appellate court libraries, libraries of accredited law schools, and land-grant college and federal libraries in independent agencies or executive department libraries should apply directly to the Superintendent of Documents. Subdivisions of agencies should apply to the secretary of their department or to the director of an independent agency, who in turn should apply to the Superintendent of Documents.

REGIONAL DEPOSITORY LIBRARIES[20]

Regional depository libraries for U.S. government publications were first officially authorized by the Depository Library Act of 1962; however, two state libraries had previously been operating experimental regional depositories under separate agreements with the Superintendent of Documents. These were the State Historical Society Library of Wisconsin, since June 1953,[21] and the New York State Library, since February 1956.[22]

In addition to fulfilling the requirements for regular depositories, regional depositories "shall receive from the Superintendent of Documents copies of all new and revised Government publications authorized for distribution to depository libraries," and they will "retain at least one copy of all Government publications either in printed or microfacsimile form (except those authorized to be discarded by the Superintendent of Documents)."[23] This means that regional depositories must select *all* depository items on the "Classified List of U.S. Government Publications," and all new items added to the list by periodic "Surveys."

During 1977, 540 new items were added, to bring the total number of active depository items to 3,838. Since regional depositories must automatically select all items, they are not required to return the item cards, as regular depositories must do in order to indicate their selections. The regional depository must retain all depository publications permanently, except for those categories which any regular depository may discard.

20. This section was written by LeRoy C. Schwarzkopf.

21. Benton E. Wilcox, "Streamlining the Depository Libraries," *Library Journal* 82 (January 15, 1967):138–40.

22. William P. Leonard, "The Federal Documents Depository System in New York: A New Approach," New York State Library *Bookmark* 15 (April 1956):153–54.

23. 44 *U.S.C.* 1912.

In addition to maintaining a complete and permanent collection of depository publications (in hard copy or microform), regional depositories "within the region served will provide interlibrary loan, reference service, and assistance for depository libraries in the disposal of unwanted Government publications." They "may permit depository libraries, within the areas served by them, to dispose of Government publications which they have retained for five years after first offering them to other depository libraries within their area, then to other libraries."[24]

How the Superintendent of Documents and the regional depositories interpret and implement these functions and responsibilities is described below.

Regional Concept

The concept of regional library service is not new. It did not originate with the depository library system, which forms a loose national network to make government documents available to the people. It had its greatest impetus in the post–World War II era with the information explosion, and more recently with the sharp rise in prices for library materials. Its basic principle is sharing library resources within a specific area (geographic or political) and thereby preventing unnecessary and costly duplication of collections, particularly of little-used or expensive materials. Regional service for government publications differs, however, in several respects, due to several significant characteristics of the depository library program.

Depository publications are furnished free by the federal government, and since 1922 a library could select the items or series it wishes to receive. Therefore the acquisition cost of the material is not a factor. But the cost of maintaining and servicing a depository collection is a critical factor, as it is for general library materials. This is compounded by a characteristic not associated with general library materials. Depository publications are legally the property of the United States government. They cannot be disposed of at will by the holding library but only as authorized by federal law. Thus a key feature in any regional scheme for sharing resources of depository publications is that it must be coupled with a provision for libraries to discard old and/or unwanted publications which occupy valuable shelf space. Both the Wisconsin and the New York experimental plans in the 1950s, which preceded formal authorization of regional depositories, included such provisions.

Under both plans, if a member depository wished to discard materials which it had held at least 25 years, it was required to send a request to the Superintendent of Documents for permission to transfer control of the materials to the central depository and loan collection. The state library would ask the discarding library to send a list of the materials, from which it would select those publications it wished to add to its own collection. It would coordinate with the discarding library the details for the physical transfer of the remaining materials to other depositories in the state. It then authorized the discarding library to dispose of any remaining materials for which no request had been received.

24. Ibid.

In the original charter from the Superintendent of Documents for these two libraries, the term "regional depository" was not used. The library was referred to as a "central state depository and loan collection." However, the term "regional depository" was used about this time, in the late 1950s, when federal legislation was introduced to provide these services. In Wisconsin, the creation of the central depository and loan collection was authorized by state law, and the State Historical Society was provided additional funds by the state legislature for its establishment and operation. Federal legislation, subsequently introduced and passed, has not provided additional federal funds for libraries which assume additional regional responsibilities. Although the retention period of 25 years appears long when compared with the more reasonable five years eventually agreed to in the 1962 act, it was apparently arrived at to allow the discarding of materials acquired before 1922, when all depositories were required to accept all depository publications.

Number of Regional Depositories

Each state, and the Commonwealth of Puerto Rico, are authorized by law to have two regional libraries, but during the legislative hearings on the act it was not expected that each state would exercise this option.[25] Eight states have two regional depositories: Alabama, Arizona, Colorado, Louisiana, Michigan, New Mexico, Texas, and Wisconsin. The two states with the largest numbers of depositories—California with 97 and New York with 77—still have only one regional depository. On the other extreme, Arizona and New Mexico, each with 10 depositories, have two regionals apiece. One of the six Nevada depositories is a regional.

The law and the implementing *Instructions* do not provide regulations or guidance on how the service responsibilities shall be divided in those states with two regional depositories. It was expected that the need for two regionals would be dictated by geography. A practical application of this is best seen in Texas, where one regional depository (Texas State Library in Austin) is in the southern portion of the state and the other regional (Texas Tech University) is in the northern portion. In five of the other states, the two regionals are located in generally the same geographical section, and in some cases very close together, as in Colorado.

The general practice in these states is to divide responsibilities by type of library: an academic regional depository serves the academic libraries and a state or public library serves the public and other types of libraries. In Colorado, a combination geographic and type-of-library split of responsibilities has been used. Responsibilities might also be split by type of service; that is, one depository could receive and initially process all interlibrary loan and reference requests, and the other depository could process all disposal requests. In any case, the two regional depositories are free to work out any mutually acceptable arrangement among themselves to divide their legal responsibilities for providing service within the state.

25. *Senate Report 1587*, pp. 11–12.

The designated regional depository in Maine (University of Maine Library) provides services to the depositories in the two nearby states of New Hampshire and Vermont. Although this situation is not mentioned in the act or *Instructions*, it had been anticipated during the hearings on the legislation that more states would follow this procedure, particularly the sparsely settled mountain and Western states which have few depositories.[26] The seven depositories in Wyoming were provided regional services on a temporary basis from 1972–74 by a regional depository (Denver Public Library) in the neighboring state of Colorado until the Wyoming State Library was prepared to assume the additional regional responsibilities. In late 1977 the University of Maryland Library agreed to provide regional services to the three non-federal depository libraries in the District of Columbia.

There are three joint regional depositories in which a designated regional depository shares its responsibilities with a cooperating library. The North Dakota State University Library shares its responsibilities with the University of North Dakota Library. The State Historical Society of Wisconsin has shared its regional responsibilities with the University of Wisconsin Library from the beginning of the experimental stage in 1953. In late 1977 the University of Nebraska Library agreed to cooperate with the Nebraska Publications Clearinghouse, which had been a regional since 1974, to establish a Joint Regional Depository.

The main division of responsibilities pertains to the selection of items and holdings of each partner to ensure that, together, they accept and permanently hold all depository publications in compliance with the law. Since each partner does not select all items, libraries with partial regional responsibilities have to return the item cards to indicate their selections, like regular depositories. In the Wisconsin partnership, this is the only division of a single responsibility. The State Historical Society accepts and processes all interlibrary loan, disposal, and reference requests; but it seeks backup support from the University of Wisconsin as needed. In North Dakota, the other responsibilities are divided as well, primarily on a geographical basis, since the two depositories are separated by 75 miles, whereas the two Wisconsin depositories are located in the same block. In Nebraska, the University of Nebraska Library has agreed to process disposal requests and to provide interlibrary loans on government documents published prior to 1974. The Nebraska Publications Clearinghouse provides all other regional services.

Organization

There are presently 51 depository libraries in 40 states which have accepted additional responsibilities, in whole or in part, of a regional depository. Sixteen, or 31 percent, are state libraries; 30, or 59 percent, are academic libraries; and 5, or 10 percent, are public libraries.[27] This illustrates the preeminence of the academic

26. U.S. Congress, House, Committee on House Administration, *Hearings, Revision of Depository Laws*, 85th Cong., 1st sess., 1958, pp. 11, 40.

27. "List of Depository Libraries as of August 1, 1977," *Monthly Catalog of United States Government Publications* (July–September 1977), D1–23.

libraries in the depository library system. On an overall basis, they account for 65 percent of all depositories, while public libraries account for only 24 percent.

These depository libraries provide service to 42 states, leaving eight states without regional service (Alaska, Arkansas, Delaware, Missouri, Rhode Island, South Carolina, South Dakota, and Tennessee), plus the Canal Zone, District of Columbia (federal libraries only), Guam, Puerto Rico, and the Virgin Islands. Regional depositories have no jurisdiction over depository libraries of federal agencies within their area. Federal libraries may dispose of unwanted depository publications at any time by first offering them to the Library of Congress and the National Archives.

Interlibrary Loans

Regional depositories are required to "provide interlibrary loan, reference service, and assistance to depository libraries in the disposal of unwanted Government publications" within the region served. The placement of the word "depository libraries" may leave a reasonable doubt as to whether regional depositories are required to provide interlibrary loan and reference service to other depository libraries only, or to all other libraries and/or citizens in their region. In his *Instructions*, the Superintendent of Documents directs that regional depositories must provide interlibrary loan and reference service to designated depository and nondepository libraries. Irrespective of the spirit and letter of the law, which is subject to interpretation, regional depositories generally provide interlibrary loans to all libraries which normally use these services of the parent library.

To understand the intent of the interlibrary loan provision, one should consider it in relation to the disposal provision, and in the anticipated effect the two provisions combined would have on the selection policies of the selective depositories. It was expected (and hoped) by the framers of the 1962 legislation that critical space problems would be alleviated for many depositories if they were assured they would be able to borrow older, lesser-used materials from a permanent central collection and could thus safely discard this type of material.[28] It was also expected that depositories would reduce the number of items selected if they had assurance of being able to borrow little-used materials. On the other hand, it was expected they might increase their selection of medium-use items, especially those of topical value. They would be able to discard these materials, following the initial period of heavy use, with the assurance of being able to borrow them later if needed for research or for historical purposes. No data have been reported to determine the effects of the interlibrary loan and/or disposal provisions on selection policy.

Interlibrary loan service for government documents at regional depositories is generally integrated into that of the parent library. The typical practice is to require that requests by depository and nondepository libraries be submitted on standard

28. U.S. Congress, Senate, Committee on Rules and Administration, *Hearings, Revision of Depository Laws*, 87th Cong., 2d sess., 1962, p. 15.

ALA-approved forms to the Interlibrary Loan Office, which initially processes the requests. The documents unit is usually asked to identify, search for or retrieve the documents, and authorize their release if they are located in a separate collection. The Interlibrary Loan Office then prepares the publications for mailing or reproduction, mails the materials, and completes the administrative aspects of the transaction (including tracers and billing for lost materials).

Regional depositories do not believe the law requires them to lend every depository publication in their collection. The Superintendent of Documents has not provided further clarification in his *Instructions*. Regional depositories generally believe that interlibrary loan requests should be limited to older or lesser-used materials. They believe that first claim on the use of the depository collection belongs to the clientele of the parent library and the citizens in the local district. Regional depositories, along with regular depositories, receive only one free copy of a government publication on depository distribution. Restrictions are placed on the loan of certain categories of materials which accord with general interlibrary loan practice: reference works, rare volumes, old or fragile materials, current Census reports, heavily used materials, *Statutes-at-Large*, the *Congressional Record*, and old Serial Set volumes.

Disposal Operations

The most significant provision of the Depository Library Act of 1962 authorizes regional depositories to permit selective depositories in their region to discard any depository publication after holding it for at least five years. The act allows federal libraries to discard any depository publication at any time after first offering it to the Library of Congress and the National Archives. Previously, all depository libraries (except those in Wisconsin since 1953 and in New York State, exclusive of New York City, since 1956) were required to hold depository publications permanently, except those categories of superseded and ephemeral publications which the Superintendent of Documents authorized for disposal in his *Instructions*. The *Instructions* provides guidance to regional depositories on how to process requests for disposal. The regional depository has authority to issue instructions governing the specific procedures to be followed in its area so long as they are in accordance with the guidelines and the mandatory requirements of the law.

Disposal operations and policy among regional depositories differ in three main areas: (1) requirement for detailed versus a general listing of unwanted publications; (2) the extent of the geographical area in which takers for discarded publications are sought; and (3) whether offerings of the unwanted materials to other depositories and libraries are made by the regional or selective depository.

LIST OF PUBLICATIONS

Preparation of a list of discards is a mandatory (and valid) requirement. The list must contain enough information so that the regional depository and any prospective recipient can identify the material. The regional depository must initially have sufficient information to identify the materials which it does not already hold or wishes to add to its collection as duplicates. It is obligated to take any publications not already in its collection, and it may wish to add duplicates for any anticipated interlibrary loan requests. As far as the selective depository is concerned, the ideal solution would be for it to prepare a general list of unwanted publications, ship all the publications to the regional, and clear its records. However, a regional is generally willing to have shipped to it only those publications which it wishes to add to its own collection. The list must therefore contain enough information and be arranged in a manner that will facilitate a check against another library's holding records or shelflist.

The Superintendent of Documents suggests a general listing, giving only the "approximate extent of the holdings." Most regional depositories are satisfied with a general list of inclusive or specific numbers for Serial Set documents, numbered publications in series, and periodicals (example: Serial Set 1107–1231; BLS *Bulletins* 1151–1638; or *Survey of Current Business*, 1961–1969). However, only a few regionals will accept a general list with approximate holdings of unnumbered or general publications with a Cutter number as the book number, or numbered publications with a complicated numbering system (example: Senate Committee on Finance, Hearings, 1959–1969, 153 pieces; or Water Pollution Control Research series, 1965–1969, 178 pieces). In the latter case, most regional depositories will require a detailed list which provides title, date, and Superintendent of Documents (SuDoc) number for each publication on the list.

The regional depository may also prescribe the order in which the entries are to be listed, that is, in item number or SuDoc classification number order, or shelflist order. It may require that the list include the issuing agency, and be prepared alphabetically by issuing agency and title rather than in shelflist or item number order. The prescribed order may be related to the type of records the regional itself maintains. Some problems may arise in listing current item number and SuDoc classification numbers. With respect to item number, the current policy of retaining the item number permanently for a particular series began with the use of item cards in 1950. Prior to the use of the card system, which allows interfiling, new item numbers were reassigned each time the Classified List was republished. Thus some items which were discontinued before 1950 may have been issued under more than one item number.

With respect to the requirement to list SuDoc numbers, there is the obvious situation in which the item may have been integrated into the library's general collection, and the library's documents records do not show this number. Or a locally devised numbering or shelving system may have been used for the separate collection, in preference to the SuDoc classification system. In these cases the regional may waive the requirement of the SuDoc number or the item number so long as the publications can be identified.

Another problem arises where there have been reclassifications in the SuDoc numbers due to reorganization in the federal government. In this case, some depositories may continue to use the old numbers, rather than make the change. Other depositories may use the new number, but may change the old numbers on all the publications and the holding records to the new number. Either practice partially destroys the value of the SuDoc classification system, which uses a permanent standard number.

When the SuDoc number is uniformly used as intended, it provides a positive identification for a particular publication, which can be recognized by any depository or other library which collects U.S. government publications.

GEOGRAPHICAL AREA

In regard to the geographical area in which offerings for discarded publications are made, the law and the implementing *Instructions* are clear on the minimum requirements. After the regional depository has approved the disposal and made its selections, the list should be offered first to all other depositories in the regional's area of responsibility and then "to some other library or educational institution in the vicinity or area . . . to which requests might be referred." Some regional depositories may require that subsequent offerings be made statewide to selected nondepository libraries and educational institutions, as well as to those in the immediate vicinity of the discarding depository. However, an outstanding difference is the commendable practice by some regional depositories to circulate these offering lists out of state, especially to other regional depositories. This goes beyond the requirements of the law.

The regional depositories often include on these lists duplicate or nondepository copies of U.S. government publications which may be less than five years old, and in any case do not have to be offered to other depositories. In some smaller or medium-size states, there are often not enough large research libraries that want these older materials. It is a shame to destroy long runs of research materials which are no longer in print when there are a number of new or expanding universities that are building up research collections. Some type of central clearinghouse is needed to obtain information on the number of such libraries and their needs, and to channel offering lists to those libraries, or to provide regional depositories with a current list of such libraries and their specific needs for retrospective documents.

OFFERINGS TO OTHER LIBRARIES

With respect to which depository (regional or selective) makes the subsequent offering of discards, differences are due to philosophical and policy considerations over the amount of assistance a regional will provide, and whether it will be active or passive. The wording of the law suggests that the discarding depository should send out subsequent offering lists. On the other hand, some regional librarians feel that it is the duty of the regional to provide the maximum assistance to selective depositories within its available resources. In this case, the regional may send offering lists to all depositories in its region, selected nondepository libraries in the state, and frequently to out-of-state libraries as well.

The items on various lists from the selective depositories may be consolidated into a single list, or the offerings of each depository may be listed separately on a consolidated list. In the former practice, the requesting library will be unable to determine the location of the materials, whether they are all at the regional or at some selective depository. These consolidated lists are usually sent at the same time to all addresses; however, to comply with the law, the following priorities are assigned in fulfilling requests: depositories in the region; libraries and other educational institutions in the district of the offering library; all other libraries in the state; and all other institutions and out-of-state libraries.

Usually, in this type of consolidated, simultaneous offering, the "some for all" rule is applied, rather than the traditional rule of "first come, first served." All addresses are given a time limit in which to reply (usually 45–60 days), after which the requests are screened by the regional depository. Priorities are then assigned and instructions are issued to the holding libraries as to where they should send the requested materials. Regional depositories that use this method have reported a higher percentage of transfers since adopting the system. It is good for both the discarding and the receiving library. Prospective takers are more likely to submit requests when they are assured that all replies will be considered if submitted within a reasonable time. They are also more likely to make a more accurate and thorough screening of their holding records, rather than a hasty return in hope of "beating out" the other libraries.

The *Instructions* also provides three other situations (not specifically mentioned in the law) where regional depositories are required to assist depositories in the disposal of unwanted publications. In case a library's depository status is terminated by request or for cause, it must request instructions from the regional depository for disposition of the publications on hand. It may keep them permanently, with the approval of the regional, or if it desires to discard them it is no longer bound by the five-year retention requirement, and the regional must issue the necessary instructions and assist in disposal of the documents.

The libraries of state appellate courts that are depositories are not bound by the mandatory retention provision. The *Instructions* allows these depositories to discard unwanted publications at any time. If the state is served by a regional, the publications should be offered to the regional depository; if the state is not served by a regional, the publications should be offered to the state library.

With respect to unwanted sample copies of new items furnished on a special survey, depositories that are served by a regional should contact the regional depository for instructions. Other depositories, not served by a regional, may simply discard the sample copies.

In the *Instructions* the Superintendent of Documents states that a "Regional Library may refuse to grant permission for disposal of any publication that it feels should be kept by one of its depositories for a longer period of time," beyond the mandatory five years. This may be done even though the selective depository has kept the publication at least five years and submitted its request in accordance with instructions of its regional depository. Such authorization does not appear to be warranted by a strict interpretation of the law. The regular depository is authorized to select the items it wishes to receive, because (presumably) it knows best the needs of the citizens in its area and its own resources for servicing a depository collection. Then, by extension, it also has the right to select those items which it wishes to retain beyond the mandatory five-year period.

Reference Service

The Depository Library Act of 1962 requires the regional depository to provide "reference service . . . within the region served." Neither the act nor the implementing *Instructions* specifically defines the term "reference service." The emphasis should probably be on the word "service" rather than "reference," and should include all other assistance not specifically concerned with interlibrary loan or disposal operations which the regional depository may provide. When used in this context, the *Instructions* mentions two areas in which regionals may provide such service, as follows: "A representative from the designated Regional Depository should make periodic visits to the various depository libraries in the State or region in order that they may be familiar with the operations and needs of the depository libraries whom they serve in this capacity." "Regional depositories in concurrence with the Superintendent of Documents may prepare guidelines and issue any special instructions which they deem necessary for the efficient operation of depositories within their jurisdiction and which will enable the library to better serve the needs of the community where it is situated."[29]

Most regional librarians would agree that periodic visits to their depositories would be beneficial. However, this raises the question of federal financial support for depository libraries in general, and for regional depositories in particular. Many regional librarians, or their library administrators, do not feel that the law, when strictly interpreted, requires them to make such periodic visits. Regional depositories have already assumed additional responsibilities, spelled out specifically in the law, with no compensation other than the good will of their fellow depository libraries. This is particularly true of state universities which ordinarily do not have responsibilities, or access to funds, for providing support to libraries statewide. It is not only a matter of travel funds, but compensation for time taken away from the regular duties of the documents librarian.

Since the Superintendent of Documents is responsible by law for making "first hand investigation of conditions" at depository libraries, he or she has a mandate for making periodic visits and inspections. In the past, the Superintendent of Documents and his staff have made few such visits or inspections. However, the Superintendent of Documents has now established a formal program to visit and inspect the depository libraries. The Depository Library Council to the Public Printer has recommended that a representative from the regional depository be in-

29. *Instructions to Depository Libraries*, revised November 1977, sec. 2.

vited to accompany the GPO inspection team on these visits.[30] Such invitations have been made, but no federal travel funds have been provided for the regional representative.

Other formal programs which regional depositories have employed to provide assistance are newsletters and workshops. (Only a few regional depositories publish a newsletter on a regular schedule.) Regional depositories will, of course, respond (within their available resources) to reference questions and other requests for assistance from depositories in their area. The main formal program for providing assistance is the workshop. The regional depository may conduct the workshop as a separate event, under its own auspices, or it may jointly sponsor and conduct a workshop with a local, state, or regional library association, including a national interest group or its local chapter. These interest groups are primarily the Government Documents Round Table of the American Library Association and the Government Information Services Committee of the Special Libraries Association.

The workshops sponsored by regional depositories are generally tailored for two types of audiences: documents specialists and nonspecialists. The first type is designed for the documents librarians at the depository libraries in the region, with a variation of this type that includes nondepository libraries with a large documents collection. The second type, for the nonspecialist, is designed to promote the use of documents in all types of libraries. It is usually designed for reference and acquisition librarians at nondepository libraries, particularly small public libraries and high school libraries, or those without a separate documents section or a regularly assigned documents librarian.

The standard schedule for the typical one-day depository library workshop consists of three parts. In the morning, formal presentations are made by invited speakers from the participating depositories and by one or more guest speakers, usually from the Government Printing Office or other federal agencies concerned with issuing or distributing widely used government publications. In the afternoon, the assembly is usually broken down in three or more discussion/work groups ("mini-workshops"), covering specific topics such as selection and acquisition, bibliographic control, interlibrary loans and cooperation, organization, and use and servicing of a documents collection. Each group has a discussion leader, usually from one of the depositories or regionals. At the end of the workshop a summary of major problems discussed by the work groups is prepared and presented, together with recommendations for further action.

Regional Depository Status

The law provides that "not more than two depository libraries in each State and the Commonwealth of Puerto Rico may be designated as regional depositories." The Virgin Islands is also allowed to have regional depositories by the Superintend-

---

30. *Documents to the People* 3 (January 1975):21, 30.

ent of Documents under provisions of section 2 of the *Instructions*. Designation must be made by a U.S. senator of the state, the resident commissioner of Puerto Rico, or the governor of the Virgin Islands. The designation must have the prior approval of the "head of the library authority of the State or Commonwealth of Puerto Rico," and the designated library must already be a depository and have signified an interest in assuming the added responsibilities of a regional depository.

As a practical matter, the initiative normally comes (and should come) from the state library authority. It should obtain a volunteer library (either itself as a state library or another research library), which should execute an agreement in writing (usually signed by the library director) that it meets the prerequisites and is willing to assume the added responsibilities of a regional depository. The state library agency should send this written agreement to one of the two U.S. senators (usually the senior senator) with a request that he or she designate the library as a regional depository. (The law does not indicate whether the senior or junior senator, or both, may make a designation.) After the designation has been made, the senator (or resident commissioner of Puerto Rico or governor of the Virgin Islands) should send to the Superintendent of Documents a copy of the designation, along with the written agreement.

If the state library cannot find a candidate in the state, it may fulfill its responsibility by making arrangements with a regional depository in a neighboring state to provide these services. Documents librarians in those states, who feel handicapped by the lack of regional services, should petition their state library agency. However, petitions to a U.S. senator are also in order in view of the provisions of the law, and may result in the senator's using his or her influence on the state library agency.

Criteria for Regional Designation

What qualifies a candidate for regional designation? Since a regional depository must accept and permanently retain all depository publications (except those authorized to be discarded by the Superintendent of Documents), it should be a large research library covering a wide range of subjects, particularly in the social sciences, technology, and science. It should preferably have been a depository for a number of years, have chosen at least 90 percent of the depository items, and have a strong retrospective collection. Since it is responsible for interlibrary loans and reference assistance on a statewide basis, it should (preferably) have similar responsibilities for general library materials within an existing regional or cooperative network.

Since the state library agencies already have responsibilities for supporting library services statewide, it was apparently expected during the 1957–58 House and the 1962 Senate hearings on depository library legislation that most state libraries would almost automatically assume the responsibilities of a regional depository. Each state has been authorized for one special designation for a "state library," and each had used it by 1962. However, the library or agency which used the "state library" designation is in many cases not the state library agency. The designation has been taken by libraries with a wide variety of functions, illustrating the diversity of organization for state library services: state supreme court library, legislative reference service, service to state agencies in the capital, library commission, historical society, general lending or traveling library, or any combination thereof. Thus many state libraries do not have (or need) a complete collection of federal documents, or a broad research collection.

The next logical candidates for regional depository designations are the state universities and/or land-grant universities. All land-grant universities are authorized a special designation, and all major state universities which are not "land grant" have achieved depository status by congressional designations. Most of the libraries at these universities consider themselves research libraries, generally select a high percentage of the available depository items, and keep them permanently. However, the state universities generally do not have responsibilities for the support of general library services statewide.

The third category of candidate for regional depository designation is the public library in the major city. Many such libraries have strong research collections, covering a broad range of subjects; have been depositories for a long period; and have a high percentage or rate of item selection. In some states these libraries also have key responsibilities for interlibrary loans within a regional network when the state library does not have the collections or organization to support this service.

These restrictive factors have not prevented some libraries from assuming the added regional responsibilities to ensure that their state is provided regional depository services. The Nebraska Library Commission obtained depository status in 1972 with a senatorial designation and the express purpose of developing a complete collection (practically from scratch) so that it could become a regional depository. It was so designated in 1974. Portland (Oregon) State University Library became a regional in 1972, only nine years after it had become a regular depository. The University of Oregon had been a depository since 1883, and Oregon State University since 1907.

For a list of regional depository libraries, see appendix 3.

Additional References

American Library Association. *Papers and Proceedings of the Thirty-fourth Annual Meeting . . . Held at Ottawa, Canada, June 26–July 2, 1912*, pp. 308–9. New York: Johnson Reprint Corp., 1963.

Buckley, Carper W. "Implementation of the Federal Depository Library Act of 1962," *Library Trends* 15 (July 1966):27–36.

———. "The Role of the Superintendent of Documents," *Drexel Library Quarterly* 1 (October 1965):19–23.

Morehead, Joe. "The Government Printing Office and Non-GPO Publications," *Government Publications Review* 1 (Fall 1973):1–5.

Schwarzkopf, LeRoy. *Regional Libraries and the Depository Library Act of 1962.* Bethesda, Md.: ERIC Document Reproduction Service. ED 066 177. 1972.
————. *Survey of Regional Depository Libraries for U.S. Government Publications.* Bethesda, Md.: ERIC Document Reproduction Service. ED 104 361. 1974.
Whitbeck, George W., Peter Hernon, and John Richardson, Jr. "The Federal Depository Library System: A Descriptive Analysis," *Government Publications Review* 5 (1978):253–67.

ORGANIZATION AND ARRANGEMENT 3

Many factors enter into a decision to separate or integrate government publications. The local library situation—size, space, organization, resources—must govern the arrangement of government documents in a given library. The wealth of government publications as an information source and how this source can best be "accessed" by the user should be the guide to the integration or separation of materials. The best arrangement is the one which meets the stated objectives of the library and ultimately the needs of the users.

It is advised that before any plan of organization is selected, a thorough study be made of the various alternatives, their advantages and disadvantages in relation to the size, circumstances, and organizational policy of the particular library situation. Consulting experienced librarians and visiting similar libraries are ways of gaining information. Since written guidelines provide a basis for the smooth functioning of library operations, the policy statement of the library should indicate how the library is organized and where government publications fit into its organizational scheme.

Whether to separate or integrate government publications has been debated over the years in library literature and in library meetings, with very strong arguments and advocates for both approaches. Generally these views have represented the extremes for one or the other type of organization. One librarian wrote in 1965: "Even a depository library should not segregate its documents in a separate room and expect them to be fully used unless they are fully cataloged and analyzed, and

The first two chapters have, by way of offering background, characterized the responsibilities of the federal government in distributing its documents. The remainder of this work describes the handling of federal documents in the library from the aspect of effective delivery to users.

The author is indebted to LeRoy Schwarzkopf for many of the ideas expressed in this chapter. The term "integrated" refers to the treatment of government publications in a similar fashion as other library materials.

this is simply never done under modern cataloging policies of economy."[1] And another, some 30 years earlier, said: "To have all the documents in one section under the supervision of an interested librarian who knows documents is the ideal administrative device."[2] For each point of view the chief arguments appear to be that those who advocate integration believe there should be no difference in treatment between materials issued by the Government Printing Office and by other printers and publishers. Those who favor separation argue that government publications are decidedly a "different" type of material, requiring special treatment.

In the lack of empirical data on reasons for separation or integration, a compromise stance, using the best features of both approaches—that is, a partially integrated collection for a large research library and a partially separate collection for the small library[3]—appears to be sound advice. The small library is usually highly selective in the acquisition of government publications while the large library, usually a research library, requires a wide range of materials to answer the variety of questions posed by its clientele. Thus the small library should exercise care about what it selects for the general collection, while the research library should be careful about what it chooses to exclude from the general collection.

In present practice, there is wide variation in the organization of government publications, with many factors affecting organizational pattern, among which are (in addition to the philosophical question) the physical layout of the library building, size of the government publications collection, depository status, and type of library.

Library Building

The physical layout of the library may restrict the separation of a collection of materials. Although occupying the same square footage or space, a separate collection will require a specially defined area. If a separate unit is serviced by special staff, it will require space for a service area, work area, office, and stacks.

Size of Collection

The size of the collection may be a controlling factor. Whether the library has depository status may influence separation or integration, since depository libraries

1. Rae Elizabeth Rips, "The Reference Use of Government Publications," *Drexel Library Quarterly* 1 (October 1965):14.

2. Lucille H. Pendell, "Use of Federal Documents," *Wilson Library Bulletin* 5 (April 1931):508.

3. LeRoy C. Schwarzkopf, "How a Library Organizes Government Documents," paper presented at GPO Regional Depository Library Workshop, New York City, July 13, 1974, p. 5 (mimeo).

must deal with a sizable amount of materials and must adhere to certain procedural regulations of the Superintendent of Documents. The Superintendent does not stipulate how a library must organize its depository collection, but it is stressed that the collection must be accessible. According to the "Biennial Report of the Depository Libraries, October 1975," issued by the Superintendent of Documents, 749, or 65.5 percent, of the responding libraries answered affirmatively to the question: "Is your documents collection a separate department in your library?" Most small nondepository libraries do not acquire more government publications than can be integrated into the general library collection.

Type of Library

A factor for separation may also be type of library. There appears to be some relationship between type of library and documents organization. Large academic libraries, which constitute about 65 percent of libraries that have depository status, tend to have separate collections. In a survey of 35 selected university depository libraries, Julien found that 25 had separate documents collections.[4] According to a survey of regional depository libraries conducted by Schwarzkopf, 40 of the 43 regional depositories (dominated by academic libraries) had separate or primarily separate documents collections.[5] Depository libraries are usually in research libraries that select a high percentage of depository items (about 90 percent or more).

The arrangement of government publications collections generally falls into one of four types: (1) integrated into the general collection of the library, (2) separated as a special collection, (3) primarily separated (partially integrated), and (4) primarily integrated (partially separated). (The listed advantages and disadvantages have no scientific basis but are often cited.)

Integrated Collection

The advocates of an integrated collection believe in the concept that no distinctions should be made between publications issued by United States government agencies and those of other publishers. As part of the general collection of the library, the same system of classification is applied to government publications, cataloged under the same policies, and materials are shelved with other cataloged titles.

---

4. Jane A. Julien, *The Organization and Administration of U.S. Government Publications in Selected University Depository Libraries: A Survey* (Flagstaff: Northern Arizona University, 1974), p. 77.

5. LeRoy C. Schwarzkopf, *Survey of Regional Depository Libraries for U.S. Government Publications* (College Park: University of Maryland, McKeldin Library, 1974), p. 17.

Advantages are:
1. Integration places government publications on various subjects with other related works.
2. There is one classification system for the library.
3. The public catalog permits access by author, title, and subject.
4. There is minimum duplication of materials.

Disadvantages are:
1. The reference staff cannot become as knowledgeable about government publications as can documents librarians who specialize in this area.
2. There is delay in cataloging and classification of materials; and the cost of full cataloging is often cited as a disadvantage.
3. There is lack of compatibility between entries in printed indexes to government publications and the entries in the card catalog. LC subject cataloging offers only limited subject access to government publications. *Monthly Catalog* subject headings are not compatible with LC subjects (prior to 1976).

Separate Collection

In a separate collection the documents are housed and serviced as a special collection, and use of a different classification scheme and recordkeeping system is not unusual. A separate documents collection can be organized as a department, division, or section, or it can be part of a larger unit such as business, economics and/or social sciences, or general reference. In a separate unit, there is usually heavy dependence on printed catalogs and indexes to access information. A separate unit is also usually responsible for the four main library functions, which are generally fragmented for regular library materials: acquisition, cataloging and serial records, reference, and circulation and stack maintenance. Carrying out these functions will require a special staff. The philosophy of a separate collection is that librarians who become specialists can provide better reference service since they handle the various library functions and consequently are knowledgeable about the materials in the collection.

Advantages are:
1. If the Superintendent of Documents classification scheme is used, it is ready made and thus can save some costs in traditional cataloging and classification. Major indexes, such as CIS and ASI, include the Superintendent of Documents classification number.
2. A special staff of documents librarians and support staff handle all publications and become intimately aware of the content of materials, whether the data are in a single-page news release, periodicals, or monographs.

3. Acquisition of materials, with or without charge, is facilitated by direct handling.
4. The patron is better served by a special collection, where staff becomes aware of user needs and can respond to them.
5. Documents librarians can make maximum use of special catalogs and indexes to government publications.

Disadvantages are:
1. Materials in subject area are separated from related materials in other parts of the library.
2. Users of the separate collection must deal with a separate classification scheme.
3. Heavy reliance must be placed on staff in other areas of the library to refer patrons to the separate unit.

To what extent the main library functions—acquisitions, cataloging, reference, and circulation and shelf maintenance—are assumed by a unit will to a large measure determine the organization of materials in the separate unit. If the unit is responsible for all or most of the library functions, the concerns of the unit head include such matters as administration, personnel, financial support, and quarters. General principles of administration should be consulted in textbooks on this subject.

Most separate units are responsible for government documents (other than federal) which include local, state, foreign, and international publications, and for related types of materials such as technical reports, maps, and legal materials. Legal materials (bills, hearings, reports, laws and statutes, administrative law, treaties, decisions of courts and regulatory agencies) are part of the depository distribution, as are some technical reports and indexes to this literature. Therefore it is logical to include these materials in a separate unit of government publications. Since Geological Survey and Army maps form the nucleus of a map collection, maps are an important addition to a separate documents unit.

Staffing patterns also vary widely because of the range in size and types of libraries that have separate collections. One depository library inspector found from one to six documents librarians in the libraries she inspected.[6]

Primarily Separate

Very few collections are totally separate, with everything published by the federal government gathered into one unit. Almost all collections have some materials integrated, with some variations as to the degree with which materials are inte-

6. LeRoy C. Schwarzkopf, "Fall 1976 Meeting of Depository Library Council to the Public Printer," *Documents to the People* 5 (January 1977):7.

grated into the general collection. If some materials must be integrated, the question of what kinds of materials can be selectively integrated should be considered. What kinds of government publications can be treated like other materials in the library?

The most logical titles are those not thought of by patrons as government publications. These include selected periodicals such as *Children Today, Business America, Federal Probation;* legal materials such as *Statutes-at-Large* and *United States Treaties and Other International Agreements;* decisions of regulatory agencies, such as *I.C.C. Reports* and *SEC Decisions and Reports*; and yearbooks such as the *Yearbook of Agriculture.* Significant general publications and monographs may also be integrated, but some criteria for judging what publications are considered "significant" should be established. Some duplication of titles is justified to provide additional access points. This is particularly true if departmental libraries are located in other areas of the campus. In the case of major works, a copy should be obtained for integration, with the depository copy, or the added copy, remaining in the separate collection. Reference titles will also need to be duplicated for the reference department and for departmental libraries. Significant reference sources are published by the federal government. Many titles, such as the *Statistical Abstract, Occupational Outlook Handbook*, and *Official Congressional Directory,* are not thought of by patrons as government publications.

Development of a clear policy statement on what materials are to be integrated and what are to be housed in the separate collection, and who will be responsible for the selection of materials, is recommended.

Primarily Integrated

A small library, particularly a small depository which selects the minimum number of items, may want to separate some series. In this case, a list of what is to be separated should be considered. Titles which have adequate indexes and access points might be separated, for example, congressional publications.

Additional References

Erlandson, Ruth M. "The Organization of Federal Government Publications in Depository Libraries," in *United States Government Publications*, by Anne Morris Boyd, Appendix B. 3d ed. rev. by Rae Elizabeth Rips, New York: Wilson, 1949.

Jackson, Ellen. "The Administration of the Government Documents Collection," *ACRL Monograph* (January 1953), pp. 5–7.

———. *A Manual for the Administration of the Federal Documents Collection in Libraries.* Chicago: American Library Association, 1955.

Knowles, Caroline M. "The Documentation Centre of the University of Guelph Library," *Government Publications Review* 1 (Spring 1974):241–50.

"Organization and Servicing of Documents," Federal Documents Regional Workshop Conference Proceedings, Kansas City, Mo., April 13–14, 1973, session 7. *Government Publications Review* 1 (Spring 1974):307–15.

Presser, Carolynne. "Organization of a Separate Government Documents Collection, University of Waterloo—A Case History," *Government Publications Review* 2 (Spring 1975):167–76.

Shaw, Thomas Shuler. "Government Documents: Part II, Arrangement," *Louisiana Library Association Bulletin* 31 (Spring 1968):21–25, 48.

Shearer, Benjamin. "Federal Depository Libraries on the Campus: Practices and Prospects," *Government Publications Review* 4 (1977):209–14.

Waldo, Michael. "An Historical Look at the Debate over How to Organize Federal Government Documents in Depository Libraries," *Government Publications Review* 4 (1977):319–29.

4
COLLECTION DEVELOPMENT

Collection development is an important function of libraries. In many respects the methods used by libraries in the selection and acquisition of government publications are unique because of the federal depository distribution system. For depository libraries, the automatic receipt of materials may alleviate some acquisition problems, but there are three large areas (outside of the GPO) which must be considered by libraries which seek to develop a well-rounded collection of government publications. These areas are non-GPO materials and technical report literature in the realm of government publications and commercial publications such as reprints and indexes and other aids which supplement or provide access to government information. Therefore, both depository and nondepository libraries must use sources in addition to the GPO for the acquisition of government publications and their tools of access.

As discussed in chapter 2, non-GPO publications have presented an acquisition problem for librarians for many years. GPO, however, is making an effort to distribute non-GPO publications (which it receives from agencies) to depository libraries through a micropublishing program, thus expanding the bibliographical control over these materials.

The character, quality, and scope of a documents collection are shaped to a large degree by the librarian/bibliographer who performs the selection function. To achieve a balanced collection, the librarian must exercise good judgment and wise selection. If special consideration is to be given to the collection of government publications, a separate acquisitions policy statement should be developed to answer such questions as: Who are to be served (the library's public)? What will be selected? Who will do the selecting? How will the materials be obtained (deposit, purchase, gifts, exchange)? Where will the materials be housed? Access to government publications in libraries in the area will affect the depth of collection development.

The acquisitions budget and number of staff will determine whether the acquisitions program will be aggressive or of limited scope. Whatever design is envisioned as the final goal, the collection development process must be a well-planned and continuing activity.

The Depository Library

A newly established depository library that needs assistance in determining what items to select can profit from a visit to one or two well-established depository libraries. *Guidelines for the Depository Library System* recommends that a depository library select at least 25 percent of all the items offered by the Superintendent of Documents. (See appendix 4.)

Annotated lists are helpful in making a decision on what items to select for a collection. The item cards contain annotations. Small and medium-sized public and college libraries will find Nancy P. Van Zant's *Selected U.S. Government Series: A Guide for Public and Academic Libraries* (Chicago: American Library Association, 1978) a useful guide. This annotated list includes about 600 of the more than 3,800 item numbers offered by the Superintendent of Documents. John L. Andriot's *Guide to U.S. Government Publications* gives annotations for important series, serials, and periodicals. Price List 36, *Government Periodicals and Subscription Services,* also gives brief annotations of periodicals and serials. A regular feature of *Government Publications Review* is an annotated list of "U.S. Government (Depository Items)," edited by Beverly Railsback and Joyce Koch. Schwarzkopf's column in *Booklist,* a regular feature, is also a valuable guide to selection.

A designated depository library has a nucleus collection of federal documents, the size and scope of which depend on the date depository status was achieved, as well as on acquisition and weeding policy. Since 1922, depository libraries have been allowed to select categories of publications. The temptation to select as many publications as possible, without charge, should be tempered by the wise advice of Ellen Jackson, who warned that careless and indiscriminate overselection should be avoided, both to save the time a library spends on handling and storage and to limit, in the public interest, the funds expended by the federal government. On the other hand, too narrow a selection may result in a collection of little immediate or future value.[1]

Regional depositories must receive and retain at least one printed or microform copy of all publications sent to depository libraries, with the exception of materials which are superseded and those that are issued in bound form at a later date. (See the section "Regional Libraries.")

The *Instructions to Depository Libraries* (appendix 3) outlines in detail the procedures to be followed by depository libraries in the selection process. Samples in-

1. Ellen Jackson, "Administration of the Government Documents Collection," *American Library Association, ACRL Monograph* no. 5 (1953), p. 2.

clude Item Card, Daily Depository Shipping Lists, Claim Sheet, Amendment of Selections, and Request for Confirmation of Classification Numbers. Only a brief discussion will be presented here.

The basis for selection is the "Classified List of U.S. Government Publications," consisting of two sets of 3 x 5 cards representing items available for selection. Each card gives distribution item number, issuing agency, series and group title, SuDoc number, and brief annotation when appropriate. An item number may represent one title or several related series, and is subject to added titles or deletions at a later date. Selection must be made by item number and not by listed series. (Shipping lists often bear the notation that a new series has been added to an item.) Item numbers nearly always remain the same, regardless of change of agency.

One set of cards of selected item numbers must be returned to the Library Division. Be sure to indicate the depository library number assigned to your library. The other set should be filed in item number sequence after each card has been stamped with date of selection. The two cards of items not selected, with notation "not selected," may be interfiled. If at a later date a not-selected item is needed, one card can be pulled and mailed to the Library Division with a request for addition of the item.

As new series are added by existing and by newly created agencies, depository libraries are given an opportunity to select them, if desired. New offerings, referred to as "Surveys," are issued approximately monthly. Two 3 x 5 cards for each item together with the sample copies[2] of titles listed on the Survey (if available), are sent. (See appendix 3, "Instructions," for sample survey.) To ensure receipt of an item, one card, marked with depository number and date selected, should be returned immediately, as GPO must submit an estimate of the number of copies needed well in advance of a printing. Only sufficient copies are printed to provide distribution to depository libraries which have selected the series or group in which a particular publication falls; no retroactive distribution of materials can be made by the Superintendent of Documents.

A library that is not served by a regional depository may retain or discard the sample copies of titles sent with the Survey and not selected. If retained, these titles should be labeled "This item number ____ not selected" and shelved. This item will serve as a sample if reinstatement is considered at a later date. The most recent instructions stipulate that depository libraries served by a regional library must contact the regional before disposition of the sample title. To terminate or reinstate an item, fill out the "Amendment of Selections Form" (see exhibit D of "Instructions," appendix 3) and mail it to the Assistant Public Printer. The file of item cards, kept up to date with notations of selections, cancellations, added or deleted titles, and discontinued items, is a valuable source.

The Library Division of the Office of the Superintendent of Documents *does not maintain a list of selections by library but by item number only*. Item numbers may be regarded as standing orders for titles represented by that number. Therefore a

2. Samples are almost always sent to the regional depository libraries; therefore if a depository library does not receive a sample, a call to the regional depository for an evaluation of the title may be desirable.

depository library will receive all titles in the selected item number until the library chooses to discontinue the item. Automation of the item number selection book is under way at GPO. In the future, libraries will not be able to cancel or reinstate items except at stated intervals, probably semiannually.

Special offerings of publications which are made available from time to time to the Superintendent of Documents by agencies, departments, and congressional committees are offered to depository libraries. Generally, not enough copies are received by the Superintendent to make a distribution to all depository libraries. These offers are therefore made through the *Daily Depository Shipping List*. Libraries which want the title should reply immediately, as the requests are filled on a first come, first served basis. If the offer is accepted, a notation of receipt by special offer should be indicated on the shelflist record or on the publication.

Depository shipments are usually mailed on a daily basis. A change in packaging depository shipments was announced in December 1974:

> In order to expedite packaging, uniformly sized cartons will be used for all shipments (excluding self-mailer items and Congressional bills and reports). Shipments are planned so that a carton will hold all the publications on a single *Daily Depository Shipping List*. Therefore, libraries receiving all items on a given list will receive one carton, containing one shipping list and all the publications on it. If a library has selected only part of the items on a given list, one or more additional lists will be included in the same carton. Each carton will contain shipping lists covering all enclosed publications, and all selected publications from a given list will be in the same carton. There will be no split shipments, with part of a list in one carton and part in another.[3]

The packaging procedure described above may change in the future, as GPO plans to ship materials in larger cartons (40 lb.), reducing the number of cartons shipped to depository libraries.

The *Daily Depository Shipping List* has been prepared by the Library Division since August 1951 and serves as an "invoice" for depository shipments. The shipping list is the focal point for the technical processing operations of a depository collection. It is also a great source of information for changes in titles and SuDoc numbers, claims, surveys, and corrections. It should be read by all librarians who handle government publications, and not only by the person who processes documents.

Shipping lists, numbered consecutively, are mailed with depository shipments on the average of twice a day. If a lapse in shipments is suspected, the regional library or a neighboring depository library should be queried. (It is useful to maintain friendly relations with depository libraries in the area. An arrangement to supply, and to be supplied with, copies of missing shipping lists is mutually beneficial.)

The receipt of shipping lists should be recorded in numerical order, which will, at a glance, indicate missing lists. A simple listing on a sheet of paper or a numbered

3. *Documents to the People* 3 (January 1975):15.

card are suggestions. Claims for materials selected but not received must be reported on a claim sheet which must be postmarked within 15 days of the date the shipment is received. Claim sheets are available from the Library Division, Superintendent of Documents. Additional copies of claim sheets are usually sent with each filled claim. In general, claims are for complete lists. If an entire shipment is missing, secure a copy of the shipping list, circle the items selected, and mail the list immediately on discovery of the defect.

Some titles are not included in the shipping lists but are mailed separately. These direct mail or automatic distribution items include 16 titles as of June 1977:

> *Average Monthly Weather Outlook* (semimonthly), Item 275–F (C 55.109:)
> *Business America* (biweekly), Item 127–A (C 1.58/2:)
> *Business Service Checklist* (biweekly), Item 127 (C 1.24:)
> *Calendar of Business* (Senate, daily), Item 998–B (Y 1.3/3:)
> *Calendars of the U.S. House of Representatives and History of Legislation* (weekly), Item 998–A (Y 1.2/2:)
> *Commerce Business Daily* (daily), Item 231–G–3 (C 57.20:)
> *Congressional Record* (daily), Item 994 (X/a:)
> *Daily Statement of the U.S. Treasury* (daily), Item 923–A–2 (T 1.5:)
> *Daily Weather Maps, Weekly Series* (weekly), Item 273–D–4 (C 55.213:)
> *Federal Register* (daily), Item 573 (GS 4.107:)
> *Federal Register Index* (monthly), Item 573 (GS 4.107:)
> *HUD Newsletter* (weekly), Item 582–L (HH 1.15/4:)
> *Internal Revenue Bulletin* (weekly), Item 957 (T 22.23:)
> *Official Gazette of the U.S. Patent and Trademark Office: Patents* (weekly), Item 260 (C 21.5:)
> *SEC Docket* (weekly), Item 998-B (Y 1.3/3:)
> *Weekly Compilation of Presidential Documents* (weekly), Item 577-A (GS 4.114:)[4]

The Nondepository Library

The scope and extent of a nondepository library's collection of government publications will depend on the size and acquisition policy of the library. It would be difficult for any library to build a sizable documents collection without depository status because of the cost of materials and processing.[5]

---

4. *Public Documents Highlights*, no. 22 (June 1977).
5. In 1972 it was estimated that to select about 95% of the depository items, it would cost about $12,000 annually for the titles alone. Processing costs were not calculated. This figure was based on costs reflected on the shipping lists for the year 1971. Since that time, the number of items offered to depository libraries has increased considerably, and GPO raised prices by about 70% in 1972.

Nondepository libraries may therefore need to be much more discriminating than depository libraries in the selection and acquisition of government publications, using the Government Printing Office and other sources (see following section). Close cooperation with a strong depository library in the area is highly recommended. Examining the documents received by depository libraries on a regular basis will give the librarian in a nondepository library knowledge of what publications are available from GPO.

Sources for Acquisition

THE *MONTHLY CATALOG*

The Government Printing Office is the major source for government publications. The *Monthly Catalog* is the selection tool used by librarians in depository as well as nondepository libraries. (See the chapter "Monthly Catalog.")

SHIPPING LISTS

The *Daily Depository Shipping List* (discussed earlier) indicates what materials have been sent to depository libraries and offers a preview of titles not yet listed in the *Monthly Catalog*. There is a four- to six-month lag between the receipt of a depository title and listing in the *Monthly Catalog*. These lists are available on a subscription basis ($141.60 per year in 1978). Nondepository libraries which cannot afford to subscribe to the shipping lists should make arrangements with the depository library in the area to examine the lists and documents on a regular basis.

SELECTED LISTS

Selected U.S. Government Publications is an advertising vehicle issued monthly by the Superintendent of Documents, and a subscription is available free upon request. Publications in this list are those which have popular appeal. The sales publications listed, 150–200 in number, may be ordered from the distribution center indicated on the order form. One should be careful to note the date of expiration. To facilitate handling of orders, the distribution center is stocked with all titles listed on each selected list for a period of only six months. After that date, all orders should be forwarded to the GPO.

PRICE LISTS AND SUBJECT BIBLIOGRAPHIES

Price lists on topics of current interest (first published in 1898) were distributed free by the Superintendent of Documents until 1973, when it was announced that the price lists were discontinued, to be replaced by subject bibliographies. Price list 36, *Government Periodicals and Subscription Services*, is the only price list, updated and issued irregularly.

The first subject lists appeared in March 1975, and there are now over 270 lists of publications on a single subject or field of interest. These lists, available without charge, indicate in-print titles as well as those which have been reprinted. An index to the subject bibliographies (SB 999) is available from the Superintendent of Documents. The former price lists are still useful for verification of titles.

SUBJECT GUIDES

Subject guides to government publications have increased in number and serve as excellent awareness and selection tools. (Many of them are listed in the bibliography section of this work.) Selected, annotated lists, published in professional journals, notably the *Booklist* (American Library Association) and *Government Publications Review*, also serve as current selection aids.

EXCHANGE LISTS

Interlibrary cooperation has long been a tradition with documents librarians. One of the least expensive methods of filling gaps is through exchange lists compiled by libraries. The regional depository library may be helpful in locating libraries which offer exchanges. *Public Documents Highlights* and *Documents to the People* often list libraries which offer exchange lists.

GPO BOOKSTORES

In the past few years, a number of attractive retail GPO bookstores have been established in major cities around the country. These are operated under the direction of the Superintendent of Documents. As the purpose of the outlet is to meet the public demand for government publications, the titles that are stocked are those which have wide appeal.

A telephone call to the local GPO bookstore (if there is one in the area) will establish whether a publication is available. If so, an order form and account number for charges will be accepted. Sending all orders through the local bookstore is not recommended, as time is wasted if the bookstore does not carry the title in question and must forward requests to Washington, D.C. For a list and the locations of GPO bookstores, refer to the most recent *Monthly Catalog*. If there is a GPO bookstore in your city, copies of brochures describing location, hours of operation, and telephone number should be requested and distributed to patrons.

INDIVIDUAL AGENCIES

Many agencies maintain mailing lists for specific titles or series. Press releases and newsletters are examples of types of materials available from agencies without charge. If the library is a member of the Documents Expediting Project (discussed below), a request to be placed on the mailing list can be made through this service. Otherwise, individual requests should be sent directly to the agency. It is helpful to maintain a simple card file, by short title and date of request, of agencies from which material has been requested on a mailing list basis.

Publications catalogs and lists issued by individual agencies and units provide a fertile field for identifying materials issued by agencies. It is not unusual for libraries to obtain—without charge from some agencies—materials for sale through the Superintendent of Documents. Major agencies issue comprehensive catalogs of publications on a continuing basis. (See the section on selected indexes and catalogs in chapter 8 for a selected list of agency catalogs.)

More agency indexes are likely to be issued as a result of the Freedom of Information Act, "which requires agencies to maintain and make available for public inspection and copying current indexes." Recent amendments[6] require publication (with some exceptions) and distribution of these indexes at least quarterly. Agencies are required to submit index titles, period covered, brief description of contents, and availability information to the Office of the Federal Register, which will compile and publish this information quarterly in the *Federal Register*. These lists should serve as checklists to keep abreast of agency indexes and catalogs as they are issued. The first list appeared in the *Federal Register* (40 [July 9, 1975]:28867–72), and annual guides to agency material, January to December 1976 and 1977, appeared in 42 (January 31, 1977):5720–37 and 43 (January 31, 1978):4155–69. Beginning in 1978, "Guide to Freedom of Information Indexes" is published in the quarterly *Federal Register Index*.

REPRESENTATIVES OF CONGRESS

Copies of bills, congressional reports, hearings and committee prints, and some departmental publications are available from members of Congress. Congress sometimes authorizes a special appropriation for the printing of certain publications for distribution to members' constituencies. A recent edition of the U.S. Department of Agriculture *Yearbook*, for example, might be distributed in bulk to members of Congress and may be acquired from them. For a list of representatives of Congress and their addresses, consult the *Official Congressional Directory*.

LOCAL LIBRARIES

In addition to requesting materials from members of Congress, contacting special libraries within the area is beneficial. Special libraries tend to discard publications after their timeliness has passed. Naturally, special libraries acquire publications which serve their own interests; therefore, personal contact with the librarians is the best way to determine what their discards may be.

6. P.L. 93–502; 88 *Stat.* 1561; 5 U.S.C. 552 (a)(2).

DOCUMENTS EXPEDITING PROJECT

The Documents Expediting Project, commonly referred to as Doc Ex, is a unique service, created by librarians to serve a definite need. It is one solution to the problem of obtaining federal documents not available through GPO or the issuing agency. The Project was established in 1946 for distribution of war documents, multilithed reports, and other publications not handled by the Superintendent of Documents (non-GPO documents). Since 1968, the Project has operated as a unit of the Exchange and Gift Division of the Library of Congress.

By reviewing the proof sheets of the *Monthly Catalog*, the staff has advance knowledge of those items which will not be distributed through the depository system. Publications are solicited by contacting various agencies. Since materials are not always available in the quantity required to serve all members, a library is placed in priority order, according to the fee it pays. Thus a library that pays the maximum fee will receive more than one that pays a lesser amount.

Membership in Doc Ex is limited to American libraries. Annual membership fees, varying from $175 to $750 in multiples of $25, are determined by the subscribing libraries.

For many years committee prints had been considered "administrative" publications by most congressional committees and very few prints were available to depository libraries. Recently, however, at the instigation of the Joint Committee on Printing, several congressional committees have agreed to make their committee prints available to depository libraries. The pivotal location of Doc Ex at the Library of Congress and the personal contacts of the staff members enables Doc Ex to secure the majority of committee prints which are usually in limited supply. For nondepository libraries, the Documents Expediting Service is the prime source for committee prints.

Other congressional publications available from Doc Ex include Senate executive reports and documents. Agency materials include materials which a library may obtain by applying directly and other materials available only from Doc Ex. Examples of titles in the latter category are publications of the Tennessee Valley Authority and the CIA Reference Aid series.

In addition to the distribution of materials, Doc Ex performs other services of value to libraries. One of the most valuable is that of searching. Doc Ex can usually track down a needed publication, current or retrospective or out of print. This special request service is offered to all member libraries on an equal basis.

Another service performed by Doc Ex is to act as an intermediary in placing the library's name on government agency mailing lists for specific serial publications.

Special offers of materials are made by Doc Ex throughout the year. Member libraries can make selections from a list of items. Requests are filled on a first come, first served basis.

Many librarians believe that Doc Ex fees are more than offset by the savings in staff time, through this centralized service. A shortcoming of the Project may be the limited selectivity of publications; Doc Ex cannot select subject areas but must accept all materials it receives (except serial titles) from a particular agency. Member libraries, however, are free to dispose of materials not needed.

Special forms are provided by Doc Ex for requesting materials. A list of sample publications, a fact sheet on the service, articles about the Project, and a list of participating libraries are available on request to Documents Expediting Project, Exchange and Gift Division, Library of Congress, Washington, D.C. 20540.

COMMERCIAL PRINTERS

In an effort to reduce overall government expenditures in printing, many agencies are turning to commercial printers as well as to professional groups. The *Bibliography of Agriculture* and *Monthly Weather Review* are two examples of publications now available from commercial and professional channels (respectively) and not from the Government Printing Office. Documents librarians should seek constantly to identify these publications.

Out-of-Print and Back Issues

GPO

The GPO has an inventory control system that uses the S/N (stock numbers) and can quickly determine if a requested title is in print. The *GPO Sales Publications Reference File (PRF)* of in-print titles also includes some 6,000 publications no longer in stock. The *PRF* provides access by S/N numbers. (See fuller discussion of this tool in the bibliography section, chapter 8.)

A memorandum issued by the Superintendent of Documents on stock retention of dated periodicals was reprinted in *Documents to the People* (5 [January 1977]: 21–27). The purpose of this memorandum is "to re-establish policy and procedure to retain sufficient back issues on all dated periodicals to handle lost claim adjustment orders and single sales orders." The list includes titles of periodicals and the number of latest issues to be retained. This can be used as a guide by librarians who may need to purchase a single issue of a periodical from the Government Printing Office.

NATIONAL ARCHIVES

The largest and perhaps the most important collection of federal government publications is now administered by the National Archives. This collection was begun in 1895 in the Office of the Superintendent of Documents to support the cataloging and indexing activities which the Superintendent of Documents was required to perform by provision of the Printing Act of 1895.

An effort by the Office of the Superintendent of Documents to collect government publications published prior to 1895 was made, and subsequently a copy of every publication cataloged or distributed to depository libraries was added to this collection. Because the collection was not a library collection in the traditional sense, it was not made available to the public for reference or research. The need to meet requests for access to this collection, coupled with the critical space problems at GPO and the concern for preservation, led to the transfer of this collection to the National Archives in 1972. This collection numbers over 2 million documents and is available for public use. The Office of the Superintendent of Documents will continue to transfer material to the National Archives collection.

The National Archives and Records Service (Washington, D.C. 20408) provides copies of out-of-print federal documents on request, if the condition of the documents is not so fragile that copies cannot be made. Formats include negative microfilm and electrostatic and special photographic copy. Deposit accounts are accepted and telephone orders may be placed.

The basic information needed on orders from libraries is the Superintendent of Documents classification number. If this number is not known, furnish as much bibliographic citation as possible, including the source of the citation. Also include a telephone number with the order so that contact can be made in case there are questions.

The normal charge for an electrostatic copy is 15¢ per copy, with a minimum order of $2. Negative microfilm is 10¢ per frame, with a $10 minimum for microfilm orders.

LIBRARY OF CONGRESS

Another source of out-of-print publications is the Exchange and Gift Division of the Library of Congress. This division will accept bids for bound volumes of a number of series.[7] All inquiries should be addressed to the Chief, Exchange and Gift Division, Library of Congress, Washington, D.C. 20540.

The Library of Congress also has a donation collection of surplus books (including government publications) not needed for the LC collection. These are available to publicly supported libraries. The publications are miscellaneous, as they are duplicates or unwanted publications of the federal agencies. There is a high turnover in content, size, and value of materials available. LC does not believe the value of the materials justifies an institution's paying the expenses of a representative to make a special trip to Washington just for the purpose of selecting titles. A representative in the Washington area may be appointed, however, or if a representative is in the Washington area on other business, a visit can be arranged.

The representative should be provided with a letter of introduction and authorization on an official letterhead, addressed to the Chief, Exchange and Gift Division, Library of Congress, Washington, D.C. 20540. Transportation of the selected materials must be arranged by the receiving library. The assistance of your congres-

---

7. See list in *Documents to the People* 3 (March 1975):39–40.

sional representatives in Washington might be sought; many of them may be able to arrange shipping the books to libraries.

UNIVERSAL SERIALS AND BOOK EXCHANGE

Since 1948, Universal Serials & Book Exchange (formerly called United States Book Exchange) has operated a cooperative exchange clearinghouse for publications, including U.S. government publications. USBE is a private, nonprofit, self-supporting corporation, sponsored by library and scholarly organizations in the United States.

Membership is open to libraries of any type, size, and subject interest, provided they can send publications on exchange (or plan to do so in the future) and that they have an interest in acquiring publications from USBE. The philosophy of USBE is that each member provides what it can on a reasonably regular basis and takes from the USBE stock whatever it needs. Lists of U.S. government publications are available on a regular basis as a part of regular membership benefits.

Membership fee is $25 for the fiscal or calendar year. Deposit accounts may be established. USBE provides bimonthly statements. Handling fees ($3.50 for periodical title, $6 for each monograph, and $7 for each government document as of June 1978) cover the cost of receiving, handling, listing, and distributing the publication on a nonprofit basis. The fees have no relation to the value of the publications distributed. Forms are provided by USBE, on which requests can be made.

USBE is an excellent source for filling monographic gaps in the collection as well as for files or single issues of periodicals. Government publications will be accepted by USBE for exchange purposes. If possible, title lists should be sent to USBE for checking in advance. Exchange shipments are sent at the expense of the library.

For information about membership and operating instructions, write to Universal Serials & Book Exchange, Inc., 3335 V Street, N.E., Washington, D.C. 20018.

COMMERCIAL SERVICES

Several dealers handle out-of-print and in-print government publications. For names and addresses, consult the advertisement sections of library periodicals. A task force group of the ALA Government Documents Round Table has compiled a directory of commercial sources.[8] For up-to-date information, write to the task force chairperson.

Reprints of government publications provide opportunities to obtain out-of-print titles. On the other hand, documents librarians should be wary of reprints appearing under a different title or series title. For example, one publisher reprinted *Negroes in the United States* (a Bureau of the Census publication) under a series title, giving the impression of a new work.

8. *Documents to the People* 5 (September 1977):209–12.

Microforms

The trend of federal agencies to cooperate with commercial enterprise in the production and sale of microform products has resulted in an increasing number of government publications that are available in microform.[9] In many instances these forms are by-products of information and data centers, such as Educational Resources Information Center (ERIC). (Technical reports and federal data bases are discussed in another chapter.)

SELECTION

The present depository law permits all depository libraries to substitute micro-facsimile copies of any holdings of U.S. government publications, provided they are properly referenced and can be located readily. The advantages of substitution are primarily concerned with the preservation of materials, conservation of space, and economics. Microforms can save valuable shelf space. Inexpensively, they can provide duplicate copies of heavily used material. Retrospective materials, not available in any other form, can be purchased in microform, and materials which have suffered deterioration of paper, caused by heavy use or age, can be replaced by microform.

The economic advantages often cited (i.e., a saving of shelf space, decreased processing costs, and less expense than hard copy) must be weighed against other considerations (such as the quality of equipment and the economics of providing and maintaining multiple readers). Capability of printing hard copy from micro-form and floor space for microform cabinets are also considerations.

Until recently, the substitution of a depository title in microform might have been influenced by acquisition costs (since depository libraries receive hard copy without charge), but the recent decision of the Government Printing Office to pursue micropublishing presents interesting and challenging choices for the future. Depository libraries may now select some items in either hard copy or microform and will receive a large quantity of nondepository titles in microfiche format.

Not all materials lend themselves to microform. Criteria used by the GPO include whether pages can be torn apart for filming, whether paper and ink are of good quality, and whether plates and foldout material can be filmed.

This program will have tremendous implications for depository libraries in terms of space, weeding, acquisition of duplicate titles, and in bringing formerly non-GPO material within the scope of the GPO distribution program.

An additional category of titles in microfiche is produced by the federal agencies in microfiche format only. There are fifteen to twenty such titles, for example: *Consolidated Master Cross Reference List* (D 7.20:) issued by the Department of Defense, *Reports and Publications* (Y 3.P84/4:) of the Board of Governors of

---

9. The term "microform" is used here to include all types of microreproduction: microfilm, microfiche, microcard, and machine-readable tapes.

the Postal Rate Commission, and *Administrative Law Judge and Commission Decisions* (Y 3.0c1:10-2) of the Occupational Safety and Health Review Commission. These titles are offered to depository libraries only in microfiche format and are for sale to the public in this format.

Libraries which circulate hard-copy government publications will need to consider the limitations of microform unless portable readers are available in quantity. The lack of compatibility in the products of micropublishing has been the chief deterrent to purchasing microforms, because the various forms require different viewing and reproduction equipment.

The large commercial sets, such as *Debates of Congress* and the *Serial Set*, are very costly. If reviews of the microform edition are not found, librarians should consult others who have purchased the titles. Often the reproductions are poor because the original work from which the reproductions were made was less than adequate. Some pitfalls can be avoided with wise advice. If a choice of form is available, the form which is most easy to use in the local situation, the quality of the product, and availability of adequate viewing equipment should govern the choice. *Microform Review* is a useful guide to reviews.

A number of agencies, such as the Library of Congress and the National Archives, offer publications on microform. These are listed in the agency catalogs. Many Department of Commerce publications, including the Census Bureau publications, are available from the National Technical Information Service in microfiche (see the chapter "Technical Reports").

CLASSIFICATION

In an integrated collection, the classification of documents in microform is dependent on the policy of the library; that is, how does the library handle other microforms? In a separate collection, the classification scheme that is used by the unit should prevail, as form of document should not make a difference in classification (with one exception, noted below). If SuDoc classification is used, the depository titles in microform should be given SuDoc numbers and arranged by this number. The shelflist or catalog record should indicate type of form—microfiche, microfilm, or microcard—and location (if the latter is necessary). The exception is the treatment of large sets, such as ERIC or NTIS reports, which arrive with identifying numbers beginning ED or PB, and should be arranged by these numbers. Indexes to these sets are usually adequate for locating these materials. Ease of access should be the determining factor in any classification system for microforms.

SPECIAL HANDLING AND EQUIPMENT

Because of rapidly changing technology in the field, those who are interested in keeping up with the current technology of microforms should attend seminars and workshops on the subject. Some sources for the evaluation of equipment, in addition to company brochures, are *Library Technology Reports* of the American

Library Association and the *ARMA Records Management Quarterly* of the Association of Records Managers and Administrators. The National Micrographics Association is also a source of information on microfilms. Regular maintenance of equipment and forms is just as necessary as their servicing.

Additional References

GENERAL

Brock, Clifton. "The Quiet Crisis in Government Publishing," *College and Research Libraries* 26 (November 1965):477–89.

Buckley, Carper W. Comment on "The Government Printing Office and Non-GPO Publications" by Joe Morehead, *Government Publications Review* 1 (Fall 1973).

————. "Implementation of the Federal Depository Library Act of 1962," *Library Trends* 15 (July 1966):27–36.

California State Library, Government Publications Section. *U.S. Government Publications: Acquisition, Processing and Use.* Proceedings of three workshops: Sacramento, May 12, 1966; Bakersfield, May 17, 1966; Anaheim, May 19, 1966. Sacramento: California State Library, 1967.

Hugerford, Anthos Farah. "U.S. Government Publications Acquisition Procedures for the Small Special Library," *Special Libraries* 65 (January 1974):22–25.

Isacco, Jeanne. "Helpful Hints for Ordering from GPO," *Documents to the People* 3 (January 1975):19.

Jackson, Ellen. *A Manual for the Administration of the Federal Documents Collection in Libraries.* Chicago: American Library Association, 1955.

Morehead, Joe. "The Government Printing Office and Non-GPO Publications," *Government Publications Review* 1 (Fall 1973):1–5.

Paulson, Peter J. "Government Documents and Other Non-Trade Publications," *Library Trends* 18 (January 1970):363–72.

Shaw, Thomas Shuler. "Government Documents: Part I, Problems in Acquisitions," Louisiana Library Association *Bulletin* 30 (Winter 1968):181–84.

Staatz, Evelyn. "Government Documents in a Non-Depository Library," Penn Valley (Pa.) Community College Library *Government Publications Review* 1 (Fall 1973):310–11.

BOOKSTORES

Barrett, William J. "GPO Bookstores," *Documents to the People* 6 (January 1978): 43.

U.S. Superintendent of Documents. *Government Printing Office Bookstores.* Washington, D.C.: Govt. Print. Off., 1968.

DOCUMENTS EXPEDITING PROJECT

Brewster, John W., "To Catch a Government Document: Doc Ex," *Wilson Library Bulletin* 44 (May 1970):941–45.

Chona, Harbans S. "Doc Ex Revisited: Does It Answer the Needs?" *Wilson Library Bulletin* 45 (January 1971):513–15.

MICROFORMS

Mawdsley, Katherine F. "Administration and Organization of Government Documents in Microform," *Documents to the People* 6 (January 1978):28–30.

"Micropublishing," in proceedings of the Federal Documents Regional Workshop, Kansas City, Mo., April 13–14, 1973, *Government Publications Review* 1 (Winter 1973):226–32.

Scott, Peter. "The Present and Future of Government Documents in Microform," *Library Trends* 15 (July 1966):72–86.

5
THE MONTHLY CATALOG

After some 80 years of existence with essentially the same features, the *Monthly Catalog of United States Government Publications* underwent radical change in 1976. Hence a separate chapter is devoted to this publication.

The *Monthly Catalog* is to government publications what the *Cumulative Book Index* is to general book publications. An indispensable source for all who work with government publications, the *Monthly Catalog* has multifaceted functions. Described as the national bibliography of United States government publications,[1] its foremost function is bibliographic control. As a catalog of publications, it is an acquisition tool for current and retrospective purchases. As an index of subjects, it is a major instrument for reference service.

The *Monthly Catalog* is distributed to depository libraries and is available on a subscription basis. The Government Printing Act of 1895 directed the Superintendent of Documents to issue "a catalog of government publications which shall show the documents printed during the preceding month, where obtainable, and the price." The *Monthly Catalog* became the vehicle used by the Superintendent of Documents for announcing government publications printed by the Government Printing Office and offered for sale.

Another function of the *Monthly Catalog* is to catalog and index the publications distributed to depository libraries, although not all depository titles and series are listed (see below). Also listed are non-GPO-printed publications sent by agencies to the Superintendent of Documents for listing in the *Monthly Catalog*.

Over the years the *Monthly Catalog* has had several title variations and some changes in content. From 1895 to June 1907 it was called the *Catalogue of the United States Public Documents*; from July 1907 to December 1939 the title was *The Monthly Catalog, United States Public Documents*; from 1940 to 1950 it was

---

1. LeRoy C. Schwarzkopf, "The Monthly Catalog and Bibliographical Control of U.S. Government Publications," *Drexel Library Quarterly* 10 (January–April 1974):80.

called *United States Government Publications: Monthly Catalog*; and since 1952 it has been known by its present title, *Monthly Catalog of United States Government Publications*. Excellent histories of the content changes are detailed in Boyd[2] and in LeRoy Schwarzkopf's article "Monthly Catalog and Bibliographical Control of U.S. Government Publications."[3] Schwarzkopf's article is an incisive analysis of the *Monthly Catalog* as a bibliographical tool.

The limitations of the former *Monthly Catalog,* and the desire to move toward a standard national bibliographic entry for government publications to improve their access, prompted the Depository Library Council to the Public Printer to recommend to the GPO Library Division an expansion of the cataloging data for entries in the *Monthly Catalog.*

The *Monthly Catalog* and OCLC

The *Monthly Catalog* was issued in a new size (10¼ x 7⅞ ") and "revolutionary" format with the July 1976 issue, reflecting greatly expanded cataloging of government publications. In March 1976 the GPO Library Division began cataloging government publications according to Anglo-American Cataloging Rules (AACR) and the Library of Congress MARC (machine-readable cataloging) format. The GPO joined the Ohio College Library Center (OCLC), a cooperative on-line shared cataloging network.

Monthly Catalog entries are placed in the OCLC data base by the catalogers at GPO, using as authority for subject headings the Library of Congress *Subject Catalog* (8th ed. and supplements). GPO adds LC and Dewey numbers only when numbers are printed in the publication as a result of the CIP (cataloging in publication) program of the Library of Congress. Those government publications cataloged by the Library of Congress with LC classification are entered into the base by the Library of Congress. As with other records, OCLC users may also enter records of government publications, including either LC, Dewey, or Superintendent of Documents classification.

Since the data base includes government publications entered by these several sources, there is a lack of uniform quality in the individual records. Some effort to correct this has been instituted by OCLC, which announced an editing plan to upgrade cataloging data (including government publications) submitted by other libraries. GPO and the Library of Congress are collaborating (to some extent) to avoid duplication in the cataloging of government publications.

Local access to the OCLC data base is through a terminal connected by telephone lines to the large computer facility at OCLC headquarters in Columbus, Ohio. After one learns the basic command language, documents may be called up

---

2. Anne M. Boyd, *United States Government Publications*, 3d ed. rev. by Rae E. Rips (New York: Wilson, 1949), p. 43.

3. *Drexel Library Quarterly* 10 (January–April 1974):79–105.

most simply by LC card number or OCLC number, and it is possible to retrieve by title and main entry (corporate author in the case of government publications, if personal author is not the main entry). Other means of access, by Superintendent of Documents number or by subject, may be forthcoming in the future. The need to access by SuDoc number is keenly felt by documents librarians, but at the moment (1978) the issue is unresolved.

One special feature of the OCLC data base is the capability of producing catalog cards that can be tailored to local needs. This feature can be used to produce shelf-list cards or cards for a public catalog. However, libraries should examine the cost-benefits of card production through this means. For example, is the cost of obtaining cards through OCLC less than the cost of producing cards locally?

The Library of Congress is investigating the feasibility of producing cards for government publications on a sale basis. Because of rapid changes in technology and in administrative decisions, the most recent information on OCLC or other networks that process GPO tapes should be sought from persons in the library who are most directly concerned with the installations. Already in the planning stages, a major change is projected in processing *Monthly Catalog* entries to a GPO in-house operation, rather than through OCLC. The implications of such a move in terms of data base access remain to be seen.

Tapes

The distribution of *Monthly Catalog* tape records in MARC II format began in April 1977, permitting libraries which have access to computer facilities (either locally or through networks) to reorganize the data to serve local or regional needs. Information on the tape-distribution service is available from the Library of Congress, Customer Services Section, Cataloging Distribution Service, Building 159, Navy Yard Annex, Washington, D.C. 20541.

A Selection and Bibliographic Tool

Even with computer access, the printed *Monthly Catalog* endures as the prime selection tool for current government publications since it is the list of new publications in print.[4] The greatly expanded entries should be of assistance in identifying a publication and should aid in the selection process. Entries are listed by Superintendent of Documents classification number order. Indexes include author, title, subject, and series/report index. Semiannual and annual cumulations are available.

---

4. It takes four to six months before a title received on deposit is listed in the printed *Monthly Catalog.*

The hard-copy *Monthly Catalog* also continues to be the primary bibliographic tool for verification and reference because not all libraries have access to an automated data base, and most of the data bases are still limited in terms of sphere of government publications.

Librarians should examine each issue of *Monthly Catalog* as soon as it is received. Those in depository libraries will want to order certain titles not received on deposit, and librarians in nondepository libraries will wish to make a selection of government publications for sale.

The inside cover gives detailed instructions on ordering publications. The printing of *Monthly Catalog* by computer, beginning in January 1974, coupled with other changes in format beginning with the July 1976 issue, have necessitated different symbols than those used for many years in *Monthly Catalog*. The black dot or "bullet," which designates depository items, was temporarily lost in July 1976 when cataloging was converted to MARC format. An outcry from librarians, who relied on the dot for reference purposes, led to its restoration with the April 1977 issue.

Order forms for sales publications distributed by GPO are included in the *Monthly Catalog*. Form 3356 (Book and Pamphlet Order Form [2 parts: original and customer's copy]) and Form 3641 (Deposit Account Order Form [3 parts: original, shipping copy, and customer's copy]) are available from the Superintendent of Documents.

Publications may be purchased in one of two ways:

1. Money order or check, written for the amount of purchase. Minimum mail order charge is $1.
2. Deposit account. A simple way to conduct business with GPO is to establish a deposit account by forwarding to the Superintendent of Documents a minimum of $50 in advance of purchase and maintaining a credit balance. A statement is issued by GPO monthly.

Unless a price is noted, publications distributed by issuing agencies may be obtained without charge from the issuing agency. Use a printed-form post card reproduced by the library (see figure 3 for sample). Although items may be listed with prices in the *Monthly Catalog,* they are often available free upon request to an agency.

Because of the limited editions of many titles listed in the *Monthly Catalog*, librarians are urged to place their orders immediately upon receipt of the catalog each month.

Serials

Beginning in 1977 a serials supplement, *Monthly Catalog of United States Government Publications, Serials Supplement*, was issued. Listed serial titles conform to CONSER (conversion of serials) standards. Before 1977 the February issue of the *Monthly Catalog* carried a list of government periodicals and subscription publications. The GPO defines a serial as any publication sold on a subscription basis or any publication issued three or more times a year.

DOCUMENTS DEPARTMENT
UNIVERSITY OF ILLINOIS LIBRARY AT CHICAGO CIRCLE
BOX 8198, CHICAGO, ILLINOIS 60680

Date _____

May we request the following publication(s) for our documents collection. Please advise us of any charge for the material before sending, and return this card with the publication(s). Thank you.

80-10-45349

Figure 3. Sample of Form Card

GPO Stock Numbers

In 1972 the GPO began the assignment of a 9-digit stock number to all publications printed for sale. These numbers serve as inventory control and should be used in ordering publications. Early in 1975, the 9-digit stock number was changed to 12 digits, allowing 6 digits to designate issuing agency (the first 3 for major agency and the next 3 for subordinate agency), 5 digits for the publication's number, and the 12th digit for checking errors.

The stock number is assigned when a publication is first printed. It remains with a document until the item is exhausted. If the publication is revised, a new number is assigned by the Superintendent of Documents. If it is "reprinted with minor changes," the old number remains.[5]

According to the *Monthly Catalog* entries, S/N numbers are hyphenated, as follows: 027-000-00435-1.

Access to bibliographic data by S/N numbers is possible through the *GPO Sales Publications Reference File* which complements the *Monthly Catalog*.

Excluded from the *Monthly Catalog*

It is important to note what kinds of publications are *not* included in the *Monthly Catalog*. As noted previously, an effort to list as many non-GPO publications as possible is being made. However, the GPO can include only those publications that are sent to them by the agencies. Except for a few technical reports published by agencies and distributed as depository items, the vast number of technical reports is excluded from *Monthly Catalog*.

Under the provisions of the Printing Act of January 12, 1895, administrative and confidential publications are excluded from listing in *Monthly Catalog*.

Categories of publications excluded from listing in *Monthly Catalog* are:

1. Classified publications—those with restricted distribution due to considerations of national security
2. Material considered administrative[6]:
   a. Anything in the nature of orders, memoranda, or specific instructions from one echelon or level of command or supervision to a lower one or between units of a department or agency
   b. Any preliminary report or draft which has not had final approval
   c. Any material concerned with personnel instruction or handling, outlining the policy of any agency to employees, and employee news organs or similar material
   d. Procedure manuals for operations within a department or agency which are of concern only to the employees and not to the public
   e. Letters to offices of agents in the field
   f. Memoranda or instructions to state or local government officials or to persons or firms working under contract with a department or agency
   g. Office directories
   h. Briefs and other such papers relating to cases being ruled upon or adjudged
   i. Reprints of articles from journals intended for internal use
3. Other material[7]:
   a. Army regulations (depository item)

5. U.S. Superintendent of Documents, *Public Documents Stock Numbering System* (1975).
6. U.S. Government Printing Office, *GPO Circular Letter* (September 12, 1973), no. 105.
7. Wellington Lewis to LeRoy Schwarzkopf, December 10, 1974.

    b. Federal specifications (depository item)

    c. Military specifications (depository item)

    d. Reprints of publications which were listed at the time of original printing (depository item)

    e. Congressional bills and resolutions (depository item)

    f. Contract publications not clearly indicating an agency.

The reason given by the Superintendent of Documents for not listing a, b, c, and e (under 3 above) is that adequate separate indexes are available for these series. Indexes to army regulations and other military publications are issued in the pamphlet series D 101.22:310-[nos.] and distributed by Headquarters, Department of the Army, Washington, D.C. In the past, these were not sent to depository libraries, but in 1977 several indexes were distributed, indicating a change in policy.

The annual *Index to Federal Specifications and Standards* (GS 2.8/2:) and its supplements are depository items, as is the *Index of Specifications and Standards* (D 7.14:) of the Department of Defense. There are a number of indexes for congressional bills and resolutions. The *Congressional Record* is one source. Another is the *Digest of General Public Bills and Resolutions* (LC 14.6:), issued in frequent cumulations by the Library of Congress and sent to depository libraries. A commercial index, *Congressional Index*, published by Commerce Clearing House, is a useful index to current bills and resolutions. (See pp. 128–30.)

Librarians should analyze the *Monthly Catalog* in terms of its potential, as well as its limitations, as it undergoes continuous scrutiny and change. (The Superintendent of Documents welcomes comments from librarians.) Projected changes include (1) addition of an authority file of corporate authors, (2) cross-references for the subject and author index, and (3) stock number index. The 1977 annual index includes a cumulated list of corrections, and a cumulation of SuDoc classes.

Looking Ahead

As this is written, it is too early to assess the full impact of the new cataloging data in the *Monthly Catalog*, although some of its features have been questioned. The most serious shortcoming, of which GPO is aware, is related to the inadequacy of LC subject headings for government publications. For these publications, which are so timely in substance, LC subject headings do not reflect the current terminology. To alleviate this situation, GPO plans to introduce additional subject access points, including "see" references.

Current GPO cataloging policies and procedures are reported in a column in *Public Documents Highlights*, issued by the Superintendent of Documents, and it should be read to keep up with new developments in *Monthly Catalog* cataloging entries. Undoubtedly, many of the problem areas of the new *Monthly Catalog* will be resolved in time, as GPO, the Library of Congress, and documents librarians work together in improving the bibliographic control of federal government publications.

As of December 1978, the *Monthly Catalog*, 1976– , became available on line from Lockheed's Dialog Information Retrieval Service. It is to be expected that this primary bibliographic tool for government publications will be accessible from several information systems in the future, making a variety of access points possible.

Additional References

Baldwin, Gil. "GPO Use of OCLC and the *Monthly Catalog*," *Documents to the People* 6 (January 1978):44–48.

Boast, Carol, and Cheryl Nyberg. "The Monthly Catalog, July 1976–August 1977, Observations, Evaluations, Congratulations," *Government Publications Review* 5 (1978):167–76.

6
CATALOGING AND CLASSIFICATION

One of the functions of cataloging and classification is the interpretation of materials for access by users. The magnitude of government publications has been at the crux of the controversy by librarians over cataloging and classification of these materials in libraries.

The literature on whether to catalog and classify government publications is often related to the discussion on arrangement and treatment of them in libraries. The small library that purchases government publications very selectively usually treats them like any other materials and shelves them with other library materials on the same subject. The depository library and other libraries that deal with a large quantity of government publications treat them more diversely, but most do not fully catalog them, presumably because of economic factors. It can be assumed that economic considerations are reflected in the cataloging practices of depository libraries, and this is borne out by the statistics. According to the biennial report of the depository libraries (1971), classification systems were reported as follows[1]:

24	No system
85	Dewey (8.19%)
53	Library of Congress (5.11%)
44	Other systems
570	Superintendent of Documents (54.4%)
240	Combination which includes SuDoc (23.5%)

1. Norman Barbee, "Government Printing Office," *Government Publications Review* 1 (Winter 1973):222–23.

Cataloging Policy

A cataloging policy statement, outlining the extent of cataloging to be provided for government publications, should be written. Some points to consider before writing such a statement are[2]:

1. Availability of funds. If cost is not a factor, a full bibliographic record for most government publications is desirable.
2. Patron use of records. How a patron uses the library, as well as how those servicing government publications use the cataloging record, should be considered. If patrons are able to take advantage of card catalog entries in extending their research, the entries should be as full as possible. Full cataloging data are desirable if special documents librarians are not servicing government publications.
3. Availability of other catalogs. If book catalogs or automated systems augment the cataloging of government publications, a full bibliographic record may not be necessary.
4. Classification system. If the classification system is to be the same as for the general collection, full cataloging is desirable.

Classification

The three schemes of classification generally used for collections of government publications are

1. Dewey Decimal or Library of Congress (subject)
2. Superintendent of Documents (issuing agency)
3. Alphabetical arrangement by issuing body.

The Dewey Decimal or Library of Congress subject classification places government publications with other publications of the same subject in the general library collection. Advantages are that there is only one classification scheme for the library and the Library of Congress cataloging copy can be used for cataloging, classification, and subject headings.

The usual arrangement of a separate government publications collection is by issuing agency, based on the principle of provenance. This principle follows an archival arrangement, rather than one by subject, and gives coherence to a body of literature produced by various agencies. There are advantages in following an

---

2. Adapted from Ruth M. Erlandson, "The Organization of Federal Government Publications in Depository Libraries," in *United States Government Publications* by Ann Morris Boyd, rev. by Rae Elizabeth Rips, 3d ed. (New York: Wilson, 1949), pp. 569–79.

archival arrangement for government publications, rather than purely by subject. The chief advantage is that all publications of an agency, whether they are one-page news releases, small pamphlets, or monographs (e.g., numbered series), are kept together. Series titles are most often requested by patrons by report or series number, and access to publications by report/series number is relatively simple in a separate collection classified by the Superintendent of Documents classification scheme.

Library of Congress Cataloging of Government Publications

There is a natural assumption that the Library of Congress is a depository library and receives and catalogs all government publications, but this is not so. The Library of Congress is not in the federal depository library system but is covered by a separate law. Title 44 of the *U.S. Code* (sections 1718 and 1719) provides for the distribution of federal publications to the Library of Congress for its own use as well as for international exchange. This statutory provision, however, does not assure the Library of Congress of receiving all government publications. Like other libraries, LC has difficulty obtaining government publications printed outside of GPO.

What government publications the Library of Congress retains for its permanent collection is not determined by law but by the library's own policy. The Library of Congress is selective in what government publications are retained and cataloged for its own collection. Schwarzkopf found that of the 16,770 entries in the *Monthly Catalog* in 1973, 20 percent indicated availability of LC printed cards.[3] There are no absolute rules on what materials are kept or cataloged, but Mather reports that LC selects for cataloging those monographs "consisting principally of important factual information concerning the economy, social environment and political life of the United States."[4]

LC normally catalogs congressional publications, a large portion of which constitutes hearings and committee prints. It catalogs final reports of the various censuses, conference proceedings and bibliographies, presidential commissions and committees, treaties, important monographic series such as the Geological Survey's *Professional Papers* and *Bulletins* and the National Bureau of Standards *Special Publications*, and the publications of the General Accounting Office (GAO). Many serials and periodicals are cataloged although they are analyzed only selectively.

Draft reports, preliminary reports, survey reports, and materials which appear later in bound form are not cataloged. Very few separates (nonserial items) are

3. LeRoy C. Schwarzkopf, "The Monthly Catalog and Bibliographic Control of U.S. Government Publications," *Drexel Library Quarterly* 10 (January–April 1974):95.

4. Alma Mather, "Federal Documents and the Library of Congress," *Illinois Libraries* 56 (April 1974):316.

cataloged. Other reports not cataloged include classified material, technical reports, reprints, noncurrent scientific and technical material, and ephemeral material.

Materials usually discarded by the library include administrative internal materials, patents, drawings and specifications, federal military standards and specifications, and summaries of reports.[5]

For the materials which LC catalogs, LC printed card numbers are assigned and reported to the Library Division of the Superintendent of Documents for inclusion in the *Monthly Catalog.*

Among measures to hasten the LC cataloging information process is a cooperative effort between American publishers and the Library of Congress to provide cataloging data in publications, called the Cataloging in Publications Program (CIP). This program is being extended to government publications, with several agencies participating.[6] The CIP, like other LC cataloging, is selective and not all publications of the participating agencies are cataloged.

The radical change in cataloging government publications according to AACR rules, as first reflected in the July 1976 *Monthly Catalog*, has greatly changed access to LC cataloging data. (See the chapter "Monthly Catalog.")

Government publications are cataloged by LC under the same rules that apply for other publications: the *Anglo-American Cataloging Rules* (AACR), adopted in 1967. The most visible change from former rules, as far as government publications is concerned, is the application of the rule affecting personal authors. Under previous rules the main entry for government publications was the corporate entry. Under present AACR rules, the main entry is personal author whenever one is indicated (see figure 4).

Another major change is the adoption of the K (Law) schedule, published in 1969. This schedule caused some changes in the classification of hearings. Before 1969, hearings were classified under available schedules by subject (see figure 5).

The K (Law) schedule provides for the classification of hearings under the broad class "law," grouping them together (see figure 6). This feature has negated the subject arrangement of hearings. In other words, hearings classified by the Library of Congress classification scheme for any given committee before 1969 are classified and shelved by subject. After 1969, the publications of any given committee are grouped together by committee and then by date. The SuDoc classification groups all hearings by issuing agency as discussed in the following section.

Committee prints, which are studies on various aspects of a subject under investigation by a committee, are usually monographic in character and are not included in the K schedule but continue to be classified under the other subject schedules.

5. Alma Mather, "Library of Congress," *Government Publications Review* 1 (Winter 1973): 220–31.

6. Linda I. Perkins, "Cataloging in Publication Program," *Illinois Libraries* 56 (April 1974): 317.

Elam, Noram E
Soil survey of Palo Verde area, California / ₋by Noram E. Elam₎, United States Department of Agriculture, Soil Conservation Service in cooperation with University of California, Agricultural Experiment Station. — ₋Washington₎ : The Service : for sale by the Supt. of Docs., U.S. Govt. Print. Off., 1974.

37 p., ₋12₎ fold. leaves of plates : ill., col. maps ; 28 cm.

Cover title.
Bibliography: p. 35.

1. Soils—California—Palo Verde Valley—Maps.   I. United States.   Soil Conservation Service.   II. California.   Agricultural Experiment Station, Berkeley.   III. Title.

S599.C2E4   631.4′7′79497   74-602707
                                                                                                MARC

Library of Congress   75

McCamman, Dorothy F   1914-
Future directions in Social Security unresolved issues : an interim staff report : prepared for the Special Committee on Aging, United States Senate / ₋ by Dorothy McCammon₎. — Washington : U.S. Govt. Print. Off., 1975.

vii, 32 p. ; 24 cm.

At head of title: 93d Congress, 2d session. Committee print.
Includes bibliographical references.
$0.50

1. Social security—United States.   I. United States.   Congress.   Senate. Special Committee on Aging.   II. Title.

HD7125.M22   368.4′00973   75-601299
                                                                                                MARC

Library of Congress   75

Figure 4. Personal Author as Main Entry

U. S. *Congress. House. Committee on Education and Labor.*

National school lunch programs. Hearings, Ninety-first Congress, first session, on H. R. 515 and H. R. 516 ... January 16 and March 6, 1969. Washington, U. S. Govt. Print. Off., 1969.

iii, 106 p. illus., maps. 24 cm.

1. School children—Food—U. S.   I. Title.

LB3479.U5A47   1969   371.7'16'0973   77–600953
MARC

Library of Congress   69 ₍8₎

U. S. *Congress. House. Committee on Government Operations.*

Consumer problems of the poor: supermarket operations in low-income areas and the Federal response. Hearings before a ₍Special Studies Committee₎ of the Committee on Government operations. House of Representatives, Ninetieth Congress, second session. October 12, November 24 and 25, 1967. Washington, U. S. Govt. Print. Off., 1968.

v, 352 p. illus. 24 cm.

1. Food prices—U. S.   2. Supermarkets—U. S.   3. Poor—U. S. I. Title.

HD9004.A5317   658.87'8'0973   68–61012

Library of Congress   ₍3₎

Figure 5. Hearings Classified by Subject before 1969

United States. Congress. Senate. Committee on Aeronautical and Space Sciences.
 Advanced aeronautical concepts : hearings before the Committee on Aeronautical and Space Sciences, United States Senate. Ninety-third Congress, second session. July 16 and 18, 1974. — Washington : U. S. Govt. Print. Off., 1974.

  vi, 375 p. : ill. ; 24 cm.

  1. Aeronautics—United States.   2. Aeronautical research—United States.   I. Title.

KF26.A3   1974d   629.13   74–603121
                     MARC

Library of Congress   74 ₍4₎

KF	Law of the United States
KF 26	Senate, standing committee
A3	By committee (Cutter assigned from key word, *Aeronautical*)
1974	Initial date of hearings
d	Letter following the date is assigned consecutively to hearings as cataloged by the Library of Congress

Figure 6. K (Law) Schedule

Superintendent of Documents Classification Scheme

The Superintendent of Documents Classification Scheme is based on the principle of provenance (i.e., place of origin). Adelaide R. Hasse is credited with development of the Documents Office Classification Scheme between 1895 and 1903. A grouping of those publications issued by the various units of government by corporate author, rather than by subject, is the basis of the scheme. The organizational status of the issuing agency, therefore, plays a crucial position in the scheme.

Because of the propensity for changes in government organization, critics of the scheme point to the latter as the fundamental weakness. However, the Superintendent of Documents Classification Scheme is an accepted national classification scheme for federal government publications. It is applied to the classification of government publications distributed and sold by the Office of the Superintendent of Documents. Major indexes to government publications, such as the *Monthly Catalog, American Statistics Index*, and the *CIS/Index*, include the SuDoc classification numbers. A large number of separate documents collections is organized by the SuDoc classification scheme.

Over the years, the basic scheme has been expanded and changed to accommodate new agencies and new subunits. (For the benefit of nondepository libraries, the most recent edition of *An Explanation of the Superintendent of Documents Classification System* is reprinted as appendix 2.) Since minor changes are made from time to time, those who plan to use the scheme should write for the latest revision.

Other explanations of the scheme have been issued. John Andriot's *Working with U.S. Government Publications, Preprint No. 1, The Superintendent of Documents Classification Scheme: An Explanation and Current Agency Outline* (McLean, Va.: Documents Index, 1973) includes more detail than the edition issued by the Superintendent of Documents. LeRoy Schwarzkopf has compiled a brief explanation, based on the two compilations mentioned above.[7]

Because of these several explanations, only a brief analysis of some of the features pointed out by Andriot and Schwarzkopf, and not included in the Superintendent of Documents' explanation, will be made.

The two major elements of the typical SuDoc classification number consist of what is called the "class stem": author (issuing agency) plus series symbols, and the book number (individual publication within the series). The notation is alphanumeric, the letters usually denoting a high-level agency, unit, or office and the numerals standing for subordinate units, series, and book numbers (see figure 7).

AUTHOR SYMBOL

Schwarzkopf states that the term "author symbol" is a misnomer because this symbol actually designates the issuing agency, which is usually the author. An

7. LeRoy C. Schwarzkopf, "Superintendent of Documents Classification System" (College Park: University of Maryland, 1974) (mimeo).

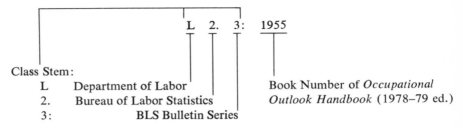

Figure 7. Major Elements of SuDoc Classification Number

example is a committee print prepared by the Library of Congress Congressional Research Service (author) for a congressional committee (issuing agency). In this case the Library of Congress enters the Congressional Research Service, or its subunit, as main entry (author). The Superintendent of Documents, on the other hand, assigns as author symbol the class number of the committee (see figure 8).

Although the agency classification is based on the structural organization of the government at the time a publication is issued, the classification has not always reflected the change. Andriot points this out with examples of the Civil Aeronautics Board, which, formerly under Commerce and now an independent agency, was assigned class number C 31.200: . The Federal Security Agency, which was abolished in 1953, continued the classification FS until late 1969, when the FS was changed to the HE (Health, Education, and Welfare) class. Another example of

77-7507

Y 4.R: 86/2:C 73/2

United States. Library of Congress. Science Policy Research Division.

Information support for the U.S. Senate, a survey of computerized CRS resources and services / prepared for the Subcommittee on Computer Services of the Committee on Rules and Administration, United States Senate by the Science Policy Research Division of the Congressional Research Service. — Washington : U.S. Govt. Print. Off., 1977.

viii, 88 p. : ill ; 24 cm.

At head of title: 95th Congress, 1st session. Committee print.

Issued Jan. 12, 1977.

Includes bibliographical references.

●Item 1046

pbk.

1. United States. Library of Congress. Congressional Research Service. 2. United States. Congress. Senate. 3. Computer input-output equipment. 4. Information storage and retrieval systems. I. United States. Congress. Senate. Committee on Rules and Administration. Subcommittee on Computer Services. II. Title.

OCLC 2810654

Figure 8. Author Symbol

a continued classification number is HH, which was the symbol for the Housing and Home Finance Agency. In 1965 the functions of this agency were transferred to the new Department of Housing and Urban Development (HH).

SERIES SECTION

The second element (based on Andriot) designates a specific series—periodical, continuation, or generic type:

.1   Annual reports
.2   General publications (monographs and publications which do not fall in any other class)
.3   Bulletins
.4   Circulars

Automatic assignment of .1 and .2 to each new agency class, whether such publications were published or not, was a common practice in the early years.

Four additional classes were added in recent years:

.5   Laws administered by the agency
.6   Regulations, rules, and instructions
.7   Press releases
.8   Handbooks, manuals, guides

Other generic types, not assigned a definite number but given a number in sequential order, are addresses (speeches), bibliographies and lists of publications, maps and charts, and posters.

MODIFICATION OF CLASS STEM

As stated earlier, the class stem is derived by combining the designations for authors and those for series published by the authors. Three types of modifications of the class stem (based on Schwarzkopf) are employed to designate the issuing agency at the third and/or fourth level in the organizational hierarchy. Examples of third-level designations are

D   Department of Defense
    D 101.   Department of Army
    D 103.   Corps of Engineers
    D 201.   Department of the Navy
    D 210.   Office of Naval Research
    D 301.   Department of the Air Force
    D 305.   Air Force Academy

In another method, the author symbol is completed in the series number:

L 36.   Department of Labor, Employment Standards Administration
  L 36.100:   Women's Bureau
  L 36.114:   Women workers in [state name]
  L 36.200:   Wage and Hour Division

A third method of designating hierarchy of third- and fourth-level units again completes the author symbol in the series number, with numbers in 1000's used for third-level agencies and 100's for fourth-level subordinate agencies, with the series symbol making up the last two digits (see HE 20.5115, below):

HE   Department of Health, Education, and Welfare
  HE 20.   Public Health Service
  HE 20.3000:   National Institutes of Health
  HE 20.4000:   Food and Drug Administration
  HE 20.5000:   Health Services Administration
  HE 20.5100:   Community Health Services Bureau
  HE 20.5115:   Neighborhood Health Centers, Summary of Projects Data

Andriot comments:
> Whether to subdivide by a group number of 10, 50, 100, or 1000 or expand on a single sequential number is probably decided on a case by case basis. Also, the rule on whether an agency is given its own agency class number or is assigned a sequential number within the parent class is not clear. One finds dozens of units of the Air Force classified within the D 301 number, while on the other extreme is the greatly expanded classification scheme of the Public Health Service under HE 20.[8]

In the beginning, sequential numbers to .4 were usually assigned to series, alphabetically by title, but now any additional series are given the next highest number in order of issuance. But there is one variation to this plan of sequential numbering: similar publications are grouped together by subject. In some cases publications are issued as parts or supplements of a main title:

  C 59.11:   *Survey of Current Business*
  C 59.11/2:   *Weekly Business Statistics* Supplement to the *Survey of Current Business*
  C 59.11/3:   *Business Statistics*, the Biennial Supplement to the *Survey of Current Business*
  C 59.11/4:   Supplement (special) to *Survey of Current Business* (example: *The National Income and Product Accounts of the United States, 1929–74—Statistical Tables*)

8. John L. Andriot, "The Superintendent of Documents Classification Scheme," p. 6.

As an example of group-related publications by subject, Andriot cites:

A 88.11:   *Cotton Quality Crop of* (year)

with some 23 additional titles tied into this basic class:

A 88.11/10:   *Prices of Cotton Cloth and Raw Cotton, and Mill Margins* (monthly)
A 88.11/10–2:   *Mill Margins Report, Cotton Cloth and Yarn Values, Cotton Prices* (annual)
A 88.11/17:   *Cotton Fiber and Processing Test Results* (semimonthly)
A 88.11/17–2:   *Summary of Cotton Fiber and Processing Test Results* (annual)

A new periodical is often assigned a sequential number (e.g., /2) to place the title adjacent to the superseded title:

BNDD Bulletin   J 24.3: (1969–73)
Drug Enforcement   J 24.3/2: (1973–   )
Children   HE 21.9: (1970–71)
Children Today   HE 21.9/2: (1972–73)

But when a structural change in organization occurs, the number is likely to change:

Children Today   HE 1.459: (1974–78). Children's Bureau
Children Today   HE 23.1209: (1978–   ). Children's Bureau is now subordinate to the Office of Human Development Services (HE 23.   ), Administration for Children, Youth and Families (HE 23.1000:   )

BOOK NUMBERS

Separating the symbols for the agency (author) and series designation is the colon (:). The symbols used for the individual publications, or book number (based on Andriot), can be numbers, dates, Cutter numbers, and other combinations:

Nos.	L 2.3:1905	*Handbook of Labor Statistics*
Dates	C 3.134:976	*Statistical Abstract* (1976)
Vols.	C 59.11:57/6	*Survey of Current Business,* vol. 57, no. 6
Cutter	HE 1.2:R88	*Rural Income Maintenance Experiment*

The exception to this rule is the Y 3. class, which usually places the : between the agency and series designated:

Y 3.P81:	Commission on Population Growth and the American Future
Y 3.P81:9	Research reports
Y 3.P81:9/1	*Demographic and Social Aspects*

LOCATING SUDOC NUMBERS FOR NONDEPOSITORY MATERIALS

Locating Superintendent of Documents classification numbers for current non-depository materials received through the Documents Expediting Service or through a mailing list can often present problems, especially for nonserial items. A listing will most probably appear in the *Monthly Catalog*, as Doc Ex sends publications to the Superintendent of Documents for listing. For committee prints, the *CIS/Index* includes a section on new classification numbers. The *Publications Reference File* is also a good tool to use for searching SuDoc numbers.

If a quantity of material is awaiting numbers, publications can be arranged on a special shelf by issuing agency in the order most likely to be listed in the *Monthly Catalog*. If the materials are date-stamped as received, frequent checks for numbers can be made. After a certain interval (one year at the most), numbers should be invented in order to get materials on shelves for use. A year's time provides for receipt of an annual cumulated index to the *Monthly Catalog*, which facilitates searching. Table 1 lists aids to locating SuDoc numbers.

INVENTED NUMBERS

Classification numbers should be invented (made up locally) only as a last resort. But if the choice is between getting materials on the shelves or holding materials for an excessive length of time for want of classification numbers, the former is more prudent. Invented numbers should avoid conflict with possible future assignments by the Superintendent of Documents staff. General publications present small problems since the titles can be assigned the General Publications series designation .2 and then Cuttered by title.

Related materials can be assigned numbers which will place them together on the shelves:

Department of Labor, Manpower Administration
Manpower Research and Development Reports (list of projects) (L 1.39/6:yr)
————. Individual reports (indexed in above)
Invented number: L 1.39/6–30: contract no. (from title page or introduction)

For serials, it is suggested that a copy of the document be sent to the Superintendent of Documents for assignment of a class stem. This procedure will bring uncataloged serials titles (GPO and non-GPO) to the attention of the Superintendent of Documents for entry in the *Monthly Catalog*.

TABLE 1 **AIDS TO LOCATING SuDoc CLASSIFICATION NUMBERS**

1789–1909	*Checklist of United States Public Documents, 1789–1909.* 3d ed. rev. and enl. 1911 (Reprint: New York: Kraus Reprint Corp., 1962).
1789–1975	*Checklist of U.S. Public Documents, 1789–1975.* Washington, D.C.: U.S. Historical Documents Institute, Inc., 1975.
1895–1924	*Monthly Catalog of Government Publications with Superintendent of Documents Classification Numbers Added, 1895–1924.* (The "Classes Added" Set) Arlington, Va.: Carrollton Press, 1975.
1924–	*Monthly Catalog of United States Government Publications.* Washington, D.C.: Govt. Print. Off. (SuDoc numbers not listed before July 1924).
1910–1924	*Documents Office Classification Numbers for Cuttered Documents, 1910–1924.* Compiled by Mary Elizabeth Poole and Ella Frances Smith. Ann Arbor, Mich.: University Microfilms, Inc., 1960.
Early to 1976	*Documents Office Classification.* Compiled by Mary Elizabeth Poole. 5th ed. Washington, D.C.: U.S. Historical Documents Institute, Inc., 1977.
1970–	For Congressional publications: *Congressional Information Service/Index (CIS/Index) to Publications of the United States Congress.* Washington, D.C.: Congressional Information Service.
1974 annual and retrospective	For statistical data: *American Statistics Index.* Washington, D.C.: Congressional Information Service.
1977–	*GPO Sales Publications Reference File.* Superintendent of Documents, 1977– .
Current and retrospective	*Price Lists* (discontinued 1974); *Subject Bibliographies*; departmental and agency catalogs.
Current	"New Classification Numbers" in *Monthly Catalog* each month; annual cumulation.
Current	*Guide to U.S. Government Publications.* Ed. by John L. Andriot. McLean, Va.: Documents Index.

For annotations, see "Selected Indexes, Catalogs . . . ," chapter 8.

AUTHORITY FILE FOR INVENTED CLASSES

It is helpful to maintain an authority file of invented classes. A title entry to publications for which numbers were invented is also useful, since there is no printed access to these materials. The shelflist card should also be identified with a notation (inv. no.) in case a true SuDoc number surfaces at a later date, and corrections can be made if necessary.

CUTTER NUMBERS

The catalogers at the Superintendent of Documents use the two-figure Cutter table. In case a place is not provided in this table, a third number can be added. Because the third place seldom appears in the SuDoc system, using a three-place number from the (three) Cutter Table for invented numbers is one way to distinguish these numbers. Using this table will further distinguish invented numbers from SuDoc numbers, even if a three-place number is assigned by SuDoc, as it sometimes does for proper names:

> Board of Governors of the Federal Reserve System
>   *Empirical Literature on the U.S. Balance of Trade.* 1966. (Staff Economic
>   Studies 35) FR 1.2:T763
>   *What Truth in Lending Means to You.* 1972. FR 1.2:T874

CHANGES IN CLASSIFICATION

A major weakness of the SuDoc system is the continued reorganization of government agencies and the attendant necessary notation changes. An example of organizational change affecting classification numbers is the Office of Civil Defense or the Defense Civil Preparedness Agency. The Office of Civil Defense has been classified under various presidential numbers: Pr 33.801:, Pr 33.1001:, Pr 34.201:, Pr 34.701:, and Pr Ex 4.; and under the Defense Department numbers D 13., D 119., and D 14.; and under its own independent number FCD 1.

The literature is filled with controversy on how best to handle these changes. Some librarians advocate reclassifying to reflect current organization; others would maintain the status quo. Reclassification should be approached with reservation, as the usefulness of indexes which include the original name of an agency, together with the original SuDoc number, will be diminished.

Documents collections are generally not browsing collections. Use of special notes, such as "for later number, see" and "for earlier number, see" on the publications and in the shelflist record serves the purpose, rather than constantly changing notations and records.

Exceptions could be made for periodical titles which often serve a browsing function and should be brought together on the shelves. *Aging*, a periodical issued by the HEW Administration on Aging, is a case in point:

FS 1.12:	June 1951–Jan. 1963
FS 14.9:	Feb. 1963–Sept. 1965
FS 15.10:	Oct. 1965–Aug. 1967
FS 17.309:	Sept. 1967–Dec. 1969
HE 17.309:	Jan. 1970–May 1973
HE 1.210:	June 1973–Dec. 1977
HE 23.3110:	Jan. 1978–

Locator blocks (or "dummy blocks," as they are sometimes called) or some other form of signage might be used in the stacks to refer patrons to the location of other issues of periodicals when the classification numbers change.

NEW CLASSIFICATION NUMBERS

The *Monthly Catalog* has included a list of new classification numbers since 1942, with a cumulation in the December issue. From 1977 the separate *Annual Cumulative Index* has included a cumulation of the new classification numbers for the year. Andriot's *Guide to U.S. Government Publications* also includes new classification numbers. Until Mary Elizabeth Poole published her first edition of *Documents Office Classification* in 1950, there was no comprehensive compilation for locating class numbers. This is an indispensable tool.

Because an increasing number of printed indexes and catalogs of government publications include the SuDoc notation, the use of this classification system for a separate government documents collection is an attractive choice. For the depository library there are several additional incentives for using this system. The *Daily Depository Shipping List* carries the SuDoc number for each title. Item cards also include numbers for each class. Transferring this notation to the document itself is a routine task which can be performed by nonprofessional staff. The Library of Congress includes SuDoc numbers on the printed cards whenever this information is available at time of printing. Printing the SuDoc number in publications (cataloging in publication) is also urged by documents librarians. Publications of the Environmental Protection Agency and some publications of the Department of Health, Education, and Welfare have appeared with SuDoc numbers printed in the publications.

Alphabetical Arrangement by Issuing Agency

For a very small collection, documents might be shelved by issuing office and title, without actual classification. Serials can be shelved without classification by title, then arranged chronologically or numerically. For nonserial-type materials, however, shelving without classification can present problems.

First, the several layers of government require time-consuming decisions as to which agency or subunit is to be the corporate entry. Here are examples of title pages which show several subunits:

> U.S. Department of Health, Education, and Welfare
>   Public Health Service   National Institutes of Health
>   Bureau of Health Manpower Education
>   Division of Nursing
>
> *Research on nurse staffing in hospitals.*
>   *Report of the Conference, May 1972.*
>   (HE 20.3102:N93/27)

> U.S. Department of Commerce
>   Domestic and International Business Administration
>   Bureau of East/West Trade
>   Office of the Joint Commission Secretariat
>   *American-Polish trade accords, 1972–73.*
>   (C 57.402:Po75/972–73)

Second, some sort of marking system should be devised for guidance in shelving and retrieving the document.

Third, frequent changes in the organizational structure of the government and in the functions among the many departments and offices add to the confusion of identifying an issuing agency.

Lastly, shelving and retrieving materials with notations takes considerably less time than interpreting textual material.

VERTICAL FILES

Among the government publications often organized without classification are those which fall into the category of ephemeral material—single pages, leaflets, and pamphlets. These are usually organized in vertical files in small, nondepository libraries. Because of the lack of access points, vertical files should be kept to a minimum.

Depository libraries must adhere to new rules regarding vertical file materials, requiring records and SuDoc classification. (See appendix 3, "Instructions to Depository Libraries.")

Other Arrangements

COMBINATION

In a library where some government publications are cataloged and integrated into the regular collection and some are maintained separately, the use of two classification systems is not uncommon. In many libraries, reference-type titles are cataloged in LC or Dewey classification and sent to the reference department. Duplicate titles, held in the documents collection, are treated like other government publications in the separate collection. (A discussion of the organization of a partially integrated collection appears in the chapter "Organization and Arrangement.")

SINGLE CLASSIFICATION SYSTEM

Since many separate collections of government publications include those of other governmental bodies (other than United States government publications), the idea of unifying the entire collection—federal, state, municipal, foreign and international (or any combination)—under one or two classification systems is intellectually appealing. Indeed, several classification systems have been reported in the literature.

Swank devised a system for state, county, and municipal documents, based on issuing agency.[9] He assigned consecutive numbers to each state and county, a device which presents problems in the accommodation of new states and counties.

Mina Pease's "Plain J" Classification system is a modification of the Library of Congress "J" class, expanded to accommodate publications of local government bodies and international governmental organizations.[10] These plans have not been adopted widely.

AUTOMATED SYSTEMS

The introduction of automation to the production of indexes and catalogs presents alternatives to the traditional card catalog. Book catalogs and indexes for government publications are increasing in number and are often by-products of machine-readable data files which can be accessed by a terminal or through a printed source. The *Monthly Catalog* and its access by a processing center, the Ohio College Library Center, was discussed in an earlier chapter.

A Canadian system, which is generating some interest in the United States, is the CODOC (Cooperative Government Documents) system. This is the system originated by the McLaughlin Library, University of Guelph, Ontario, and further developed for general use by the Office of the Library Coordination, Council of Ontario Universities. CODOC is a computer-based programming and retrieval system that is based on country and issuing agency as the basis for organization. Processing, bibliographic control, and access to government publications are provided through eight printed or COM lists: shelf, title, corporate author, corporate author index, personal author, series, serials, and a KWOC (Key-Word-Out-of-Context based on the title) index. Written in standard COBOL language, the CODOC program is available through a leasing arrangement. Further information

9. Raynard Swank, "A Classification for State, County, and Municipal Documents," *Special Libraries* 35 (April 1944):116–20.

10. Mina Pease, "'The Plain J': A Documents Classification System," *Library Resources and Technical Services* 16 (Summer 1972):315–25.

is available from the Council of Ontario Universities, Suite 8039, 130 St. George Street, Toronto, Ontario, Canada M58 2T4.[11]

This very brief mention of CODOC does not do justice to the technical capabilities and advantages of this system. It is mentioned only to recognize its existence—and that of other automated systems—in the bibliographic control of government publications. Those who are interested are urged to read the literature.

PRINTED INDEXES

Because government publications rarely are fully cataloged in any library, the use of printed indexes and catalogs is essential. The number of specialized indexes to government publications has increased rapidly in recent years, significantly closing the large gap in bibliographic control reported in the literature of earlier years. The limitations, as well as the strengths, of each index must be fully understood in order to exploit the potential of these sources. Chapter 8 lists and annotates selected indexes and catalogs to government publications.

Additional References

Campbell, Grace A. "Study of the Extent to Which Existing Printed Government Indexes and Catalogues Can Replace the Card Catalogue in Making the Contents of Federal Documents Available," *Library Bulletin* no. 7, vol. 36 (November 1939) (Stillwater, Oklahoma A and M College).

"Classification Abstracts," *Documents to the People* 3 (May 1975):36.

Feinberg, Hilda. *Title Derivative Indexing Techniques: A Comparative Study.* Metuchen, N.J.: Scarecrow Press, 1973.

Knowles, Carolyn M. "The Documentation Centre of the University of Guelph Library (Its Functions and Position with the Library Organization)," *Government Publications Review* 1 (Spring 1974):241–50.

Lyle, Jack W. "Utilizing the Superintendent of Documents System without Reclassification," *Library Resources and Technical Services* 16 (Fall 1972):497–99.

———. "Reply to R. M. Simmons," *Library Resources and Technical Services* 16 (Spring 1971):95–97.

Presser, Carolynne. "CODOC: A Computer-Based Processing and Retrieval System for Government Documents." *College and Research Libraries* 39 (March 1978):94–98.

Schwarzkopf, LeRoy. "Comments on 'Handling Changes in Superintendent of Documents Classification' by R. M. Simmons," *Library Resources and Technical Services* 16 (Winter 1972):95–97.

———. "The Monthly Catalog and Bibliographic Control of U.S. Government Publications," *Drexel Library Quarterly* 10 (January–April 1974):79–105.

Simmons, R. M. "Handling Changes in Superintendent of Documents Classification," *Library Resources and Technical Services* 15 (Fall 1971):241–44.

11. "COU Develops CODOC," *Government Publications Review* 3 (1976):347–48.

7

TECHNICAL REPORTS, MACHINE-READABLE DATA BASES, AND INFORMATION SERVICES

Federal funding of research is resulting in an ever-increasing volume of technical report literature in a wide array of fields of knowledge. The only solution in dealing with the sheer size of this output is to apply computer technology to the bibliographical control of this material. There is a proliferation of data bases,[1] and on-line searching is becoming more accessible to the public through all types of libraries. As a result, patrons are requesting the documents cited in these searches. A librarian must identify who produced the report, where it is indexed, and how to locate or purchase a copy. Since the production, acquisition, and servicing of these publications differ from other government publications, an understanding of technical report literature is important to facilitate document delivery to patrons.

Technical Reports

Within the world of government publications, but deserving a separate chapter because of its importance, is a large body of literature known as technical reports. These reports have assumed increasing importance as access to the report literature is greatly facilitated through use of computers. Historically, technical reports evolved as a result of massive government support of research and development in science and technology prior to and immediately following World War II, altering traditional ways of reporting results of research. The technical report in part replaced the journal article as a means of communication between scientists, chiefly because of the versatility of the technical report form. The technical report can be

---

1. Very simply stated, a data base contains bibliographic or other data in machine-readable form and can be comprised of one or several data files. A data file is a set of records with similar characteristics.

produced quickly; it can be classified, if necessary, to be read by authorized personnel only. Many research reports during World War II were classified for security reasons. As these reports were declassified and the results of research made available to the public, numerous agencies outside of GPO assumed responsibility for the control, announcement, and distribution of reports.

In the context of scientific reporting, a technical report is defined as "work done on a research project, which a scientist compiled to convey information to his employers and also to other scientists working in the same or related field."[2] Since World War II, government sponsorship of research, or contract research, has permeated areas other than science and technology. Therefore, in a larger context, a technical report can be defined as "a detailed account of the work done on a research project, designed to relay information to a parent corporation and to others working in the same or related field."[3]

Technical reports may be final reports of completed investigations or progress reports issued at certain intervals. The research may typically be conducted under government contract by an individual or by a team of researchers in private industry, universities, or government research units. Reports resulting from these research efforts are channeled to a variety of information centers.

The volume of research reports published each year is of staggering proportions. One information center, the National Technical Information Service, adds some 60,000 reports annually to a data base of over 800,000 reports. The importance of report literature can be measured by the increasing demand for these reports, stimulated by computer-based information services. No library can afford to acquire the total output; on the other hand, no library can afford to acquire none. Librarians should become thoroughly familiar with the idiosyncrasies of report literature, its availability and control.

This chapter emphasizes government-sponsored reports which are not printed and distributed by the Government Printing Office, although many of the indexes to this report literature are printed by GPO. The *Monthly Catalog* lists a few series of technical reports printed by the GPO (examples are the National Bureau of Standards *Technical Notes* and the Bureau of Mines *Report of Investigations*), but these are depository items. Some technical reports, formerly available only from the National Technical Information Service, are now distributed to depository libraries and are listed in the *Monthly Catalog*. This action was the result of the Comptroller General's decision of June 27, 1975, which emphasized that NTIS publications "issued primarily for the general benefit of the public" may be distributed free to depository libraries.[4] (See pp. 96–98 for a discussion of the NTIS *Government Reports Announcements & Index*, which indexes and abstracts technical reports, and tells the public how to purchase reports.)

2. Bernard Houghton, *Technical Information Sources; A Guide to Patents Standards and Technical Reports Literature* (Hamden, Conn.: Archon Books, 1967), p. 78.

3. Hanna Agonis, "Technical Research Reports in Government Publications and External Literature" (master's thesis; New Haven: Southern Connecticut State College, 1970), p. 1.

4. *Documents to the People* 4 (May 1976):33.

Microforms, report literature, machine-readable data bases, and computerized information services interweave inextricably. Therefore, a discussion of machine-readable data bases and computer-based information systems is included in this chapter. (Microforms as a substitute for government publications in paper copy are discussed in chapter 4.)

BIBLIOGRAPHIC CONTROL

Computerized data bases (discussed later) are an important source for identifying technical reports. For those who have access to machine-readable files, any of a variety of terms (author, title, accession numbers, etc.) will call up a bibliographic citation immediately. Computer-based literature searches place increasing demands on librarians to locate the documents cited. As a natural extension of services provided by librarians, document delivery of technical report literature should present few problems if librarians become familiar with the availability and acquisition processes related to the literature cited in a computer-based literature search.

For those who must rely on conventional manual methods of access, special problems surface. Because of their volume and format, technical reports are not listed in the usual book-trade publications which deal primarily with monographs. Nor are they included in the major subject indexes and abstracts, concerned primarily with periodical literature. The approach, then, is to consult specialized indexes that have been compiled to bring some control over this literature. Over the years, variations in the abstracting and indexing of technical reports have occurred. Some of the abstracts have been consistently indexed from their beginnings; others have changed over the years in content and scope. To fill gaps in the approaches to technical report literature, nongovernmental groups have issued specialized and retrospective indexes to be used in conjunction with government-sponsored indexes.[5] As an aid in identifying some abstracts and indexes to technical reports, a chronological guide appears on pages 100–5.

AVAILABILITY

Libraries may purchase technical reports in several formats from various information centers. Reports can be purchased in paper copy or in microform (microfiche, microfilm, or microprint). Other formats include magnetic tapes and punched cards. Many libraries purchase individual reports on demand; others purchase reports on a standing order basis for a class, or reports by subject or for the total collection. Standing orders may be placed for reports on a topic or a selected group of topics. This service assures automatic receipt of publications as they are published and at less cost per report (for microfiche) than purchasing individual

5. Nancy G. Boylan, "Identifying Technical Reports through U.S. Government Research Reports and Its Published Indexes," *College & Research Libraries* 28 (May 1967):175–76.

reports. Most distributors of technical reports welcome the establishment of deposit accounts, facilitating the ordering process. Pre-addressed order forms are available from some sources.

Interlibrary loan channels should not be overlooked as a way of borrowing technical reports. Knowledge of the holdings of technical reports in libraries in the local area (public, academic, state, systems libraries, school, federal, and special) and in the state will provide access to reports through interlibrary loan. Visiting libraries in the area, attending meetings of local library groups, and interacting with documents librarians are some ways to gain this knowledge. An increasing number of libraries are purchasing all categories of reports, or reports on selected topics, and will lend them to other libraries. Obtaining materials this way is often faster than ordering them from the distributor.

TREATMENT

Libraries which acquire only a few reports in hard copy can treat them as individual monographs, integrating them into the total collection of the library. The paper-copy technical reports which are produced from microfiche are often of poor paper quality and may require binding. Because of the highly specialized nature of some of the reports, it is not uncommon for libraries to give the reports to the patron rather than spend time and money in processing them. The likelihood of another patron's requesting the same report is minimal. Many libraries cannot be so generous, however, and some means of storing and possibly retrieving the reports must be devised. If paper-copy technical reports are maintained in a separate collection, they can simply be recorded and shelved by accession number: AD xxx xxx, ATI xxxxx, PB xxx xxx, TT xx-xxxxx, and so on. "Accession numbers" are assigned to the documents as they are received, and have no bearing on subject matter. A public catalog of the holdings by author, title and subject may promote access. Whether the time and effort that is necessary for this process is worthwhile must be determined by local circumstances.

TYPICAL ACCESSION NUMBERS
AD: Accession number for Armed Services Technical Information Agency (ASTIA) documents. ASTIA is a predecessor of the present Defense Documentation Center (DDC). In January 1975, a prefix *A* was added to the AD numbers (i.e., AD-A000 001) to begin a new 6-digit series.
ATI: An early ASTIA accession number, used between 1947 and 1953 for the *Air Technical Information/Index*. With some exceptions, ATI documents are held and distributed by DDC.
ED: Accession number applied to reports entered into ERIC, the Educational Resources Information Center.
EJ: Accession number for periodical articles listed in *Current Index to Journals in Education* (*CIJE*).

PB: Accession number applied to documents issued by the Publications Board, the first of a succession of agencies which led to the present National Technical Information Service. The PB designation continues to be used for documents accessioned, indexed, and distributed by NTIS. Because PB numbers (PB xxx xxx) were also applied to some documents which already carried the DDC accession number, AD xxx xxx, the use of correlation indexes is helpful. See table 2.

TT: Technical Translations, TT–yr–xxxxx.

ACRONYMS AND CODES

The profuse use of acronyms for technical reports adds to the difficulties of identifying reports. The following publications may help.

U.S. Department of Defense, Institute for Defense Analysis. *How to Get It—A Guide to Defense-related Documents.* October 1973. Available from NTIS. AD 769 220. Prepared by the Committee on Information Hangups and "intended for all who have to identify or acquire government published or sponsored documents of interest to the defense community." Entries by document acronym, series designation, or short title. A very handy compilation.

U.S. Defense Documentation Center. *Government Acronyms and Alphabetic Organizational Designations Used in DDC.* August 1977. Available from NTIS. AD–A044 000.

For a guide to the codes used by the former Atomic Energy Commission, now the Department of Energy, see

U.S. Atomic Energy Commission. Technical Information Center. *Report Number Codes Used by the USAEC Technical Information Center in Cataloging Reports.* December 1974. Available from NTIS. TID–85–R11. Frequently revised.

Machine-Readable Data Bases and Information Services

The major conclusion of the report of the President's Science Advisory Committee (published in 1963) had a profound influence on the bibliographic control and availability of information generated under government contract:

Transfer of information is an inseparable part of research and development—individual scientists and engineers, industrial and academic research establishments, technical societies, Government agencies—must accept responsibility for the transfer of information in the same degree and spirit that they accept responsibility for research and development itself.[6]

For many years this concern of government for technical communication encouraged the financial support and development of computerized information systems by many federal agencies. Although the federal government was responsible for the generation and processing of large data bases, the trend now is a balancing of federal with private-sector interests. Not only state government but the commercial sector is increasingly assuming the data processing and distribution functions.[7]

Information systems vary widely in their missions; some serve a specific technical community, others a larger community of users. Not all are equipped to serve a clientele outside the sponsoring agency, but most of them give service to the general public, to other federal agencies, and to state and local governments. Most centers not only collect data but also analyze, evaluate, condense, and synthesize them. This information is then stored and selected portions can be retrieved by computer.

In addition to literature searches, information centers may prepare custom computer-generated bibliographies or provide consulting services. Many of the data bases now available have resulted from the application of computer technology to produce hard-copy indexes and abstracts. In general terms, data bases are marketed as information services, information systems, technical information services, data services, information centers, or information analysis centers. The name of a group does not always indicate the nature of services or products available.

Some data services provide citations to current literature as it is published and make lists available to users periodically. Users who file a profile of interest areas will be notified of new material entered into the system, referred to as the Selective Dissemination of Information (SDI) service. SDI service is usually available on a subscription basis. Custom bibliographies can be requested from most data services.

Literature searches and information retrieval services are available to users upon request. Users must define the data required, geographical areas of concern, desired format and must fully describe the problem for which the data are required. Responses can be meaningful only when the user understands what is available and when the data center understands user needs. Organizations which provide computerized searches of data bases will define the population served and method of inquiry (mail, telephone, or walk-in). The services provided by a data center should be confirmed before a user request is initiated. This may be achieved most satisfactorily through a personal contact with the information center's personnel. The same criteria for selecting hard-copy indexes and abstracts apply to the selection of data bases: content, scope, searching features, format, update schedule, and cost.

6. U.S. President's Science Advisory Committee, *Science, Government and Information: The Responsibilities of the Technical Community and the Government in the Transfer of Information* (Washington, D.C.: Govt. Print. Off., 1963), p. 1.

7. Martha E. Williams, "Criteria for Evaluation and Selection of Data Base Services," *Special Libraries* 66 (December 1975):562.

DATA BASES

Data bases are now available in a variety of subject areas: applied and pure sciences, social sciences, business, law, and others. Essentially, there are two kinds of data bases: nonbibliographic or "primary" and bibliographic or "secondary," with the former referring to original research and the latter to indexes and works providing controls to the literature generated by the original research. The nonbibliographic data bases are best illustrated by Census-type data. Librarians are most familiar with the second type of data base, the bibliographic, as exemplified by the Library of Congress MARC (machine-readable cataloging) tapes.[8]

Single-point access to several data bases is increasingly available from government and commercial search services. Among the commercial vendors providing on-line access to federal data files are Lockheed Missiles and Space Company's Dialog Information Retrieval Service (3251 Hanover Street, Palo Alto, Calif. 94304), which includes several federal data files: NTIS (National Technical Information Service), ERIC (Educational Resources Information Center), MGA (Meteorological and Geoastrophysical Abstracts), and NAL/CAIN (National Agricultural Library). Systems Development Corporation's SDC Search Service (2500 Colorado Avenue, Santa Monica, Calif. 90406) has CAIN, ERIC, IDC/LIBCON (Library of Congress Cataloging from Information Dynamics Corp.), NTIS, and SSIE (Smithsonian Science Information Exchange). These two services also include two government information data bases: the CIS (Congressional Information Service) and ASI (American Statistics Index). The file of federal data bases of the Bibliographic Retrieval Services (Corporation Park, Building 702, Scotia, N.Y. 12302), has CAIN, ERIC, MEDLARS (Medical Literature Analysis and Retrieval System of the National Library of Medicine), NTIS, and National Agricultural Library Serials File. Since these services are likely to add and subtract files at any time, the most recent information about their services should be sought. As this book goes to press, Lockheed has announced the addition of the GPO *Monthly Catalog* data base to its Dialog Information Retrieval Service.

Government agencies are also providing "one stop" information retrieval services. An example is the Oceanic and Atmospheric Scientific Information System (OASIS), which provides access to atmospheric, marine, and solid earth bibliographic information files.

ON-LINE SEARCHES

A data base with on-line capability can be queried by a terminal located in the library. This kind of interaction produces a citation for immediate viewing on a cathode-ray tube (CRT), a Teletype, or other receiving equipment. An interactive system gives opportunity for interaction between the requester and the data base being searched. The services of a skilled operator who can identify the most specific

---

8. Vivian S. Sessions, "Primary and Secondary Data Base Professionals: Time for Rapprochement?" *Public Data Use* 3 (January 1975):1–3.

and pertinent descriptors (subject headings) related to the search question will keep costs to a minimum. If a printing capability is installed, a printout of the citations is possible immediately. If not, printouts of searches may be requested off-line, to be mailed at a later date. In many instances, orders for future delivery of the full text of the cited reference in paper copy or microform (usually microfiche) can be placed with the data facility.

BATCH MODE SEARCH

For data bases which do not have the capability of on-line searches, a batch method is possible. In this method, search requests are "batched" and run at one time. Printouts of the results are received at stated intervals. This method does not allow for interaction with the data base at the time a request is made for a search. Consequently, the request should be as specific as possible.

RETROSPECTIVE SEARCHES

A search request for past files may be made if the information is not immediately required. The turn-around time, or the elapsed time between submission of a request and reply, could vary with the nature of the request and the method of distribution of the reply.

COSTS PER SEARCH

Costs per search vary widely, from no cost to a specified fee. Cost of services is determined by type of search requested and number of data files to be searched. A simple search may be as low as $5, while an average search may cost around $50. Elements in the cost figures usually include the following:

1. Cost of data base times the number of minutes of connect time (range: $25–$150 per hour)
2. Cost of the communication network (range $10–$11 per hour)
3. Cost of citations printed (on-line or off-line) (range: 4¢–50¢ per citation)[9]

Costs to the institution providing services will include the lease or purchase of a terminal, salaries for qualified personnel, rental of space, and connect time.

IDENTIFYING DATA FILES

The identification of data files and data products for purchase has been a problem for librarians. Three directories which will assist are

9. Information from Professor Martha E. Williams, director, Information Retrieval Research Laboratory, University of Illinois at Urbana-Champaign.

Sessions, Vivian, ed. *Directory of Data Bases in the Social and Behavioral Sciences* (New York: Science Associates/International, 1974). Includes entries for data files produced by federal agencies.

U.S. National Technical Information Service. *Directory of Computerized Data Files, Software & Related Technical Reports* (1978). Available from NTIS: SR 78/03, $50. This is the third such compilation.

Williams, Martha E., and Sandra H. Rouse. *Computer Readable Bibliographic Data Bases—A Directory and Data Sourcebook* (Washington, D.C.: American Society for Information Science, 1976).

Another problem is to determine which systems and services provide access to data bases. An attempt to centralize this information through mechanized means is being made by the National Bureau of Standards, Systems and Software Division, and its first catalog has been issued:

U.S. Department of Commerce, National Bureau of Standards, *A Mechanized Information Services Catalog,* NBS Technical Note 814 (Washington, D.C.: Govt. Print. Off., 1974).

The products of an increasing number of federal data bases are being managed by commercial firms which contract to manufacture such products, reproducing documents in paper copy or microfiche. These firms usually handle all sales of the products. The ERIC data products are available from a commercial source—an example of cooperative efforts between government and commercial interests.

Commercial packages, time-sharing facilities, and inexpensive nationwide communications networks and local and regional library networks place computer-based information within the reach of most libraries. Thus librarians must be alert to the growing number of machine-readable files and data-based information centers and seek ways to extend reference service through automated means to supplement manual searches.

Gaining some knowledge of what computers can do and becoming familiar with the vocabulary will be useful prior to investigating a data base. Library schools offer seminars and workshops on information retrieval. Many provide opportunity for "hands on" experience at a terminal.

In the space allotted, only a few selected information centers which should be familiar to all librarians can be described, namely, the Defense Documentation Center, Department of Energy, Educational Resources Information Center, Joint Publications Research Service, National Aeronautics and Space Administration, National Technical Information Service, American Statistics Index, and the Congressional Information Service. Detailed information is available from each source.

Defense Documentation Center

Technical reports produced by U.S. military organizations and their contractors are handled by the Defense Documentation Center (DDC), an activity of the Department of Defense, Defense Supply Agency. DDC is an outgrowth of several organizational changes:

1941   Office of Scientific Research and Development (OSRD)
1945   Air Documents Division, Army Air Force, Air Materiel Command Intelligence Department
1947   The Air Force and Navy combined and formed Central Air Documents Office (CADO)
1950   Army joined CADO
1951   Armed Services Technical Information Agency (ASTIA) established to serve all three military departments (merged CADO and Navy Research Section in the Library of Congress operated by the Office of Naval Research)
1963   Name changed to Defense Documentation Center and operational control transferred from Air Force to Defense Supply Agency, Department of Defense

Defense facilities and their contractors are required to submit to DDC copies of each report which record scientific and technical results of research. After screening, they are assigned an AD (accession document) number and processed.

REGISTRATION WITH DDC

Federal government agencies and their contractors, subcontractors, and grantees who are conducting defense-related government-sponsored research are eligible to register for services provided by DDC, the National Security Agency Reference Center for Scientific and Technical Information (NSAREF), and the Department of Defense Information Analysis Centers (IAC's). Libraries (through faculty or staff members who are grantees) may take advantage of these services by registering with DDC. Research and development organizations that do not have current contracts may be declared eligible by a military service under the Defense Potential Contractor's Program. The DDC manual, *Registration for Department of Defense Scientific and Technical Information Services* (DSAM 4185.3), outlines procedures for registering and has a set of registration forms.

INDEXES

Classified and unclassified reports of limited distribution are announced in DDC *Technical Abstract Bulletin* and *TAB Index*. Unclassified materials that have no distribution limitation are announced in the NTIS *Government Reports Announcements & Index*.

AVAILABILITY OF PUBLICATIONS

Organizations that are registered for DDC services may request copies of the classified technical reports in either full-size hard copy or microfiche. There is a service charge for all reports. DDC has contracted with NTIS for the reproduction of reports; therefore DDC users with NTIS deposit accounts can reduce response time in filling requests.

Order forms are available from the Defense Documentation Center, Cameron Station, Alexandria, Va. 22314. Unclassified reports are available from NTIS. Each DDC request must include the user code and Department of Defense contract number. The NTIS order forms have spaces for this information. The accession series prefix, identifying documents distributed by DDC and its predecessors, is AD xxx xxx.

An early ASTIA accession prefix, used between 1947 and 1953 for the *Air Technical Information/Index,* was ATI xxxxx. With some exceptions, ATI documents are held and distributed by DDC. (For guides to acronyms, see p. 85.)

Department of Energy

On August 4, 1977, the President signed PL 95–91 which created the new cabinet-level Department of Energy. Abolished by this law were the Federal Energy Administration (FEA), the Energy Research and Development Administration (ERDA), and the Federal Power Commission (FP). (ERDA had replaced the former Atomic Energy Commission in 1974.) In addition, the new agency took over energy programs scattered in several other agencies.

The Technical Information Center of the Department of Energy continues to handle the bibliographic control of energy research.

INDEXES

Reports of the former ERDA and AEC were indexed in *Nuclear Science Abstracts* from 1948 to June 30, 1976, which included abstracts of books, conference proceedings, individual conference papers, patents, and journal literature. Reports were also indexed in the NTIS *Government Reports Announcements & Index.* For full abstracts, one must consult *Nuclear Science Abstracts. Nuclear Science Abstracts* was discontinued with the publication of volume 33 (no. 12, dated June 30, 1976) and replaced by *Atomindex,* published by the International Atomic Energy Agency and a product of the International Atomic Information System (INIS). The latter provides literature coverage, scope, and abstracting and indexing that is essentially identical with that of the former *Nuclear Science Abstracts. Atomindex* is available on a subscription basis from UNIPUB, P.O. Box 433, Murray Hill Station, New York, N.Y. 10015.

The Department of Energy Technical Information Center publishes *Energy Research Abstracts (ERA),* which contains abstracts and indexes to all literature of departmental origin, as well as to non-nuclear information generated by foreign countries with which the department has cooperative agreements. *ERA* is available to government agencies and, on an exchange basis, to universities, research institutes, industrial firms, and publishers of scientific information. Information about *Energy Research Abstracts* is available from Technical Information Center, Department of Energy, P.O. Box 62, Oak Ridge, Tenn. 37830.

AVAILABILITY OF PUBLICATIONS

Public availability of the former ERDA reports is indicated in the report number index to *Nuclear Science Abstracts* (before June 1976) and the *Energy Research Abstracts.* Unclassified technical reports on energy are distributed by NTIS. Information on the availability of published literature, including published conference papers, may be obtained from the Technical Information Center.

Reports of the former Atomic Energy Commission may be found in AEC depository libraries which received free microfiche copies of reports until 1968. A list of these libraries can be found in various issues of *Nuclear Science Abstracts* that cover this period. In 1968 AEC discontinued its free distribution of reports in favor of contractual arrangements with a commercial firm to sell the reports at special rates to certain classes of customers. This arrangement still continues (1977).

Libraries which subscribe to the complete set of reports are listed in the inside front cover of *Energy Research Abstracts.* The former AEC and ERDA reports are identified by a unique report number, consisting of a code plus sequential number (i.e., ORNL–5007). In this case, ORNL identifies the Oak Ridge National Laboratory as the originating installation. (For a guide to the codes used by the former Atomic Energy Commission, see p. 85.)

DATA BASE

The Division of Technical Information Extension offers a computer search service called RESPONSA and an on-line service for current files called AEC/RECON. Tape distribution to outside facilities is limited. The Department of Energy is continuing to add to the AEC data base on energy information, and in the future the data base will be made available to the private sector through sale of magnetic tapes.

Educational Resources Information Center

The first nationwide, comprehensive information network designed to serve American education is the ERIC system, established in 1966 by the U.S. Office of

Education. Currently under the auspices of the National Institute of Education, ERIC Central (headquarters) operates as a coordinating agency for reports emanating from research and development activities in education. The National Institute of Education was established as part of the Education amendments of 1972[10] and became the research and development arm of a new Education Division in the Department of Health, Education, and Welfare. Not limited to federally sponsored research, ERIC includes a broad range of subjects in conference proceedings, bibliographies, professional papers, and curriculum-related materials.

ERIC is a decentralized operation with four units: ERIC Central at NIE headquarters; the various clearinghouses, usually near university campuses; the ERIC facility which contracts for a centralized computer and services; and the ERIC Document Reproduction Service. The clearinghouses, each responsible for a specialized educational area, gather information, then evaluate, abstract, and index the data.

Unlike some information centers which accept and process all reports received, ERIC maintains quality control over the literature input into the ERIC system through evaluation undertaken by the clearinghouses. Each clearinghouse has the responsibility for selecting significant and relevant material. The clearinghouses also prepare newsletters, bulletins, and bibliographies. A list of clearinghouses appears on the inside back cover of the monthly *Resources in Education* (formerly called *Research in Education*).

The number of clearinghouses has fluctuated with the changing needs of the educational community. Note the special announcements in the monthly issues that report the creation, discontinuance, and realignment of clearinghouses.

ERIC Central collects reports from federal agencies and other organizations engaged in education-related research and receives from the specialized clearinghouses all data processed by them.

INDEXES

Each document is listed in the monthly abstract journal, *Resources in Education*. Periodical literature is listed in *Current Index to Journals in Education (CIJE)*. Both are available to the public on a subscription basis. The accession series prefix for the report literature is ED; for *CIJE, EJ*.

AVAILABILITY OF REPORTS

Reports indexed in the monthly abstract journals are available on microfiche or hard copy, with the exception of most copyrighted material. Reports can be purchased individually or on a standing order subscription basis for selected clearinghouse areas. Complete sets of reports are also available on standing order. Libraries which have a heavy demand for the reports will find there is considerable

10. 86 *Stat.* 327; 20 *U.S.C.* 1221e.

savings of cost, time, and effort in placing a standing order for all categories. Information on how to order documents is included in the monthly *Resources in Education*.

The cost of a subscription to all ERIC reports, announced in each *Resources in Education*, is approximately $160 per month (1978), at the rate of about 8.7¢ per microfiche. The pricing schedule of individual reports is included in each issue of *Resources in Education*.

DATA BASE

Basic files are available in ERIC format (IBM 360 OS) or in the Library of Congress MARC II format. Files include the complete resumé, including document description, indexing, and abstract or annotation of each document announced in accession number order.

Commercial on-line search service of the ERIC data base is available from the Systems Development Corporation (SDC) Search Service, Lockheed's Dialog Information Retrieval Service, and Bibliographic Retrieval Services (BRS).

Many local information centers have developed retrieval computer programs by the use of ERIC tapes. Therefore, access to the ERIC data base is widespread. For a list of organizations which currently provide computerized searches of the ERIC data base, see *Survey of ERIC Data Base Search Services* (Washington, D.C.: National Institute of Education, 1976). The *Survey* is organized geographically by state and city. Information includes organization, population served, files available, how to submit an inquiry, and what product may be expected. It also includes cost data and turnaround time, and identifies the computer program used to process searches.

Joint Publications Research Service

The Joint Publications Research Service (JPRS) was established in 1957 as a component of the Department of Commerce to provide English-language translations of books, newspapers, and articles to federal agencies. The early translations were primarily in the field of science but, in time, materials in the social sciences were added. By October 1958, many translations were made available to the general public and listed in the *Monthly Catalog*.

AVAILABILITY OF REPORTS

Certain segments of the JPRS reports became depository items (1067–L 1–13) in 1978. The following series are available in microfiche: translations on Eastern Europe, the Far East, Japan, Latin America, the Near East and North Africa, Sub-Sahara Africa; Telecommunications Policy, Research and Development; Environ mental Quality; Law of the Sea; Narcotics and Dangerous Drugs; *People's Republic of China Scientific Abstracts;* and *World Epidemiology Review.* Each series may be selected separately since each has its own item number.

There are several other sources for obtaining JPRS reports. NTIS is a major source for individual reports or for standing orders. The *Monthly Catalog* cautions: "when ordering Joint Publications Research Service Publications from the National Technical Information Service, give the JPRS number in the order. Do not include *Monthly Catalog* entry numbers or the Superintendent of Documents Classification Number." For information on areas covered and cost of publications, write to NTIS.

Some JPRS translations are published by the commercial press. A microprint edition of the reports can be purchased from the Readex Microprint Corporation, New York. The Readex set is arranged by *Monthly Catalog* entry numbers. An index that correlates the JPRS report numbers with the *Monthly Catalog* entry numbers, prepared by Mary Elizabeth Poole, is available from the Readex Microprint Corporation. Some libraries will lend reports in microprint.

From 1962 to 1975, the CCM Information Corporation, New York, issued monthly indexes to the JPRS translations. Four bibliographies and indexes to the U.S. JPRS translations—China and Asia, East Europe, International Developments, and the Soviet Union—were issued from 1962 to 1970. In 1970, these were superseded by a computer-based index, *TRANSDEX: Bibliography and Index to the United States Joint Publications Research Service (JPRS) Translations.* CCM announced discontinuance of this service in 1975.

Indexes to the JPRS reports (by key word, author, personal names, title, and series) are (as of 1978) available from Bell and Howell, Old Mansfield Road, Wooster, Ohio 44691. For information on matters other than procurement of reports, write to JPRS, 1000 North Glebe Road, Arlington, Va. 22201.

National Aeronautics and Space Administration

On March 3, 1915, the Advisory Committee for Aeronautics (later known as the National Advisory Committee for Aeronautics, or NACA) was established as a rider to the Naval Appropriations Act "to supervise and direct scientific study of problems of flight and to direct and conduct research and experiment in aeronautics."[11] NACA was terminated in 1958 and its functions were transferred to the National Aeronautics and Space Administration.[12] Among the functions of NASA are "to conduct research for the solution of problems of flight within and outside the earth's atmosphere . . . and to provide for the widest practicable and appropriate dissemination of information concerning NASA's activities and their re-

11. 38 *Stat.* 930, as amended; 50 *U.S.C.* 151.
12. 72 *Stat.* 426; 42 *U.S.C.* 2451 et seq., as amended.

sults."[13] The NASA Scientific and Technical Information Facility (STIF) abstracts and indexes technical report literature on the science and technology of space and aeronautics.

INDEXES

Technical report literature is abstracted in *Scientific and Technical Aerospace Reports (STAR)*. Reports are also indexed in the *Government Reports Announcements & Index,* but for the abstracts, *STAR* must be consulted. A companion publication, *International Aerospace Abstracts,* includes journal articles, books, conference papers, proceedings, translations, and certain foreign dissertations. *STAR,* together with *International Aerospace Abstracts (IAA),* attempts to cover worldwide literature in aerospace.

Both publications are basically identical in indexing style. According to a survey of special libraries that use *STAR,* this index is a prime source in its subject field, with accurate and complete citations and consistency of entries over the years.

STAR is available to the public on a subscription basis from the Superintendent of Documents, Government Printing Office, Washington, D.C. 20402.

AVAILABILITY OF PUBLICATIONS

Nonclassified publications may be ordered from NTIS. For classified documents, registration with the Defense Documentation Center is required. For details, write to NASA/STIF (National Aeronautics and Space Administration, Scientific and Technical Information Facility), Baltimore-Washington International Airport, Md. 21240.

National Technical Information Service

The National Technical Information Service, formerly the Clearinghouse for Federal Scientific and Technical Information (CFSTI), is a centralized information system, reportedly the largest in the world. A number of organizational and name changes prior to NTIS includes Publication Board (PB), 1945–46; Office of Technical Services, 1946–64; and Clearinghouse for Federal Scientific and Technical Information, 1964–70.

As a component of the United States Department of Commerce, NTIS is the major source for government-sponsored research and development reports prepared by federal agencies and their contractors or grantees. Its stated mission is "to collect and disseminate scientific, technical and engineering information."[14] However, a wide range of Department of Commerce publications, some of which do not fall within the scope of "research and development" reports as defined, are also entered

13. *United States Government Manual,* 1976–77, pp. 563–66.
14. 64 *Stat.* 823.

into the NTIS data base. The services of NTIS include processing, announcing, selling documents, and providing computer searches.

NTIS processes all reports received from some 300 federal agencies and from state, local, private, and foreign sponsors. Because no law requires agencies to send results of federally sponsored research to NTIS, it must seek reports through its own acquisition program.

The pricing of each report is based on page count, content, and expected demand. There is some concern among librarians that an increasing number of publications, formerly available without charge from various federal agencies, are now available only from NTIS.

INDEXES

Reports are listed in the combined *Government Reports Announcements & Index*. Prior to April 1975, reports were listed in *Government Reports Announcements (GRA)*, an abstract journal issued biweekly, and *Government Reports Index (GRI)*, published concurrently with *GRA*.

The index section merges the machine-readable records generated by several agencies: Department of Energy (includes the former Energy Research and Development Administration, which superseded the former Atomic Energy Commission), the National Aeronautics and Space Administration, the Defense Documentation Center, and the National Technical Information Service. Therefore, this single source indexes the reports included in the individual agency abstracts, that is, *Energy Research Abstracts* of the Energy Research and Development Administration (ERDA), *Scientific and Technical Aerospace Reports* of NASA, and the unclassified and unlimited reports of the Defense Documentation Center (DDC). For detailed abstracts, the individual abstracting journals must be consulted.

There is some duplication of entries in the *Monthly Catalog* and *Government Reports Announcements & Index,* particularly for Department of Commerce publications, but the *GRAI* refers users to the GPO for hard copy and NTIS makes microfiche copies available. Critics of the NTIS indexes point to overlapping with other indexes, unpredictable coverage, inconsistent bibliographic entries, and the inclusion of excessive numbered series. Despite its criticisms, *GRAI* is the primary bibliographic tool for a large segment of the technical report literature. *GRAI* is available to the public on a subscription basis from NTIS.

AVAILABILITY OF REPORTS

Full texts of most of the documents abstracted in *GRAI* are available in a variety of forms—paper, microfiche, magnetic tape for computer input, and microfilm. Automatic distribution of reports in subject categories is provided by a standing order service called Selected Resources in Microfiche (SRIM). This service requires a deposit account.

Order forms for reports may be obtained from NTIS, Department of Commerce, Springfield, Va. 22161. Orders will be delayed if the full NTIS accession number is not cited. NTIS will send pre-addressed order forms to facilitate handling. Payment may be made by check, money order, or American Express card. A deposit account cuts processing time, and one may be established with a deposit of $25. A service charge is made for orders which must be billed. An up-to-date pricing schedule can be found in the most recent issue of *Government Reports Announcements & Index.*

DATA BASE

All federally sponsored research projects completed since 1964 may be accessed on-line through a service called NTISearch, and is available to the public by telephone call or correspondence with NTIS. Additions to the data base are announced in *Weekly Government Abstracts (WGA)* and *Government Reports Announcements & Index.* Searches are priced (1977) at $50 for up to 100 abstracts, with added charges for additional abstracts. Access to the Smithsonian Science Information Exchange's (SSIE) current research information file is also available to NTISearch users. A combined NTIS-SSIE search is $85 for the first 125 abstracts and 25¢ for each additional abstract (1977).

Direct access to the on-line NTIS data base is possible through several vendors, the Systems Development Corporation (SDC) Search Service, Lockheed's Dialog Information Retrieval Service, and Bibliographic Retrieval Services (BRS).

Searches (already completed) may be purchased at a package price of $25 (1977) per search. A complete listing of search titles is available from NTIS.

Two information retrieval systems, available commercially from Congressional Information Service, are included since they deal primarily with government information.

CIS/Index

The need for a comprehensive index to congressional information was met by the Congressional Information Service with its publication of the *CIS/Index,* beginning in 1970. Publications of the United States Congress are indexed, abstracted, and listed in the *CIS/Index.* Included are hearings, reports, committee prints, and other congressional papers. Full information on content and how to use the *Index* is contained in the introductory pages of each *Index.* (See also p. 128.)

INDEX

An index book and an abstracts book are published monthly, covering publications issued during the previous month. Each quarter a cumulative index of materials covered during the previous quarter is issued. The *CIS/Annual* cumulates all abstracts issued during the year. A 1970–74 cumulation is also available.

AVAILABILITY OF REPORTS

The CIS Microfiche Library offers complete texts of indexed materials on a subscription basis. Individual titles may be purchased (on microfiche) on a demand basis. A deposit account may be requested.

DATA BASE

Searching the *CIS/Index* is available on-line (AcCIS) through the facilities of the Systems Development Corporation. For information about this service, write to the Congressional Information Service, P.O. Box 30056, Washington, D.C. 20014.

American Statistics Index

The *American Statistics Index* is an index to the statistical publications of U.S. government agencies. When first issued in 1973, the scope of the coverage was limited to social and socioeconomic statistics. By 1974, however, the coverage was extended to the full range of federal statistical publications.

INDEXES

American Statistics Index 1974 Annual and Retrospective Edition supersedes the 1973 annual and covers current statistical publications. Significant publications issued since 1960 are also included in this index. Monthly supplements, an index book and an abstracts book, provide up-to-date information on changes in publications since the 1974 edition. The supplements serve as an adjunct to the annual. Each monthly supplement contains notes on retention of issues. Full information on content and how to use the *ASI* are contained in the introductory pages of the *Index*.

AVAILABILITY OF REPORTS

The ASI Microfiche Library provides complete texts of the reports on a subscription basis. Individual titles may be purchased (on microfiche) on a demand basis. A deposit account may be requested.

DATA BASE

Searching the *American Statistics Index* is available on-line through the facilities of the Systems Development Corporation. For information about this service, write to the Congressional Information Service, P.O. Box 30056, Washington, D.C. 20014. (See also p. 122.)

TABLE 2   **CHRONOLOGICAL GUIDE TO SELECTED INDEXES TO TECHNICAL REPORTS**
(Numbers in parentheses refer to citations)

SUBJECT AREA	DATE	TITLE	ACCESS	COMMENTS
General scientific and technical reports	1895–	Monthly Catalog of U.S. Government Publications (28)	Subj., pers. auth. 1963– ; title since 1974; ann. cum. (see also 34)	
	1946–49	Bibliography of Scientific and Industrial Reports (BSIR) (18)	Subj., nos., s.a. cum. (see also 29–31, 33)	Includes R&D from foreign govts. and captured foreign documents
	1949–54	Bibliography of Technical Reports (BTR) (19)	Subj., nos., s.a. cum. (see also 30–33)	Replaced BSIR
	1954–64	U.S. Government Research Reports (USGRR) (22)	Subj., nos., s.a. cum., corp. auth. 1959– ; no cum. index for 1964 (33)	Replaced BTR; includes Technical Abstract Bulletin (TAB) sec., 1961–67
	1962–63	Keywords Index (20)	KWIC format; corp. auth., pers. auth., 1963; no cum.	Experimental index; related to USGRR
	1965–71	U.S. Government Research and Development Reports (USGRDR) (6)	Jan.–Mar. 1965 cum., 1965–67, see GWI; no cum. until 1968	Replaced USGRR; 1965–June 1966, each issue had index
	1965–67	Government-wide Index (GWI) (5)	Subj., nos., corp. auth., pers. auth.; no cum.	Indexed USGRDR, STAR, NSA, Technical Translations
	1968–71	U.S. Government Research and Development Reports Index (USGRDR–I) (6)	Subj., nos., corp. auth., pers. auth., ann. cum.	Replaced GWI; indexed government-sponsored reports in STAR, USGRDR, NSA
	1971–75	Government Reports Announcements (GRA) (15)	See GRI	Replaced USGRDR
	1971–75	Government Reports Index (GRI) (16)	Subj., nos., corp. auth., pers. auth., ann. cum.	Replaced USGRDR–I; indexes GRA, STAR, NSA
	4/1975–	Government Reports Announcements & Index (merged GRA and GRI)	Bi-w.	
Aeronautics and space	1915–58	Index of NACA Technical Publications (11)	Subj., pers. auth.	

			publications
1958–62	Technical Publications Announcements (TPA) (14)	Subj., nos., pers. auth., corp. auth., cum.	Title varies; international scope
1962–63	Keywords Index (20)	KWIC; corp. auth., pers. auth. 1963 only	Includes NASA research reports
1963–	Scientific and Technical Aerospace Reports (STAR) (13)	Subj., nos., pers. auth., corp. auth.; ann. cum.	Replaced TPA; international scope; NASA and contractors' reports
1961–	International Aerospace Abstracts (35)	Subj., nos., pers. auth., s.a., ann. cum.	Abstracts journals, books, conference papers, proceedings, journal translations, certain foreign dissertations; complements STAR
Military reports			
1946–54	BSIR and BTR (See entry under General Scientific and Technical Reports [18, 19])		
1950–65	Air Force Scientific Research Bibliography (2)	Subj, nos., pers. auth.	All publications of Air Force Office of Scientific Research; listing continued in USGRDR
1953–	Technical Abstract Bulletin (TAB) (7)	Subj., nos., title, pers. auth., corp. auth., ann. cum. 1960–	Title varies; available only to qualified users
1954–64	USGRR (See entry under General Scientific and Technical Reports [22])		Includes unclassified TAB section
1959–68	OAR Cumulative Index of Research Results (1)	KWIC; nos., pers. auth., corp. auth.; AD nos. 1965–68	All reports published by Air Force Office of Aerospace Research
1962–63	Keywords Index (See entry under General Scientific and Technical Reports [20])		Includes ASTIA documents
1965–71	USGRDR (Reports and Index) (See entry under General Scientific and Technical Reports [6])		TAB section discontinued in 1967
1971–	GRA, GRI, and as of 4/75 combined GRA and GRI (See entry under General Scientific and Technical Reports [15, 16])		

TABLE 2 (cont.)

SUBJECT AREA	DATE	TITLE	ACCESS	COMMENTS
Nuclear science	1946–48	Guide to Published Research on Atomic Energy (4)		Includes non-AEC reports
	1947–48	Abstracts of Declassified Documents (3)	Cum. ind.	Indexed AEC reports
	1948–76	Nuclear Science Abstracts (NSA) (9)	Subj., pers. auth., corp. auth., nos., ann. cum., 5-yr. & 15-yr. cum.	Replaced above titles; international scope; replaced by Atomindex (37)
	1976–	Energy Research Abstracts (ERA) (36)	Subj., pers. auth., corp. auth., nos., ann. cum.	Includes all DOE reports
	1954–	USGRR (See entry under General Scientific and Technical Reports [22, 6, 15, 16])		
	1962–63	Keywords Index (See entry under General Scientific and Technical Reports [20])		Includes all AEC research reports
Patents	1790–	Patent Number Sequence Classification Record (24)	Original and cross-reference classifications	NTIS microfilm reels arranged in patent number sequence
	1790–1977 (updated periodically)	U.S. Patent Classification—Subclass Listing (27)	Classification numbers arrangement	Includes original and all cross-reference classifications; NTIS microfilm PB 269 981; updated by Index of Patents
	1872–	Official Gazette (26)	Classification, patentee	Announces all patents issued; includes claims and/or abstracts and diagrams
	1872–1925	Annual Report of the Commissioner of Patents (23)	Patentee, subj.	Includes annual index to Official Gazette
	1920–	Index of Patents (25)	Patentee, subj.	Title index to 1954; class. index 1954–
	1946–54	BSIR, BTR (See entry under General Scientific and Technical Reports [18, 19])		Includes German patents after World War II
	1947–76	NSA (See entry under Nuclear Science [9])		International coverage of nu-

	1969–	STAR (See entry under Aeronautics and Space [13])	Subj., nos., pers. auth., corp. auth.	NASA-owned patents and patent applications abstracted
Educational research	1956–65	Office of Education Research Reports (17)		Research sponsored by OE Bureau of Research; includes Cooperative Research Program reports
	1966–	ERIC—Resources in Education (RIE) (8)	Subj., nos., pers. auth., corp. auth., s.a. and/or ann. cum.	Title varies
Translations	1946–54	BSIR, BTR (See entry under General Scientific and Technical Reports [18, 19])		Especially captured foreign documents
	1948–76	NSA (See entry under Nuclear Science [9])		
	1954–58	USGRR (See entry under General Scientific and Technical Reports [22])		
	1958–	Monthly Catalog (See entry under General Scientific and Technical Reports [28])		JPRS reports from Communist bloc countries; Poole Index to Readex Microprint Edition of JPRS Reports (1958–) gives JPRS nos. and Mo. Cat. entry nos. for Readex Microprint edition
	1959–67	Technical Translations (21)	Subj., pers. auth., nos., s.a. cum.	Translations prepared by government and private sources; includes JPRS social science reports, 1965–67
	1959–68	OAR Cumulative Index of Research Results (See entry under Military Reports [11])		
	1963–	STAR (See entry under Aeronautics and Space [13])		
	1965–67	GWI (See entry under General Scientific and Technical Reports [51])		Includes Technical Translations
	1968–	USGRDR & I, GRA & I (See entry under General Scientific and Technical Reports [6, 15, 16])		All technical translations sponsored by U.S. govt.

Prepared with the assistance of Marjorie Bengtson, assistant documents librarian, Library, University of Illinois at Chicago Circle, Chicago.

TABLE 2 (cont.)

ABBREVIATIONS

ann.	annual
arr.	arrangement
auth.	author
bi-w.	bi-weekly
class.	classification
cum.	cumulations
corp.	corporate
KWIC	key word in context
mo.	monthly
nos.	numbers
pers.	personal
s.a.	semi-annual
s.mo.	semi-monthly
subj.	subject

AEC	Atomic Energy Commission
ASTIA	Armed Services Technical Information Agency
BSIR	Bibliography of Scientific and Industrial Reports
BTR	Bibliography of Technical Reports
DOE	Department of Energy
GRA	Government Reports Announcements
GRI	Government Reports Index
GWI	Government-wide Index
IAA	International Aerospace Abstracts
JPRS	Joint Publications Research Service
Mo. Cat.	Monthly Catalog of U.S. Government Publications
NACA	National Advisory Committee on Aeronautics
NASA	National Aeronautics and Space Administration
NSA	Nuclear Science Abstracts
NTIS	National Technical Information Service
OAR	Office of Aerospace Research
RIE	Resources in Education
STAR	Scientific and Technical Aerospace Reports
TAB	Technical Abstract Bulletin
TPA	Technical Publications Announcements
USGRDR	U.S. Government Research and Development Reports
USGRDR-I	U.S. Government Research and Development Reports Index
USGRR	U.S. Government Research Reports

2. ——. Office of Scientific Research. *Air Force Scientific Research Bibliography.* 1950–65 (D 301.45/19–2:700/v.1–8)

3. U.S. Atomic Energy Commission. *Abstracts of Declassified Documents.* 1947–48 (Y 3.At7:11)

4. ——. *Guide to Published Research on Atomic Energy.* 1946–48 (Y 3.At7:7)

5. U.S. Clearinghouse for Federal Scientific and Technical Information. *Government-wide Index to Federal Research and Development Reports.* 1965–67 (C 51.9:)

6. ——. *U.S. Government Research and Development Reports* and *Index.* 1965–71; *Index,* 1968–71. (C 41.21:) (C 51.9/3:) (C 51.9/2: Ind.)

7. U.S. Defense Documentation Center. *Technical Abstract Bulletin.* 1953– (D 10.8:)

8. U.S. Educational Resources Information Center. *Resources in Education.* 1966– . Formerly *Research in Education,* 1966–74 (FS 5.77:) (HE 5.77:) (HE 18.10:) (HE 19.210:)

9. U.S. Energy Research and Development Administration. *Nuclear Science Abstracts.* 1948–76. Replaced by *Atomindex* (37) and *Energy Research Abstracts* (36) (Y 3.At 7:16/) (ER 1.10:)

10. U.S. Joint Publications Research Service. *JPRS Reports.* 1958– (Y 3.J66:)

11. U.S. National Advisory Committee for Aeronautics. *Index of NACA Technical Publications.* 1915–58 (Y 3.N21/5:2 T22/915–49) (Y 3.N21/5:2 T22/949–55) (Y 3.N21/5:17/955–58)

12. U.S. National Aeronautics and Space Administration. *Index of NASA Technical Publications.* 1958–61 (NAS 1.9/2:T22/) (NAS 1.21:9)

13. ——. *Scientific and Technical Aerospace Reports.* 1963– (NAS 1.9/4:)

14. ——. *Technical Publications Announcements.* 1958–62 (NAS 1.9:)

15. U.S. National Technical Information Service. *Government Reports Announcements.* 1971– (C 51.9/3:)

16. ——. *Government Reports Index.* 1971– Merged with *Government Reports Announcements* to form *Government Reports Announcements & Index* (C 51.9/4:)

17. U.S. Office of Education. Bureau of Research. *Office of Education Research Reports.* 1956–65 (FS 5.212:12028) (FS 5.212:12029)

18. U.S. Office of Technical Services. *Bibliography of Scientific and Industrial Reports.* 1946–49 (C 35.7:)

19. ——. *Bibliography of Technical Reports.* 1949–54 (C 35.7:)

20. ——. *Keywords Index to U.S. Government Technical Reports.* 1962–63 (C 41.21/5:)

21. ——. *Technical Translations.* 1959–67 (C 41.41:)

22. ——. *U.S. Government Research Reports.* 1954–64 (C 41.21:)

23. U.S. Patent and Trademark Office. *Annual Report of the Commissioner of Patents.* 1872–1925 (I 23.1/1:) (C 21.1:)

... NTIS on microfilm, PB 269 331

25. ——. *Index of Patents.* 1920– (I 23.1/1:date/2) (C 21.5/2:)

26. ——. *Official Gazette of the United States Patent and Trademark Office.* 1872– (I 23.8:) (C 21.5:)

27. ——. *U.S. Patent Classification–Subclass Listing.* 1977. Available from NTIS on microfilm, PB 269 981

28. U.S. Superintendent of Documents. *Monthly Catalog of United States Government Publications.* 1895– (GP 3.8:)

29. Special Libraries Association. *Numerical Index: Bibliography of Scientific and Industrial Reports.* v. 1–10, 1946–48. New York, Special Libraries Association. v. 11– issued by Office of Technical Services. Arranged by PB number and refers to appropriate BSIR issue for abstract (C 35.7/3:11–)

30. Special Libraries Council of Philadelphia and Vicinity. *Correlation Index, Documents Series and PB Reports.* New York, Special Libraries Association. 1953

31. U.S. Armed Services Technical Information Agency. *Correlation Index of Technical Reports (AD-PB reports).* 1958 (PB 151 567S). Two indexes (30) and (31) correlate the report numbers and/or AD number with the PB number to locate abstract in BSIR. Should be used in conjunction with the *Numerical Index* (29)

32. ——. *Subject Index to Unclassified ASTIA Documents, Index to ASTIA's AD's 1 through 75,000.* 1960 (PB 151 567). Supplemented by *Correlation Index* (31)

33. Bradshaw, Nina H., comp. *PB-AD Reports Index, 1946–67.* Washington, D.C.: Technical Information Service, 1968. Includes BSIR, BTR, USGRR, and USGRDR. Arranged in PB number order with corresponding AD or ATI report number

34. *Cumulative Subject Index to the Monthly Catalog of United States Government Publications, 1900–1971,* compiled by William W. Buchanan and Edna A. Kanely. Washington, D.C.: Carrollton Press, 1975. *Cumulative Subject Index . . . 1895–1899,* compiled by Edna A. Kanely. Carrollton, 1977.

35. American Institute of Aeronautics and Astronautics. *International Aerospace Abstracts.* 1961– . New York. American Institute of Aeronautics and Astronautics

36. U.S. Department of Energy. *Energy Research Abstracts.* Jan. 1976– . Department of Energy, Technical Information Center, P.O. Box 62, Oak Ridge, Tenn. 37830 (ER 1.15:) (E 1.17:)

37. International Atomic Energy Agency and International Atomic Information Systems (INIS). *Atomindex.* July 1976– (Replaced *Nuclear Science Abstracts*). Available from UNIPUB, P.O. Box 433, Murray Hill Station, New York, N.Y. 10015.

Additional References

GENERAL

Association of Research Libraries. Office of University Library Management Studies. *On-Line Bibliographic Search Services.* Occasional paper no. 4. Washington, D.C.: Association of Research Libraries, June 1976.

Boylan, Nancy. "History of the Dissemination of PB (Publication Board) Reports," *Journal of Library History* 3 (April 1968):156–62.

———. "Technical Reports, Identification and Acquisition," *RQ* 10 (Fall 1970): 18–21.

Fass, Evalyn M. "Government Information Services: or, Of Needles and Haystacks," *Drexel Library Quarterly* 10 (January–April 1974):123–46.

Herner, Saul, and Matthew J. Vellucci. *Selected Federal Computer-based Information Systems.* Washington, D.C.: Information Resources Press, 1972.

Kates, Jacqueline R. "Cataloging Government Technical Reports," *Special Libraries* 65 (March 1974):121–23.

Rowe, Judith. "The Use and Misuse of Government Produced Statistical Data Files," *RQ* 14 (Spring 1975):201–3. See also regular column by Judith Rowe on government-produced data files in *Government Publications Review.*

Shaw, Thomas S. "Distribution and Acquisition," *Library Trends* 15 (July 1966): 37–49.

U.S. Library of Congress. *Federal Government: A Directory of Information Resources in the United States, with a supplement of Government-sponsored Information Analysis Centers.* Washington, D.C.: Library of Congress, 1974.

Williams, Martha E. "Use of Machine-readable Data Bases," chapter 7 in *Annual Review of Information Science and Technology.* Vol. 9, pp. 221–84. Washington, D.C.: American Society for Information Science, 1974.

———. "Criteria for Evaluation and Selection of Data Bases and Data Base Services," *Special Libraries* 66 (December 1975):561–69.

———. *The Impact of Machine-readable Data Bases on Library and Information Services.* National Program for Libraries and Information Services. Related Paper No. 26. Washington, D.C.: National Commission on Libraries and Information Science, 1975 (Bethesda, Md.: ERIC Document Reproduction Service. ED 114 103).

DDC

Committee on Information Hang-ups. *Especially DDC: Users Look at the DoD Information Process.* Springfield, Va.: National Technical Information Service, 1975 (NTIS. AD–A005 400).

———. *Information Hang-ups: Problems Encountered by Users of the Technical Information Services Offered by DDC and CFSTI, with Recommendations for the Future.* Washington, D.C.: Committee of DDC Users in the Greater Washington, D.C., Area, 1969 (Bethesda, Md.: ERIC Document Reproduction Service. ED 044 156).

Rea, Robert H. "Defense Documentation Center," *Drexel Library Quarterly* 10 (January–April 1974):21–38.

U.S. Department of Defense, Defense Supply Agency. *Defense Documentation Center: Its Programs and Services.* Updated frequently.

ERIC

Fry, Bernard M., and Eva L. Kiewitt. "The Educational Resources Information Center: Its Legal Basis, Organization, Distribution System, Bibliographic Controls," *Drexel Library Quarterly* 10 (January–April 1974):63–78.

U.S. Department of Health, Educations, and Welfare. *Office of Education, Support for Research and Related Activities.* Rev. April 1969 (FS 5.212:12025–B).

U.S. National Institute of Education. *ERIC, a Profile.* Washington, D.C.: Govt. Print. Off., 1974.

JPRS

Lucas, Rita, and George Caldwell. "Joint Publications Research Service Translations," *College and Research Libraries* 25 (March 1964):103–10.

NTIS

Committee on Information Hang-ups. *Distinction Is All: NTIS from a Technical Librarian's Point-of-View.* Washington, D.C.: Committee on Information Hang-ups, 1971 (Bethesda, Md.: ERIC Document Reproduction Service. ED 058 913).

Meredith, J. C. "NTIS Update: A Critical Review of Services," *Government Publications Review* 1 (Fall 1974):343–61.

Thott, Bo W. "The National Technical Information Service," *Drexel Library Quarterly* 10 (January–April 1974):39–51.

THE DOCUMENTS LIBRARIAN AND REFERENCE SOURCES

8

In reference work the process of selection and organization of government publications is directed toward the goal of bringing these materials to the library's public. The most important aspect of handling government documents is the servicing of them. This is the area which requires the full talents and skills of a librarian whose professional education, temperament, and experience must synthesize to bring government information to the patrons. The quality of documents reference service provided in a library is measured by the caliber of the librarians who give this service. The various techniques that are used in reference service deserve a full monograph and will not be dealt with in this book.

The number of librarians specializing in government publications is ever increasing as the demand for documents librarians rises. Specialization can best be acquired in library schools which offer courses in government publications. A strong subject background (at the master's level) in almost any of the disciplines, but particularly in the social sciences, is additional preparation listed as desirable by many academic libraries. There is no substitute, however, for "learning on the desk," as the various ramifications of working with government publications cannot be taught in the library school curriculum. A few library schools give an opportunity for field work in a practical situation. In-service training programs in libraries which have separate collections of government publications allow for an enriching experience for those interested in this area.

Continuing education in government publications can be pursued by attending workshops on the subject offered by various state and regional library groups. Personal involvement in a national library association (such as the American Library Association, Special Libraries Association, and the Association of American Law Libraries) that have organized groups for those interested in government publications is a way to keep up with developments in the field.

Reference Service

In an integrated collection, the reference librarians in the general reference department or in departmental libraries will assume the documents reference function, treating government reference sources as regular library reference materials. In a separate collection or unit, the documents librarian assumes the role of a specialist in type of publication. The contents of government publications, however, are enormously interdisciplinary. Although the documents librarian serves as a specialist, the fact that government publications cover such a wide array of subjects means that the documents librarian must also be a generalist for all areas of knowledge. Exposure to all aspects of handling government publications, from the time of their selection and arrival in the library to their placement on the shelves, provides documents librarians in a separate unit with an added dimension which is not possible in an integrated collection.

All librarians involved in documents reference service should have an opportunity to examine government publications as they are received in the library. In a separate collection, this procedure can be managed more easily than in an integrated collection, where many of the functions are handled by different units of the library. After processing, a shelf of new documents could be set aside for reference and documents librarians to examine before the documents are shelved in the stacks. If documents are treated in a separate unit, close cooperation with the library reference staff and departmental librarians is essential since these librarians are usually the first contact point with patrons. Keeping reference librarians informed of new titles and new developments in government publications (i.e., new specialized indexes) will assist them in making proper referrals to the documents unit. Inviting each reference librarian to participate as staff in the documents unit on a rotating basis is one of the most effective ways of keeping reference librarians informed and interested in the library's separate collection of government publications. In a large library, it may not be possible or practical to invite all reference librarians to examine new titles. In this case, a selection of major titles should be made by the documents librarian and routed to the reference department for reference librarians' perusal.

Knowledge of the patrons' needs and continuing surveillance of incoming materials can provide that special service to users. A current-awareness service, notifying a patron of a particular title which has come in, will extend reference service beyond the normal face-to-face service. In a separate collection, librarians who review new documents can identify them for interested patrons at the point of examination.

If government publications are not entered in the main card catalog of the library, reference form cards in the catalog and in the serials record, directing patrons to the documents unit, will provide a link to the separate collection or unit.

Documents librarians must also refer patrons to reference and other appropriate areas of the library when there are additional sources to supplement government information. Therefore, knowledge by the documents librarians of the collections in other public service units of the library is crucial if the patron is to be fully served.

All reference librarians must be acquainted with the kinds of knowledge available in different formats.

Literature

The librarian who gives reference service in government publications should keep abreast of current events through the various media. Reading the daily *Congressional Record, Weekly Compilation of Presidential Documents, Federal Register*, and the *CQ Weekly Report* will also give awareness of the current governmental scene. The past few years have seen the birth of several specialized publications designed to communicate activities in government publications to the librarians who service them. These should be read thoroughly.

> *Public Documents Highlights.* No. 1, 1973– . Bimonthly. Issued by the Superintendent of Documents and sent to depository libraries. Reports activities of the Superintendent related to federal depository libraries. Librarians in non-depository libraries will find this of interest as well. Available on request from Superintendent of Documents.

> *Documents to the People.* Vol. 1, 1972– .
> Issued six times a year by ALA Government Documents Round Table.
> Sent to members of the Round Table; available on subscription ($10 per year). Substantive reports on current activities of the Round Table. Includes announcements and information of interest to all librarians who handle government publications. Informative for those who do not. An outstanding publication.

> *Government Publications Review.* Vol. 1, 1973– .
> A quarterly professional journal providing a forum for discussion of all aspects of government publications, domestic and international. Subscription rates from Pergamon Press, Maxwell House, Fairview Park, Elmsford, N.Y. 10523.

Reference Aids

To answer recurring and other reference questions quickly, locally developed aids are often devised. The nature of these aids will vary with the situation. One way is to maintain a small, informal, information file on 3 x 5 cards, indicating where timely (or obscure) information might be found (Helsinki Agreement, Coleman Report, Ozone). This kind of file should be kept to manageable size (not more than two shoe boxes) and should be weeded constantly.

The disadvantages of an in-house tool are (1) undue reliance by staff on titles in the file, rather than use of comprehensive indexes, and (2) difficulty of establishing uniform subject headings which are known to all staff who use the file.

If a file is maintained, a staff member could be assigned the responsibility of flagging the titles for a subject entry card at the time that current documents are examined. The typed subject cards should be routed to all users of the file before filing, so that the subject headings will be familiar to those who service the collection. If a large number of recurring questions comes to the desk, the advantages of this kind of file definitely outweigh the disadvantages noted above.

Promoting Use

Needless to say, promoting the use of government publications should be a continuing activity in libraries. Many innovative programs can be developed, since government publications cover a wide spectrum of subject areas. Participating in instructional programs in school and academic libraries, preparing exhibits on topics of current interest, creating displays of new acquisitions, and distributing free materials (such as income tax forms) are some of the ways to publicize government publications.

The possibilities of outreach are limited only by the lack of imagination of the staff. And no one can disagree with one librarian's advice that the best way to advertise the government publications collection is to maintain a well-organized collection, display a variety of reference tools for access to the collection, and recruit an interested, alert staff to service the materials.[1]

Search Strategy

Search strategies are so varied, with the level of each question and the available resources within a library, that it would be presumptuous to suggest a preferred approach in answering reference questions. The key to good reference service is the use of reference tools. In many respects, reference service is only as good as the bibliographic tools available in a library. This is true of documents more than any other field, because so much government information is found primarily in nontraditional sources and is not indexed in any standard reference source or bibliographic tool. A unique feature of government publications is the wealth of information to be found in nonconventional sources, such as one-page news releases, annual reports, technical reports, and congressional hearings and reports.

1. Catharine J. Reynolds, "Discovering the Government Documents Collection in Libraries," *RQ* 14 (Spring 1975):228–31.

Special access tools exist to gain entry to government information, and librarians must learn how to use them, as well as be able to teach patrons how to use them. The number of tools has increased in recent years and their quality has improved as documents librarians and publishers work together to fill gaps in the bibliographic apparatus.

Guides, Catalogs, and Indexes

Whether a library has a separate or an integrated documents collection, basic guides, catalogs, and indexes are essential for acquisition, verification, and reference work. Because of the growing importance of government publications, the following bibliography can only serve as an introduction. It is selective and includes those sources, current and retrospective (some of which have become classics), that should be familiar to librarians working with government publications. Librarians must not only be alert to new sources but should themselves produce sources and guides to fill any gaps in the tools to gain access to government information. Careful examination and evaluation of each work to determine special strengths, weaknesses, and unique features are, of course, essential before using any reference tool.

Many of these titles can become the core of a reference collection of government publications. In a separate collection, a working reference collection will include many other works of reference value, such as the *Statistical Abstract, Economic Report of the President*, and *Budget of the United States Government*. Selection of these tools can be made from some of the sources listed.

SELECTED INDEXES, CATALOGS, CHECKLISTS, AND OTHER SOURCES USEFUL IN REFERENCE SEARCHES AND IN VERIFICATION OF TITLES

Contents

Prepared with the assistance of Michele Strange, assistant government publications librarian, Northwestern University Library, Evanston, Ill.

II. CATALOGS AND INDEXES
    A. General
    B. Specialized catalogs and indexes
    C. Departmental and agency catalogs
    D. Departmental library catalogs

III. SOURCES
    A. Census and vital statistics
    B. Congressional publications
        1. General catalogs and indexes
        2. Laws, statutes, etc.
        3. Hearings
        4. Committee prints
        5. Congressional reports and documents
        6. Congressional set or serial set
        7. Conference reports
        8. Debates of Congress
        9. House and Senate Journals
    C. Publications of the President of the United States
    D. Administrative regulations
    E. Judicial decisions

IV. CLASSIFICATION SCHEDULES

V. OTHER SOURCES

I. GUIDES TO THE LITERATURE

Guides and manuals are useful for researchers, librarians, and library school students as aids to other sources, such as bibliographies, and for information in a subject field. (Quotations are taken from the introductory material of the works cited.)

I.A. GENERAL

Boyd, Anne Morris. *United States Government Publications.* 3d ed. Rev. by Rae Elizabeth Rips. New York: H. W. Wilson, 1949.
This is still an outstanding basic guide, and now considered a classic. Excellent historical data on government organization and publications. Earlier editions also useful for historical information.

Brown, Everett S. *Manual of Government Publications: United States and Foreign.* New York: Appleton-Century-Crofts, 1950.
General guide to U.S., foreign, and international organizations' publications. Although dated, still useful for historical data.

Harleston, Rebekah M., and Carla J. Stoffle. *Administration of Government Documents Collections.* Littleton, Colo.: Libraries Unlimited, 1974.

Written as a successor to Ellen Jackson's *Manual for the Administration of the Federal Documents Collection in Libraries.* Chicago: American Library Association, 1955. A practical manual, particularly for samples of records maintained by one library. See also Morehead and Schmeckebier.

McCamy, James L. *Government Publications for the Citizen.* New York: Columbia University Press, 1949.

Examines role of public libraries in dissemination of information in government publications to the citizen. Discusses character, distribution, and library's use of government publications. Indexed.

Merritt, LeRoy Charles. *The United States Government as Publisher.* Chicago: University of Chicago Press, 1943.

A thorough study. Gives general picture of output of federal government, with departmental, functional, and subject analyses of publications. Indexed.

Morehead, Joe. *Introduction to United States Public Documents.* Littleton, Colo.: Libraries Unlimited, 1975. 2d ed., 1978.

The first textbook for use in government documents courses in library schools, written in Morehead's inimitable style. An excellent work, covering publications of governmental units. Good descriptions of agency activities in first edition. See also Harleston and Schmeckebier.

Schmeckebier, Laurence F. *Government Publications and Their Use.* 2d rev. ed. Washington, D.C.: Brookings Institution, 1969.

Basic guide "to the acquisition and use of government publications." Excellent information on the publishing history of series, bibliographies, catalogs, congressional publications, laws, and court decisions.

I.B. BIBLIOGRAPHICAL

These bibliographical aids to selected publications are useful as an indication of the variety of government publications available. Note that the guides are for selected publications and are not complete. Many are useful as a starting point in the preparation of topical bibliographies.

Body, Alexander C. *Annotated Bibliography of Bibliographies on Selected Government Publications and Supplementary Guides to the Superintendent of Documents Classification System.* Kalamazoo, Mich.: Western Michigan University, 1967. Supplements, 1968, 1970, 1972, 1974.

An excellent selection of pertinent bibliographies on various subjects issued by agencies. Arranged by Superintendent of Documents classification.

Childs, James B. *Government Document Bibliography in the United States and Elsewhere.* 3d ed. Washington, D.C.: Govt. Print. Off., 1942.

A bibliography of bibliographies on government publications of the United States, Confederate States, and foreign countries. See new edition by Palic.

Hirshberg, Herbert S., and Carl H. Melinat. *Subject Guide to United States Government Publications.* Chicago: American Library Association, 1947.

Covers period 1927–47. Lists publications by subject, with "emphasis on serials, directories, bibliographies and handbooks." Still a useful guide because many publications are of continuing interest.

Jackson, Ellen. *Subject Guide to Major United States Government Publications.* Chicago: American Library Association, 1968.

Annotated "listing, under subject headings, of some of the works of permanent value that the compiler found useful." Good for basic sources of information on topics of general interest.

Leidy, William P. *A Popular Guide to Government Publications.* 3d ed. New York: Columbia University Press, 1968.

Publications of a popular nature issued primarily between 1961 and mid-1966, with some older titles. Arranged by broad subject with detailed subject index.

Palic, Vladimir M. *Government Publications: A Guide to Bibliographic Tools.* 4th ed. Washington, D.C.: Govt. Print. Off., 1976.

The comprehensive guide to official publications issued by the United States, foreign, and international governmental organizations. Includes references to catalogs, checklists, price lists, and other indirect aids. Excellent section on publications of departments and agencies. Earlier editions by J. B. Childs. See also Brown (sec. I.A).

Schorr, Alan. *Government Reference Books 74/75: A Biennial Guide to U.S. Government Publications.* 4th ed. Littleton, Colo.: Libraries Unlimited, 1970. 1968/69 to 1972/73 editions by Sally Wynkoop.

Annotated subject guide to current reference works. "Reference work" is defined as including bibliographies, directories, handbooks and guides, indexes, statistical compendia, dictionaries and gazeteers. A good tool for selecting reference works.

Sheehy, Eugene P. *Guide to Reference Books.* 9th ed. Chicago: American Library Association, 1975.

Basic guide to the major reference sources. Good annotations. Lists the more important reference works issued by the federal government; also lists guides, bibliographies, etc., concerning government publications. Previous editions by Constance M. Winchell, Isadore Mudge, and Alice B. Kroeger.

U.S. Superintendent of Documents. *Price Lists*. Washington, D.C.: Govt. Print. Off., 1898–1974.

These numbered lists were revised at irregular intervals. Each provided a subject bibliography of materials of general interest to the public. Entries often annotated. Except for *Price List 36* (Government Periodicals and Subscription Services), which continues to be issued, these lists were discontinued in 1974 and replaced by *Subject Bibliographies*.

———. *Subject Bibliographies* (SB 001–). 1975– .

A successor to *Price Lists*. Each bibliography covers a specific topic. Over 270 different lists include materials in print and reprinted titles. Sent to depository libraries. Available to other libraries on request, without charge. An index to the bibliographies is also available. See pages 43–44 for fuller description.

———. *Selected U.S. Government Publications*. 1928– . Issued monthly.

Booklet listing materials of general interest to public and to small libraries. Entries are by broad subject and most are annotated. Publications can be ordered through Public Documents Distribution Centers. Free on subscription basis. Good current-awareness tool for small nondepository libraries.

Wynkoop, Sally. *Subject Guide to Government Reference Books*. Littleton, Colo.: Libraries Unlimited, 1972.

"Identifies some of the major reference publications of the federal government in all subject areas. . . . The emphasis is on comprehensive works and serial publications." Arranged by General Works, Social Sciences, Science and Technology, and Humanities. Broken down to specific subjects and types of publication. Annotated entries. Author, title, and subject index.

II.   CATALOGS AND INDEXES

II.A. GENERAL

To locate government publications of a general nature, the following sources are suggested. Depending on the nature of the question, use of one or more sources may be necessary. Because the time frame of an index is important to a search, a chronological list of selected catalogs and indexes is appended as table 3, and the following sources are listed in chronological order.

1774–1881

Poore, Benjamin Perley. *A Descriptive Catalogue of the Government Publications of the United States, September 5, 1774–March 4, 1881.* 48th Congress, 2d sess. Senate Misc. Doc. 67. Washington, D.C.: Govt. Print. Off., 1885. Reprinted, Ann Arbor, Mich.: Edwards, 1953.

Cited as *Poore's*. Chronological listing with index of authors, agencies, and subjects. One of a kind for time covered. Emphasis on congressional publications.

TABLE 3   CHRONOLOGICAL GUIDE TO SELECTED CATALOGS AND INDEXES
TO U.S. GOVERNMENT PUBLICATIONS (Dates indicate coverage)

	1775	1800	1880	1890	1900	1930	1940	1970	1975–
Poore's	1774 ———————— 1881								
Greely (congressional)	1789 — 1817								
Checklist	1789 ———————————— 1909								
Tables and Annotated Index	1789 ———————— 1893								
CIS U.S. Serial Set Index	1789 ————————————————— 1969								
Ames			1881 — 1893						
Document Catalogue				1893 ————————— 1940					
Document Index				1895 ———— 1933					
Monthly Catalog (GPO)				1895 —————————————————					
Cumulative Subject Index to Monthly Catalog (Carrollton Press)					1900 ——————— 1971				
Price Lists					1898 ———————————— 1975				
Numerical Lists (congressional)						1933 ————			
Congressional Index (CCH) (bills and resolutions)						1937 ————			
Guide to U.S. Government Publications (Andriot)							1946 ————		
ASI American Statistics Index (statistics)								(1960) 1974 ——	
CIS Index (congressional)								1970 ————	
Subject Bibliographies									1975—
GPO Sales Publications Reference File (publications in print)									1977

Note: Listed by popular and short titles. For complete title entries, see section "Selected Indexes, Catalogs, Checklists, and Other Sources." This table is an updated version of one which first appeared in *A Guide to Selected United States Government Publications*, compiled by Yuri Nakata (Chicago: University of Illinois at Chicago Circle Library, 1970).

1789–1909

U.S. Documents Office. *Checklist of U.S. Public Documents, 1789–1909*. 3d ed. rev. and enl. Washington, D.C.: Govt. Print. Off., 1911. Reprinted, New York: Kraus, 1962.

Cited as *Checklist*. Most useful retrospective bibliography for departmental publications. Informative notes on history of departments and their publications. Tables for documents and reports of 1st–60th Congresses. Particularly helpful are the references from departmental to congressional editions (serial numbers provided). Superintendent of Documents numbers given. Index of departments, bureaus, etc.

Update of this publication, *Checklist of United States Public Documents, 1789–1975 (Checklist '75)*, is available from Carrollton Press. Over 1 million shelflist cards, maintained by the Office of the Superintendent of Documents, were microfilmed on 118 reels (arranged in SuDoc classification order). Five index volumes in hard copy accompany the microfilm. Updated semiannually.

1881–93

Ames, John G. *Comprehensive Index to the Publications of the United States Government, 1881–1893* 58th Congress, 2d sess. House Doc. 754. Washington, D.C.: Govt. Print. Off., 1905. Reprinted, Ann Arbor, Mich.: Edwards, 1953. 2 vols. in 1.

Cited as *Ames.* Alphabetical index by subject with personal index. Emphasis on congressional publications. Arranged in columns, giving author or department, document by key word, reference to Congress, session, and series volume for documents in serial set.

1893–1940

U.S. Superintendent of Documents. *Catalogue of the Public Documents of the [53d–76th] Congress and of All Departments of the Government of the United States for the Period from March 4, 1893, to December 31, 1940.* Washington, D.C.: Govt. Print. Off., 1896–1945. 25 vols. Biennial.

Cited as *Document Catalogue.* The first and most comprehensive dictionary catalog of federal publications. Entries are by subject, author, agency, and often by title. Gives reference to serial set for congressional publications.

1895–

U.S. Superintendent of Documents. *Monthly Catalog of United States Government Publications.* Washington, D.C.: Govt. Print. Off., 1895– .

Title varies. The major current listing of federal government publications. Arranged by issuing agency with bibliographic and ordering information. Monthly and annual indexes include subjects, some titles for various years. Beginning in January 1974, three separate indexes: author, title, subject. In July 1976, when cataloging was converted to MARC format, a series/report index was added. An index to S/N numbers is projected.

Listing of Superintendent of Documents numbers began in 1924. Until 1977, February issues contained list of periodicals and subscription titles. As of 1977, an appendix issue, *Monthly Catalog of United States Government Publications, Serials Supplement*, is published annually. Entries conform to CONSER standard.

Supplements to *Monthly Catalog* published in 1947–48: *Monthly Catalog of United States Publications Supplement* (1941–42, 1943–44, 1945–46). *Decennial Cumulative Indexes,* covering 1941–50 and 1951–60, appeared in 1953 and 1968.

Cumulative indexes for 1961–65 and 1966–70 were published in 1976 (2 vols.) and 1977 (2 vols.). In preparation is an index covering 1971–75.

See also *GPO Sales Publications Reference File.*

1895–99

Cumulative Subject Index to the Monthly Catalog of United States Government Publications, 1895–1899.
Compiled by Edna A. Kanely. Washington, D.C.: Carrollton Press, 1977. 2 vols.

1900–71

Cumulative Subject Index to the Monthly Catalog of the United States Government Publications, 1900–1971. Compiled by William W. Buchanan and Edna A. Kanely. Washington, D.C.: Carrollton Press, 1975. 15 vols.

A cumulative index to biennial *Document Catalogue* (1900–40), decennial cumulative indexes to *Monthly Catalog* (1941–60), and annual indexes to *Monthly Catalog* (1961–71). Entries refer to *Monthly Catalog* by year and entry or page numbers. Despite limitations of indexes to *Monthly Catalog,* this cumulation is a monumental work and an essential tool.

1956–67

U.S. Library of Congress. *National Union Catalog, 1956 through 1967. A Cumulative List Representing Library of Congress Printed Cards and Titles Reported by Other American Libraries.* Totowa, N.J.: Rowman and Littlefield, 1970–72. 125 vols.

Combines 4th and 5th supplements to *NUC* with additional locations through 1967. Continues the title below. Continued by original cumulations of *NUC*.

Pre-1956

U.S. Library of Congress. *National Union Catalog. Pre-1956 Imprints. A Cumulative Author List Representing Library of Congress Printed Cards and Titles Reported by Other American Libraries.* London: Mansell, 1968– (in progress).

Supersedes Library of Congress *Catalog of Books*, its *Supplement* (1942–47); *Library of Congress Author Catalog, 1948–1952, National Union Catalog, 1952–1955 Imprints,* and *National Union Catalog . . . 1953–1957* (excluding motion pictures, filmstrips, and recordings). Once the U.S. volumes are published they will be helpful for verifying government publications not in *Monthly Catalog* and other indexes. Until that time the original catalogs will have to be used.

1973–

Andriot, John L., ed. *Guide to U.S. Government Publications.* McLean, Va.: Documents Index, 1973– .

Previous editions under title *Guide to U.S. Government Serials and Periodicals*, 1959–73. Issued as loose-leaf service from January 1973 to June 1976. Superseded by four volumes completed in 1978. Frequent updates are projected.

Cited as *Andriot*. Annotated guide to publications from existing and abolished agencies, arranged by SuDoc numbers with agency and title indexes. Classification numbers cross-referenced. Notes give agency history.

An outstanding and indispensable reference tool to keep on a dictionary stand, close to the reference desk. Title and agency indexes especially helpful as quick-finding aids.

1977–

U.S. Superintendent of Documents. *GPO Sales Publications Reference File* (*PRF*). 1977– . Bimonthly.

A file of some 19,000 titles in stock, 6,000 no longer in stock, and 400–500 titles and publications newly available for sale. A "books in print" list on approximately 110 microfiches in 48x reduction ratio available as selection item (552B) by depository libraries.

File is in three sections: stock number order, SuDoc number order, and alphabetical sequence (a dictionary arrangement of all titles, series, key words, key phrases, subjects, and personal author). Subjects based on key words and thesaurus of the Congressional Reference Service of the Library of Congress.

Subject access superior to LC subjects in *Monthly Catalog*. File maintained by computer and continuously updated. *PRF User's Manual; How to Use the Microfiche File* accompanies first shipment of microfiche.

Depository libraries that select this tool, and other libraries that subscribe to it, receive the entire *PRF* six times a year (January, March, May, July, September, and November). The PRF supplement, entitled *GPO New Sales Publications*, is distributed to depository libraries monthly and is available to other libraries on a subscription basis. In title sequence only, the Supplement lists newly priced and new-in-stock publications, including reprinted titles. In months when the entire set is not distributed, separate microfiche is sent.

For sale on a subscription basis: $50 for the bimonthly file; single set available at $10. Supplement is available at $5 per year. *PRF* is an indispensable verification and reference tool, complementing *Monthly Catalog*.

II.B. SPECIALIZED CATALOGS AND INDEXES

Several specialized indexes assist in locating publications by special characteristics such as author, declassified documents, popular names, statistics, and articles in periodicals.

Author

Monthly Catalog of United States Government Publications. Decennial Cumulative Personal Author Index, 1941–1950. Ed. Edward Przebienda. Ann Arbor, Mich.: Pierian Press, 1971.

————. *Decennial Cumulative Personal Author Index, 1951–1960.* 1971.

————. *Quinquennial Cumulative Personal Author Index, 1961–1965.* 1971.

————. *Quinquennial Cumulative Personal Author Index, 1966–1970.* 1972.

Broad interpretation of authorship, editors, indexers, and translators. Especially useful for period 1947–63, when *Monthly Catalog* did not index by author. Useful also since 1963, as GPO indexes by first author only.

Declassified Documents

Declassified Documents Quarterly Catalog, vol. 1, no. 1, January–March 1975– . Washington, D.C.: Carrollton Press, 1975.

Cumulative Subject Index to the Declassified Documents Quarterly Catalog, vol. 1, no. 1, January–March 1975– . Washington, D.C.: Carrollton Press, 1975.

Lists top-secret, secret, and confidential documents as they are declassified. Full text of the documents is also offered in microfiche sets.

Periodical Articles

Index to U.S. Government Periodicals. Infordata International, Chicago, 1974– .

A computer-generated quarterly index to some 160 selected government periodicals. Articles indexed by author and subject. Annual cumulations. Retrospective volumes for years 1970–74 available; others in preparation. Indexes government periodicals not indexed elsewhere.

Government periodicals are also indexed in varying degrees in the standard subject indexes. Public Affairs Information Service *Bulletin* (*PAIS*) includes wider coverage than most.

Periodicals and Subscription Services

U.S. Superintendent of Documents. *Government Periodicals and Subscription Services.* Price List No. 36. 171st ed. Washington, D.C.: Govt. Print. Off., 1978.

Frequently revised. "A listing, alphabetically by title, of all periodicals and other serials available for sale . . . on a subscription basis." Full bibliographic information plus annotations. Serials listings in *Andriot* and February (prior to 1977) issue of *Monthly Catalog* are more extensive and list items other than GPO and subscription titles.

See also *Monthly Catalog of United States Government Publications, Serials Supplement.*

Popular Names

U.S. Library of Congress. *Popular Names of U.S. Government Reports: A Catalog.* 3d ed. Compiled by Bernard A. Bernier, Jr., Katherine F. Gould, and Porter Humphrey. Washington, D.C.: Library of Congress, 1976.

Since many patrons refer to publications by popular name, this is a very handy list of reports by the personal names associated with a study. Entries are reproductions of LC entry cards. Index by subject and corporate entry. The 3d edition includes SuDoc classification numbers, a feature which improves the usefulness of this edition over the others.

Statistics

Congressional Information Service. *American Statistics Index.* 1974–   . Washington, D.C.: Congressional Information Service, 1974–   .

The key to statistical data in government publications. The *1974 Annual* is retrospective. Includes index and abstract. Annual volumes and periodic updates throughout year. Covers broad range of federal statistical publications, both current and older publications of lasting research value. Includes statistics in all printed forms and some statistics-related material. Analyzes periodical issues, series, and monographs, giving information on each table and all other statistics. Indexed by subject, author, title, agency report number, and category (i.e., sex, age, city). Gives SuDoc classification numbers. ASI data base is accessible through a terminal. (See chapter 7.)

Andriot, John L. *Guide to U.S. Government Statistics.* 4th ed. McLean, Va.: Documents Index, 1973.

"Annotated guide to over 1700 U.S. government publications from 1-page releases to huge compilations of historical data." Also gives individual titles in series. Arranged by SuDoc number. Information similar to that in author's *Guide to U.S. Government Publications.* Author-title-subject index. Useful for historical data. Now superseded by *American Statistics Index.*

II.C. DEPARTMENTAL AND AGENCY CATALOGS

The following represent a selective list of the more substantial catalogs of publications issued by agencies and departments. These are comprehensive listings, updated frequently, which cover the publishing history of an agency. Since all agencies are required to publish lists of their publications in the *Federal Register*, there are many other lists, varying in scope, that can be helpful in verifying and ordering titles. Such limitations as irregular and outdated catalogs should be taken into consideration.

U.S. Bureau of American Ethnology. *List of Publications of the Bureau of American Ethnology, with Index to Authors and Titles.* Washington, D.C.: Smithsonian Institution Press, 1971 (Bulletin 200).

Lists and annotates all publications of the bureau during its existence. Good index of authors and titles.

U.S. Bureau of Labor Statistics. *B.L.S. Publications, 1886–1971.* Washington, D.C.: Govt. Print. Off., 1972 (Bulletin 1749).
Catalog of major publications that highlight series, which are listed by number. Subject index to bulletins and reports. Updated periodically.

U.S. Department of Commerce. *United States Department of Commerce Publications.* Washington, D.C.: Govt. Print. Off., 1952.
Catalog of selected publications from 1790 to October 1950.

———. ———. Supplement 1951–52– . Washington, D.C.: Govt. Print. Off., 1954– .
Annual supplements to basic volume. Cumulates biweekly *Business Service Checklist.*

U.S. Geological Survey. *Publications of the Geological Survey, 1879–1961.* Washington, D.C., 1962.
Catalog of books, maps, and charts with subject, geographic, and author indexes.

———. *Publications of the Geological Survey, 1962–1970.* Washington, D.C., 1972.
Supplements basic catalog above. Also annual catalogs and monthly *New Publications of the Geological Survey.*

U.S. Bureau of Mines. *List of Publications, July 1910–January 1, 1960.* Washington, D.C.: Govt. Print. Off., 1960.
Updated by monthly *New Publications—Bureau of Mines* and supplemented by annual and five-year cumulations.

U.S. National Bureau of Standards. *Publications of the National Bureau of Standards* (1901 to June 30, 1947). Washington, D.C.: Govt. Print. Off., 1948.
Updated periodically.

II.D. DEPARTMENTAL LIBRARY CATALOGS

These catalogs, covering departmental library collections, contain many nongovernment titles. However, for verification of older government publications they can be helpful "last resorts" for searches.

U.S. Department of Health, Education, and Welfare. *Author/Title Catalog of the Department Library.* Boston: G. K. Hall, 1965. 29 vols.
Reproduction of the card catalog for books, papers, government documents, etc. Particularly strong in education, law, and social sciences. Most journal titles are not listed.

———. *Subject Catalog of the Department Library.* Boston: G. K. Hall, 1965. 20 vols.
"Includes subject cards for books, pamphlets, documents and serial publications."

U.S. Department of the Interior. *Biographical and Historical Index of American Indians and Persons Involved in Indian Affairs.* Boston: G. K. Hall, 1966. 8 vols.

Subject index to department collection as well as journal articles, books, and documents in other collections. Emphasis is on persons and tribes. Covers "biography, history and social conditions during the latter half of the nineteenth century and the first part of the twentieth century."

U.S. Department of the Interior. *Catalog of the United States Geological Survey Library.* Boston: G. K. Hall, 1964. 25 vols.

Indexes bound volumes, periodical titles, pamphlets, and maps (only when accompanied by some kind of text). Inclusion of analytics depends on importance of material. Covers authors, titles, and subjects in most areas of geology.

U.S. Department of the Interior. *Dictionary Catalog of the Department Library.* Boston: G. K. Hall, 1967. 37 vols.

Reproduction of the card catalog (author, title, subject), comprising books, government publications, unpublished materials, and foreign publications in natural resources, conservation, and reclamation. Some journals and most serials are analyzed. Particularly strong in mining, geology, wildlife, and land policies. Much material that is not indexed elsewhere.

————. ————. 1st supplement. 1969. 4 vols.
2d supplement. 1971. 2 vols.
3d supplement. 1973. 4 vols.
4th supplement. 1975. 8 vols.

U.S. Housing and Urban Development Department. *The Dictionary Catalog of the United States Department of Housing and Urban Development, Library and Information Division.* Boston: G. K. Hall, 1972– . 19 vols.

Reproduction of HUD card catalog, representing all forms of material on urban affairs and community development. Includes federal, state, and local documents. Includes subject headings and periodicals list. Vol. 19 has KWIC and geographic indexes to Comprehensive Planning Assistance (701) reports.

————. ————. 1st supplement. 1974. 2 vols.
2d supplement. 1975. 2 vols.

III.   SOURCES

III.A. CENSUS AND VITAL STATISTICS

Census and vital statistics data are diverse and important reference sources. A large number of the reference questions deal with statistical data and particularly with aspects of census and vital statistics. Because of wide-ranging nature of these statistics, only a brief discussion can be attempted here. The comprehensive compilations of census data are available every five and ten years, as shown in table 4.

TABLE 4. **SUBJECTS AND FREQUENCY OF CENSUS COMPILATIONS**

CENSUS	FREQUENCY YEARS	RECENT CENSUSES	NEXT CENSUS
Agriculture	5	1969, 1974	1978*
Construction Industries	5	1967, 1972	1977
Governments	5	1967, 1972	1977
Manufactures	5	1967, 1972	1977
Mineral Industries	5	1967, 1972	1977
Retail Trade	5	1967, 1972	1977
Selected Service Industries	5	1967, 1972	1977
Transportation	5	1967, 1972	1977
Wholesale Trade	5	1967, 1972	1977
Population and Housing	10	1960, 1970	1980

*Schedule changed to align with other economic censuses taken every five years, for years ending in 2 and 7.

Beginning in 1985, the population and housing censuses will be available every five years. The *Census of Business* for 1972 includes the *Census of Retail Trade, Census of Wholesale Trade,* and *Census of Selected Service Industries*. Data are available by states.

Reports between censuses are available in the form of current reports dealing with population, manufacturing, commodity production, retail and wholesale trade, housing characteristics, and state and local government finances. These reports are extremely important and should be used to update the comprehensive compilations mentioned above. Particularly popular are the Current Population Report series (C 3.186:):

P-20   School Enrollment
        Educational Attainment
        Characteristics of Persons, Families and Households
        Fertility
        Mobility Status of Population
        Residence
        Voters and Voting
P-23   Special Studies
P-25   Population Estimates and Projections
P-26   Federal–State Cooperative Program for Population Estimates

For a list of these reports, consult pages 328–56 in the catalog issued by the Bureau of the Census, and annual updates:

Bureau of the Census Catalog of Publications, 1790–1972. Washington, D.C., 1972. (C 56.222/2–2:). Updated by annuals (C 3.163/3:). "Part 1" is a reprint of the classic *Catalog of United States Census Publications* (cited as *Dubester*), 1790–1945, and "Part 2," which is a compilation of the annual catalogs, 1946–72. Arranged by subject fields with sections on guides, methodological studies, and foreign-country studies. Includes subject and geographic indexes (*ASI* has better subject approach). All entries are annotated. SuDoc numbers are provided for most of the titles listed in "Part 2." *Dubester* is an indispensable catalog with an excellent index. Librarians should annotate this catalog to indicate holdings and location of materials.

An excellent guide to contents of the large census compilations is another publication issued by the Bureau of the Census:

Guide to Programs and Publications—Subjects and Areas, 1973. Washington, D.C.: Govt. Print. Off., 1974. (C 56.209:P94)

Vital Statistics

For vital statistics, the annual cumulation is

National Center for Health Statistics. *Vital Statistics of the United States.* Washington, D.C., Govt. Print. Off. Annual. (HE 20.6210:yr/v/pt.) In several volumes. Vol. 1 is on natality; vol. 2, parts A and B, is on mortality; and vol. 3 is on marriage and divorce.

Prior to 1937, vital statistics were published in two annual volumes, *Birth, Stillbirth and Infant Mortality Statistics* (since 1915) and *Mortality Statistics* (since 1900). From 1937–49, published in two parts annually, *Vital Statistics of the United States:* part 1, *Natality and Mortality,* data by year of occurrence, and part 2 by place of residence.

For current information see

Monthly Vital Statistics Report, Provisional Statistics. Covers births, marriages, divorces, and deaths. (HE 20.6217:v/no.)

Special supplements on marriage, divorce, natality, and other subjects are issued irregularly. An example is

Teenage Childbearing, United States, 1966–1975. September 1977. (HE 20.6217:26/5/supp.)

Vital and Health Statistics Series (HE 20.6209:series/no.) is another important series.

For a subject approach to census data and vital statistics, the best source is *American Statistics Index.*

III.B. CONGRESSIONAL PUBLICATIONS

The publications of Congress generally include bills and resolutions, hearings, committee reports, committee prints, and debates.[2] These are among the most important and the most sought after government publications. Citations to congressional publications presented by patrons are often vague and incomplete, causing difficulties in the identification of titles. Nongovernmental sources are often helpful in giving a brief summary of legislation or some other issue discussed by Congress. Recommended sources are

> *Congressional Quarterly Almanac* (annual) and *CQ Weekly Report.* Washington, D.C., Congressional Quarterly.

These two publications are must reading for librarians who work with government publications. Coverage includes Congress, government, and politics. Handy source for votes in Congress. The *Almanac* is a "facts on file" that can be used as a starting point for general questions on congressional action. Very useful for tracing legislative history.

III.B. 1.   GENERAL CATALOGS AND INDEXES TO CONGRESSIONAL PUBLICATIONS (in Chronological Order)

1789–1817

> Greely, Adolphus Washington. *Public Documents of the First Fourteen Congresses, 1789–1817. Papers Relating to Early Congressional Documents.* 56th Cong., 1st sess., Senate Document 428. Washington, D.C.: Govt. Print. Off., 1900.
>
> ———. *Supplement.* 1904. Reprinted, New York: Johnson, 1963. 2 vols. in 1.
> Cited as *Greely.* Arranged by Congress, with name index. No subject index. Useful introduction.

1789–1893

> U.S. Superintendent of Documents. *Tables of and Annotated Index to the Congressional Series of U.S. Public Documents.* Washington, D.C.: Govt. Print. Off., 1902. Reprinted, Waltham, Mass.: Mark Press, 1963.
> Covers congressional set through 52d Congress. Includes *American State Papers.* An author, title, and subject index to important documents. Tables are repeated in *Checklist.* Superseded by *CIS U.S. Serial Set Index, 1789–1969* (see III.B.6).

1895–1933

> U.S. Superintendent of Documents. *Index to the Reports and Documents of the 54th Congress, 1st Session–72d Congress, 2d Session;*

---

2. For a comprehensive discussion of congressional publications, see "Congressional Publications" in *United States Government Publications* by Anne Morris Boyd and Rae Elizabeth Rips, 3d ed. (New York: Wilson, 1949), pp. 47–82.
For a list of the sessions of Congress, with dates, see appendix 5.

December 2, 1895–March 4, 1933. Washington, D.C.: Govt. Print. Off., 1897–1933. 43 volumes.

Cited as *Document Index.* Continues index of *Tables of and Annotated Index.* Includes a numerical list and schedule of volumes for each session.

1933–

U.S. Superintendent of Documents. *Numerical Lists and Schedule of Volumes of the Reports and Documents of the 73d Congress.* Washington, D.C.: Govt. Print. Off., 1934.

Cited as *Numerical Lists.* Continues listings in *Document Index.* Also included in *Document Catalogue* until its discontinuance in 1940. See also *CIS U.S. Serial Set Index, 1789–1969* (see III.B.6).

1970–

Congressional Information Service. *CIS/Index to Publications of the United States Congress.* Washington, D.C.: Congressional Information Service, 1970– .

Abstracts and index volumes. Monthly issues with annual cumulations. Abstracts congressional publications with analytics for hearing testimony. Annual volumes contain legislative histories for the year's laws. Detailed indexes of subjects, names, and bill, report and document numbers. An outstanding and indispensable work. The most comprehensive and useful tool for locating congressional information. Includes SuDoc numbers.

For indexes to hearings and committee prints prior to 1970, see Indexes to Hearings (table 5). The CIS data base is accessible through a terminal (see chapter 7).

III.B. 2.   LAWS, STATUTES, ETC.

The chief function of Congress is the making of laws, but the procedural steps in the legislative process are complicated, especially to the uninitiated. Two excellent publications describing the process are

How Our Laws Are Made. Revised frequently.
Example: House Document 259, 95th Cong., 1st sess.

Enactment of Law. Revised frequently.
Example: Senate Document 152, 94th Cong., 2d sess.

These are available from your Congressman or from the Superintendent of Documents.

Bills and resolutions originate in Congress and are first printed when referred to a committee. A bill originating in the House of Representatives is designated by the letters "H.R." followed by a number that it retains throughout its legislative stages. A Senate bill is designated as "S." Amendments are printed separately and are given the bill number. To locate the bill number of a piece of legislation or to find a bill's status, several tools can be used:

Congressional Index. 75th Congress, 1937/38– . Chicago: Commerce Clearing House, 1937– .

Weekly loose-leaf service indexing all bills and resolutions by subject, author, and bill number. Gives progress of bills, information on committees, voting records, enactments, treaties, and nominations. A quick-finding aid for current bills and their status.

The *Congressonal Record Index,* issued fortnightly for the unbound edition of the *Congressional Record,* is an aid in tracing legislation. The bound edition of the *Index* may be a separate volume or it may be bound with the *Appendix* volume. The *Index* is in two parts: (1) "Index to the Proceedings" and (2) "History of Bills and Resolutions." The first is indexed by subject, author, and names of individuals and committees. Bill numbers as well as names of individuals who introduced legislation can be identified in the "Index to the Proceedings." To trace legislation further, turn to "History of Bills and Resolutions," which includes such information as title of bill, action taken, report numbers of committee reports, and page reference to *Congressional Record* where action on legislation was taken. The "History of Bills and Resolutions," does not include references to hearings. For this information consult indexes to hearings (see table 5) prior to 1970 and the *CIS/Index* thereafter.

For the legislative history of current bills, the *Daily Digest* of the *Congressional Record* lists action taken on bills.

Also for current status of bills see the *Calendars of the House of Representatives and History of Legislation,* published each day the House is in session, with weekly subject index and cumulated index at the close of a session. The *Calendar* lists bills of both houses with their legislative histories.

Other sources are

U.S. Library of Congress. Congressional Research Service. *Digest of Public General Bills and Resolutions.* Washington, D.C.: Govt. Print. Off., 1936– .

Five or more cumulative issues with biweekly supplements, as needed, with final issue at the end of each session of Congress. Presents in summary form essential features of public bills and resolutions. The digests are well written and complete. This is a major source for a record of all laws introduced in Congress. An outstanding feature is the legislative history of public laws. Well indexed by sponsors, short title, and subject.

Congressional Information Service. *CIS/Index to Publications of the United States Congress.* Washington, D.C.: Congressional Information Service, 1970– .

The section "Index of Bill, Report and Document Numbers" includes numbers of all public bills that are the subject of hearings, reports, and other publications appearing in the *Abstract* section. All bills are cross-referenced to the *CIS/Abstract* serial numbers.

Individual bills are available from your congressman, clerk of the Senate, or clerk of the House. They may be examined at depository libraries which select this item.

After a bill becomes law—that is, is passed by both houses and is signed by the President—it is printed in a form known as a slip law (GS 4.110:nos) and given consecutive numbers by Congress, such as Public Law PL 95–114 (114th public bill signed in the 95th Congress). Slip laws are indexed in the *Monthly Catalog* and are available from your congressman or the Superintendent of Documents. At the close of each session, all laws are printed in the permanent edition, called *Statutes-at-Large* (GS 4.111:vol.). The codification of laws appears in the *United States Code: The General and Permanent Laws of the United States in 50 Titles* (Y 1.2/5:yr/vol.).

III.B. 3.   HEARINGS

House and Senate committees may hold hearings on bills (or on any subject) to give opportunity to citizens to participate in the process of legislation. Hearings (a record of testimony) are almost always held on controversial issues. Congressional hearings prior to 1970 are especially difficult to identify; they were not analyzed until the *CIS/Index* appeared in 1970. If hearings are not listed in the general catalogs to government publications (most currently the *Monthly Catalog*) try the indexes to hearings (table 5). These indexes indicate if a certain hearing was published. Arrangement is by committee of the Senate or House and a subject index is included in each volume. Since 1970, the *CIS/Index* is the best source for locating hearings.

III.B. 4.   COMMITTEE PRINTS

Congressional committees have legal and research staffs to assist in conducting studies under investigation by a committee. The Congressional Research Service of the Library of Congress is also called upon to conduct research for congressional committees. These studies are issued as committee prints. Because most committee prints were not depository items until the early 1970s, very few committee prints are listed in the *Monthly Catalog* for earlier years. The same sources for locating hearings should be used for committee prints.

III.B. 5.   CONGRESSIONAL REPORTS AND DOCUMENTS

Following the hearings on a bill, the congressional committee is expected to report to the house where the bill was introduced. These reports are issued as separates in four series:

Senate reports and House reports are individual reports of committees of the Senate and House, numbered by Congress and report number. Examples: Senate Report 95–1; House Report 95–5 (*95* stands for the 95th Congress and reports are numbered consecutively in each house).

Senate documents and House documents cover a wide variety of subjects, such as reports of investigations, messages from the President, and annual reports of executive departments and independent establishments (government and nongovernment), which are required to report to Congress. Examples: Senate Document 95–1; House Document 95–5. These reports are indexed in the *Monthly Catalog* and the *CIS/Index*. A search strategy for locating a House document appears in figure 9. The separates may be discarded, or kept as circulating copies, after the Congressional Set volumes are received.

The same procedure can be followed for locating Senate reports, House reports, and Senate documents. Those who have the *CIS U.S. Serial Set Index* can use this source for locating reports in the Serial Set, 1789–1969.

TABLE 5 **INDEXES TO HEARINGS**

1824–1958	*Printed Hearings of the House of Representatives Found among Its Committee Records in the National Archives of the United States, 1824–1958* (Special List No. 35). Washington, D.C.: National Archives and Records Service, General Services Administration, 1974.
Prior to March 4, 1935	*Index to Congressional Committee Hearings . . . prior to March 4, 1935, in the United States Senate Library.* Washington, D.C.: Govt. Print. Off., 1935. Reprinted, New York: Kraus Reprint Co., 1969.
1935–59	*Cumulative Index of Congressional Committee Hearings* [not confidential in character] *from Seventy-fourth Congress (January 3, 1935) through Eighty-fifth Congress (January 3, 1959) in the United States Senate Library.* Washington, D.C.: Govt. Print. Off., 1959.
1959–62	*Quadrennial Supplement to Cumulative Index of Congressional Committee Hearings* [not confidential in character] *from Eighty-sixth Congress (January 7, 1959) through Eighty-seventh Congress (January 3, 1963) Together with Selected Committee Prints in the United States Senate Library.* Washington, D.C.: Govt. Print. Off., 1963.
1963–66	*Cumulative Index of Congressional Hearings* [not confidential in character], *Second Quadrennial Supplement from Eighty-eighth Congress (January 3, 1963) through Eighty-ninth Congress (January 3, 1967) Together with Selected Committee Prints in the United States Senate Library.* Washington, D.C.: Govt. Print. Off., 1967.
1967–71	*Cumulative Index of Congressional Committee Hearings* [not confidential in character] *from Ninetieth Congress (January 10, 1967) through Ninety-first Congress (January 2, 1971) together with Selected Committee Prints in the United States Senate Library.* Washington, D.C.: Govt. Print. Off., 1971.
1970–	*CIS Index*, Congressional Information Service.

Note: To locate the Superintendent of Documents number for a hearing cited, refer to Poole's *Documents Office Classification* (p. 140). Search should begin with the index to the volumes. (Example: To find the class number of the Senate Committee on Haiti and Santo Domingo, look under *Haiti*, class number Y 4.H12:).

Question: How do I find House Document 254, 94th Congress, listed in *Monthly Catalog,* July 1976, p. 199?

HOUSE DOCUMENTS

76-1318

94-1:H.doc.254

National Advisory Council on International Monetary and Financial Policies.

  Replenishment of resources of Inter-American Development Bank : communication from the Secretary of the Treasury transmitting a special report of the National Advisory Council on International Monetary and Financial Policies on the proposed replenishment of the resources of the Inter-American Development Bank, September 15, 1975. — Washington : U.S. Govt. Print. Off., 1975.

  [8], 85 p. ; 24 cm. — (House document - 94th Congress, 1st session ; no. 94-254)

  Item 996

  1. Inter-American Development Bank. I. Title. II. Series: United States. 94th Congress, 1st session, 1975. House. Document ; no. 94-254.

  OCLC 2058245

Senate reports, House reports, Senate documents, and House documents are issued as separates and then included in the bound edition of the Congressional Set (Serial Set). Therefore, if the separate is not available, check for document in Serial Set.

Check *Numerical Lists,* 94th Congress, 1st session (GP 3.7/2:94–1), under House document which will refer to serial set volume 13109–5.

No.	HOUSE DOCUMENTS	Vol.; serial
250.	8th annual report of National Advisory Council on Economic Opportunity	12–2; 13120–2
251.	Cumulative report on rescissions and deferrals of budget authority, Sept. 1975	1–4; 13109–4
252.	Actions on recommendations of President's Advisory Council on Management Improvement, March 26, 1975	1–4; 13109–4
253.	Resolved, that Federal Government should adopt comprehensive program to control land use in U.S., intercollegiate debate topic, 1975–76	2–7; 13110–7
254.	Replenishment of resources of Inter-American Development Bank	1–5; 13109–5

Other approaches to this document:

  By corporate author, title, or subject; see *Index* to the *Monthly Catalog* by author, title, or subject.

  By report number; consult series/report section of *Index* to the *Monthly Catalog.*

Figure 9. Search Strategy for Locating House Document

III.B. 6.   CONGRESSIONAL SET OR SERIAL SET

At the close of the congressional session, these reports (above) are brought together and issued in the numbered Congressional Set, popularly known as the Serial Set. The *CIS U.S. Serial Set Index, 1789–1969* provides the best access to these publications. Use the *CIS/Index* (1970–) for current publications. Those who do not have access to this set may use the *Monthly Catalog* and the *Numerical Lists* as access tools (see figure 9) and the early catalogs listed in III.B.1.

> Congressional Information Service. *CIS U.S. Serial Set Index, 1789– 1969.* Washington, D.C.: Congressional Information Service, 1975– 79.
>
> Published in 12 groups, each with two parts: (1) subject index, (2) finding list. The index has subject and key-word terms derived from the individual report and document titles. The finding list contains the numerical lists and schedule of volumes plus an index to individuals and organizations cited in reports on private bills. This is a long-awaited index to the Congressional Set.

III.B. 7.   CONFERENCE REPORTS

When a bill is not accepted by both houses, a conference with representatives from each house is held. The report that is agreed upon, usually a compromise, is called a "conference report." If the report is not located as a House or Senate report, try the *Congressional Record.* Conference reports often appear in the *Record.*

III.B. 8.   DEBATES OF CONGRESS

Debates and proceedings of Congress are available in printed form since 1789.

1789–1824   *Annals of Congress* is the short title for *The Debates and Proceedings in the Congress of the United States,* with an appendix containing "Important State Papers and Public Documents," and all the laws of a public nature, with copious index (1st to 18th Congress, 1st session; March 3, 1789–May 27, 1824). Compiled from authentic sources. Gales and Seaton. 1834–56. 42 vols.

1824–37   *Register of Debates in Congress,* comprising the leading debates and incidents of the second session of the 18th Congress (December 6, 1824, to first session of the 25th Congress, October 16, 1837), together with appendix containing most important state papers and public documents to which the session has given birth; to which are added the laws enacted during the session, with a copious index to the whole. Gales and Seaton. 1825–37. 14 vols. in 29.

1833–73   *Congressional Globe . . .* (23d Congress to 42d Congress; December 2, 1833, to March 3, 1873. 1834–73. 46 vols. in 109.
Appendixes (with own index) cover other material:
1833–68 Messages of Presidents and reports of heads of departments

1833–61 Text of laws passed during sessions
1853–73 Statement of appropriations

1873– *Congressional Record*. Published daily and bound with an index and "History of Bills and Resolutions" at close of each session of Congress.

III.B. 9.   HOUSE AND SENATE JOURNALS

Until 1925 the House and Senate *Journals* were included in the Congressional Set. They are now issued as separates. The *Journals*, issued at the close of a session, are comparable to minutes of meetings. Roll call votes may be found in the *Journals*.

III.C.   PUBLICATIONS OF THE PRESIDENT OF THE UNITED STATES

The President serves as the head of the executive branch of government. One of the important publications issued by each President is

Economic Report of the President, transmitted to Congress with the report of the Council of Economic Advisers (1947–date). Required at the beginning of each regular session of Congress.

The *Economic Report of the President* is a transmittal message on the economic accomplishments of the year. The Report of the Council of Economic Advisers is a detailed review of economic conditions and the outlook for the following year. Includes numerous tables and charts covering (among other statistics) national income (GNP), price deflators, savings, unemployment, consumer price index. Many of the tables cover a number of years (25 to 30 in some instances).

The Superintendent of Documents number assigned to publications of Presidents is Pr 1– (Washington). Each administration has its own number. For example, President Jimmy Carter is the 39th President and his personal publications are assigned the number Pr 39. (See appendix 5 for a list of Presidents and their terms of office.)

The best source for current documents of the President is

Weekly Compilation of Presidential Documents, 1965–
(GS 4.114:).
Published every Monday by the Office of the Federal Register. Contains addresses and remarks, announcements, appointments and nominations, bill signings, communications to Congress, executive orders, news conferences, White House statements, checklist of White House press releases, and digest of other announcements.

In 1961 the Executive Office of the President was established to handle the continuing activities of the President's office (Pr Ex). Following is a
In 1961 the Executive Office of the President was established to handle the continuing activities of the President's office (Pr Ex). Following is a
selected list of the publications of the major continuing units of the President's office.

Office of Management and Budget (OMB)

Since 1939 the OMB has been under the Office of the President. Two major publications issued by this office are

> *Budget of the United States Government* (includes the President's budget message). Annual. *Appendix* is the detailed budget. (Pr Ex 2.8:date)
>
> *Catalog of Federal Domestic Assistance* (Pr Ex 2.20:). Describes the types of federal domestic assistance available from various agencies. Those seeking grants will find this reference tool invaluable.

Council of Economic Advisers (CEA)

As noted earlier, the *Economic Report of the President* is assigned the individual President's number Pr 36.9:, Pr 38.9: and so on. Since the *Economic Report of the President* is published together with the Annual Report of the Council of Economic Advisers to the President, libraries that follow the Superintendent of Documents classification system may wish to bring a duplicate set of the reports together under the class number assigned to reports of the Council: Pr Ex 6.1:year.

National Security Council, Central Intelligence Agency (CIA)

> *CIA Maps and Atlases* (of foreign countries) (Pr Ex 3.10/4:)
> *CIA Reference Aid* (Pr Ex 3.11:) and subseries:
>> *Handbook of Economic Statistics* (year) provides statistics for non-Communist countries and Communist countries. Includes statistics on areas such as Soviet economic performance, aid, energy, transportation, communications, minerals and metals, chemicals and rubber and agriculture.

> *Chiefs of State and Cabinet Members of Foreign Governments.*
>> Directory that identifies officials in foreign governments recognized by the United States. Completely revised edition issued each month.

Public Papers of the President

Publication of the public papers of the Presidents was authorized in 1958, and the papers are issued by the General Services Administration. Public papers are published annually, covering a year's period. Texts of official communications to the Congress, addresses, transcripts of press conferences, messages and executive documents are included in the papers and are arranged in chronological order. The following papers have been published to date (1978):

> Herbert Hoover, 1929– 3 vols. (series extended to include earlier period)
> Harry S. Truman, 1945–52 8 vols.
> Dwight D. Eisenhower, 1953–60 8 vols.
> John F. Kennedy, 1961–63 3 vols.
> Lyndon B. Johnson, 1963–69 10 vols.
> Richard Nixon, 1969–74 6 vols.
> Gerald Ford, 1974–75 2 vols.

These volumes are available from the Superintendent of Documents and are distributed to depository libraries.

Many of the papers of the Presidents prior to 1945 were commercially printed. The presidential papers in the collection of the Library of Congress are available on microfilm from the Photoduplication Service, Library of Congress. Schmeckebier describes these as covering "certain loose documents on presidential papers."[2] Since some of the commercially published sets include papers not printed as government publications, they should be consulted in any serious research. See *Schmeckebier* for a list of the commercially available sets.

The presidential papers in the Library of Congress collection include those of

Chester A. Arthur	James Madison
Grover Cleveland	William McKinley
Calvin Coolidge	James Monroe
James A. Garfield	Franklin Pierce
Ulysses S. Grant	James K. Polk
Benjamin Harrison	Theodore Roosevelt
William H. Harrison	William Howard Taft
Andrew Jackson	Zachary Taylor
Thomas Jefferson	John Tyler
Andrew Johnson	George Washington
Abraham Lincoln	Woodrow Wilson

In-print indexes to the papers (LC 4.7:   ) are available from the Superintendent of Documents. Those not in print may be ordered from the Photoduplication Service of the Library of Congress (electrostatic prints).

Executive Orders and Proclamations

The President is also concerned with laws and issues executive orders which have the force of law. He aso issues proclamations to deal with matters of general interest; these seldom have the force of law.

Since 1936, executive orders and proclamations have appeared in the *Federal Register*. Title 3 of the *Code of Federal Regulations* lists all executive orders and proclamations issued the previous year. For current executive orders and proclamations the best source is

Weekly Compilation of Presidential Documents, v.1, August 2, 1965– .
Office of the Federal Register. (GS 4.114:   )
Published every Monday, includes transcripts of presidential news conferences, messages to Congress, executive orders and proclamations, published speeches, and White House releases.

Compilations of executive orders are issued frequently by the Office of the Federal Register: 1936–38, 1938–43, 1943–48, 1949–53, 1954–58,

2. Laurence F. Schmeckebier and Roy B. Eastin, *Government Publications and Their Use,* 2d rev. ed. (Washington, D.C.: Brookings Institute, 1969), p. 314.

1959–63, 1964–65, 1966–70, 1971–75. Also available are *Consolidated Tables, 1936–1965* and *Consolidated Indexes, 1936–1965.*

Two compilations are available from Princeton Datafilm, Inc., Box 231, Princeton Junction, N.J. 08550.

> *Presidential Executive Orders: Numbered 1–8030 (1862–1938).* Vol. 1, the list, and vol. 2, the index. New York: Historical Records Survey, 1944.

> *List and Index of Presidential Executive Orders: Unnumbered Series (1789–1941).* New Jersey Historical Survey, WPA, 1943.

III.D.   ADMINISTRATIVE REGULATIONS

The federal agencies are responsible for implementing legislation. Their rules and regulations are published in two important documents: the *Federal Register (FR)* (GS 4. 107:) and the *Code of Federal Regulations (CFR)* (GS 4.108:).

> *Federal Register*, 1936–. Issued 5 times a week.

The *Federal Register* makes available to the public regulations and legal notices issued by the executive branch and federal agencies, including proclamations, executive orders, and other documents having general applicability, legal effect, and public interest. The *Federal Register* includes proposed rules and notices of hearings and investigations, and committee meetings. The *Federal Register* updates the *Code of Federal Regulations.*

The *Code of Federal Regulations* is revised and published at least once a year at quarterly intervals. The *CFR* codifies the general and permanent regulations into 50 titles (subject areas). The *CFR* is for administrative procedure what the *United States Code* is for statutory law. The *CFR* and the *FR* must be used together.

Following are some finding aids from *The Federal Register: What It is and How to Use It; A Guide for the User of the Federal Register-Code of Federal Regulations System* (GS 4.6/2:F31) (available from the Office of the Federal Register).

Daily Publications

These finding aids are published daily in the *Federal Register* and can be found in the pages preceding the body of the agency documents:

1. *Highlights*   This is a selected list of documents in the issue that are determined to have wide public interest.
2. *Contents*   This is a comprehensive list of documents in the issue and their page numbers arranged by agency and type of document (rule, proposal, or notice).
3. *List of CFR Parts Affected*   Rules and proposals that appear in the issue arranged by part number.

4. *Cumulative List of Parts Affected—Monthly*   Rules and proposals that have appeared so far in that month's *Federal Registers*.
5. *Reminders*   A daily list of public laws and a list of rules going into effect on the day of the issue. Each Wednesday three more categories are added: Next Week's Deadlines for Comments on Proposed Rules; Next Week's Meetings; and Next Week's Public Hearings.
6. *Federal Register Pages and Dates*   A parallel table of the inclusive pages and corresponding dates for the *Federal Registers* of the month.

Monthly Publications

7. *Federal Register, First Issue of the Month*   The first *Federal Register* issue of the month contains several additional aids, including a *Table of Effective Dates and Time Periods* for the month, a list of *Agency Abbreviations Used in Highlights and Reminders*, and the *CFR Checklist*, which shows the revision date and price of CFR volumes issued to date.
8. *Federal Register Index*   A list of all the documents which appeared in the *Federal Registers* of a given month arranged alphabetically by agency name and thereunder by rules, proposed rules and notices. Broad subject headings are inserted alphabetically among the agency headings. The FR Index also includes a *Cumulative List of Parts Affected* for the time period covered, a list of *Privacy Act Publications*, and a table which shows the relationship between *Federal Register* dates and pages.
9. *Cumulative List of CFR Sections Affected*   Rules and proposed rules that have been changed since the last revision of the CFR.

Quarterly Publications

10. *Federal Register Index*   The *Federal Register Index* is cumulated quarterly.

Annual Publications

11. *Federal Register Index*   The *Federal Register Index* is cumulated annually.
12. *Cumulative List of CFR Sections Affected*   There is no longer a single annual issue of *Cumulative List of CFR Sections Affected*. Four publications must be saved: the December issue is the annual for Titles 1–16; the March issue is the annual for Titles 17–27; the June issue is the annual for Titles 28–41; the September issue is the annual for Titles 42–50.
13. *CFR Index*   The *CFR Index* lists specific subjects as well as agencies, with references to the *CFR* Titles and Parts where the information appears. It also includes a table of United States Code

citations that have been cited as authority for regulations in the *CFR*, as well as a complete list of *CFR* titles, chapters, and parts.
14. *CFR Volumes, Finding Aids Section*   The back of every *CFR* volume contains: a table of *CFR* titles and chapters; an alphabetical list of agencies appearing in *CFR;* and a list of *CFR* sections affected, divided into yearly units.

III.E.   JUDICIAL DECISIONS

Many commercially published services supplement government publications in the areas of judicial decisions. Because of the very specialized nature of legal reports, no attempt is made to list more than the reports of the Supreme Court (heavily used in most libraries). Guides to legal literature should be consulted for a comprehensive treatment of judicial publications. The official opinions and decisions of the Supreme Court are published in

> U.S. Supreme Court. *United States Reports: Cases Adjudged in the Supreme Court at October Term* . . . V. 1–date. 1790–date. Washington, D.C.: Govt. Print. Off. (Ju 6.8:)

The reports are published in two preliminary forms: (1) slip opinion (Ju 6.8/b:) and (2) *Official Reports of the Supreme Court* (Ju 6.8/a:), issued irregularly, which includes several cases with indexes. Only the final volumes, the *United States Reports*, contain the corrected versions.

Two commercial sources for reports of the Supreme Court are West Publishing Company's *Supreme Court Reporter* and *United States Law Week*, published by the Bureau of National Affairs.

To locate specific cases, find the citation to the *U.S. Reports* in a table of cases. One compilation is the *United States Supreme Court Digest*, table of cases, volume 14; St. Paul, West Publishing Company. Updates published frequently.

> *United States Reports* are cited as 354 U.S. 45. (*354* represents the volume number and *45* the page).

For cases bearing significantly upon the analysis and interpretation of the Constitution, consult the table of cases in

> *Constitution of the United States, Analysis and Interpretation.* Annotations of cases decided by the Supreme Court of the United States to June 29, 1972. 92d Cong., 2d sess., Senate Document 82. Washington, D.C.: Govt. Print. Off., 1973. Serial 12980–7. Supplement issued as Senate Document 134, 93d Cong., 2d sess. 1974.

IV.   CLASSIFICATION SCHEDULES

The following sources may be used for locating Superintendent of Documents classes and numbers. See also table 1, page 75.

Poole, Mary Elizabeth, and Ella Frances Smith, comp. *Documents Office Classification Numbers for Cuttered Documents*, 1910–24. Ann Arbor, Mich.: University Microfilms, 1960. 2 vols.

Supplies SuDoc numbers for the period between the *Checklist of U.S. Public Documents, 1789–1909* and the first listings of numbers in the *Monthly Catalog* in 1924. Arranged alphabetically by SuDoc number, giving only title and date. Not to be considered a complete list.

Poole, Mary Elizabeth, comp. *Monthly Catalog of Government Publications with Superintendent of Documents Classification Numbers Added, 1895–1924*. Arlington, Va.: Carrollton Press, 1975. 30 vols.

Since Superintendent of Documents numbers are not available prior to 1924 in the GPO *Monthly Catalog,* this work adds numbers to the early volumes.

Poole, Mary Elizabeth, comp. *Documents Office Classification, Including an Explanation of the Superintendent of Documents Classification System and an Alphabetic Index of U.S. Government Author Organizations*. Arlington, Va.: United States Historical Documents Institute, 5th ed. 1976. 3 vols.

This is the 5th edition of the Documents Office Classification, compiled by Poole and based on the shelf list of the Office of the Superintendent of Documents; it updates information through June 1976. Spaces are provided to keep the work current. A monumental compilation and indispensable tool for locating class numbers.

U.S. Office of the Assistant Public Printer (Superintendent of Documents). *List of Classes of United States Government Publications Available for Selection by Depository Libraries*. Washington, D.C., Govt. Print. Off. Revised frequently.

List of depository items in Superintendent of Documents number order. Also gives item numbers.

U.S. Office of the Assistant Public Printer (Superintendent of Documents). *Inactive or Discontinued Items from the 1950 Revision of the Classified List*. Rev. March 1977. Washington, D.C., Govt. Print. Off.

Lists inactive or discontinued items in item number order.

U.S. Superintendent of Documents. *Classified List of U.S. Government Publications,* Rev. Washington, D.C.: Govt. Print. Off., 1950.

Issued in card form known as "item cards." Forms basis of selection of depository items. Updated by monthly *Surveys* of new items available on deposit.

U.S. Superintendent of Documents. *Daily Depository Shipping List*. Washington, D.C., Govt. Print. Off.

A list by item number of materials sent in each depository shipment. Gives title, series, date, price, and Superintendent of Documents number. This list is available on subscription basis. Nondepository libraries that purchase a quantity of documents should subscribe to this service although it is expensive. Titles on the shipping list will not appear in the *Monthly Catalog* for several months. The shipping lists include informative notes on availability of titles. For example, because of short supply some titles are sent only to regional depository libraries and these are noted.

V.   OTHER SOURCES

Following are sources for locating names and addresses of documents librarians and congressmen. The *Government Manual* is the first source for information about current government organization.

American Library Association. Government Documents Round Table. *1978 Directory of Government Document Collections and Librarians.* Washington, D.C.: Congressional Information Service, 1978.

Gives information on "collections . . . institutions, organizations, agencies and individuals concerned with document librarianship, publication, or related activities." Gives categories of collections, depository status, and staff for each library. Staff, document, and special collections indexes. Lists library school instructors and others connected with government publications.

U.S. Congress. *Official Congressional Directory.* Washington, D.C.: Govt. Print. Off., 1809– . Usually issued for each session.

Gives organization and personnel information for executive, legislative, and judicial branches, with emphasis on Congress. Biographies of members of Congress, information on committees, and data on others associated with Congress. Information on diplomats and international organizations. Individual index. See also CCH *Congressional Index* (III.B.2) for list of current members of Congress and committees of Congress.

U.S. Office of the Federal Register. *United States Government Manual.* Washington, D.C.: Govt. Print. Off., 1935–. Annual. Formerly *U.S. Government Organization Manual.*

Official organizational handbook, giving information on personnel, structure, and activities in all departments, boards, commissions, etc. Includes international organizations. Of particular help are organization charts and appendix of abolished and transferred agencies. Name, subject, and agency indexes.

The following instructions and information are available from the Office of the Superintendent of Documents, Washington, D.C. 20402:

1. *Instructions to Depository Libraries.*
2. *Chapter 19, Depository Library Program.* Excerpt from Title 44, *U.S. Code:* Public Printing and Documents.
3. *Public Documents Stock Numbering System.* 1975.
4. *An Explanation of the Superintendent of Documents Classification System.*

5. *Government Depository Libraries: The Present Law Governing Designated Depository Libraries.*
6. *Public Documents Highlights.*
7. *Inspection of Depository Libraries.* Questionnaire filled out by inspector during inspection visit.
8. *Guidelines for the Depository Library System.* Adopted by the Depository Library Council to the Public Printer, October 18, 1977.

Additional References

Hernon, Peter. "The Role of Academic Reference Librarians Concerning Government Publications, with Special Emphasis Given to Municipal Publications," *Government Publications Review* 2 (1975):351–55.

Hernon, Peter, and Sara Lou Williams. "University Faculty and Federal Documents: Use Patterns," *Government Publications Review* 3 (1976):93–108.

McCaghy, Dawn, and Gary R. Purcell. "Faculty Use of Government Publications," *College and Research Libraries* 33 (January 1972):7–12.

Packard, Sarah R. "The Use of United States Government Publications in Small and Medium-Size Public Libraries." University of Chicago, master's thesis, 1967.

Whitbeck, George W., and Peter Hernon. "The Attitudes of Librarians toward the Servicing and Use of Government Publications: A Survey of Federal Depository Libraries in Four Midwestern States," *Government Publications Review* 4 (1977): 183–99.

———. "Bibliographic Instruction in Government Publications: Lecture Programs and Their Evaluation in American Academic Depository Libraries," *Government Publications Review* 4 (1977):1–11.

Yannarella, Philip A., and Ral Aluri. "Circulation of Federal Documents in Academic Depository Libraries," *Government Publications Review* 3 (1976): 43–49.

RECORDS, ROUTINES, AND DOCUMENTS REQUIRING SPECIAL HANDLING

In her excellent work, *Library Records for Government Publications,* Markley states the philosophy of maintaining records: "Documents records should be designed to serve the acquisition policy of the Library and the type of reference use and services that is expected of the collection."[1] Therefore the kinds of records maintained by individual libraries will be circumscribed by the scope, arrangement, and objectives of the documents collection. Records should be as simple as possible, yet detailed enough to impart the information necessary.

A statement of policy should be formed on what kinds of records will be kept and how they should be developed for the procedures manual. A manual, kept up to date, will assist staff members in following policy and routines established by the unit. The manual should include detailed procedures on all aspects of the operation within the unit. An example is a statement on circulation policy concerning a list of restricted titles, length of circulation, handling of overdues, and who may borrow. Those who establish a new collection should give considerable thought to types of records required, and those in established situations should continuously evaluate the types of records maintained to see if routines that are not required are being continued. New depositories should consider on-line access and machine-readable records, rather than perpetuate manual files. Experts in these areas should be consulted.

Harleston and Stoffle's *Administration of Government Documents Collections*[2] and Morehead's *Introduction to United States Public Documents*[3] give good examples of types of records maintained by libraries. Depository libraries should read

1. Anne E. Markley, *Library Records for Government Publications* (Berkeley: University of California Press, 1951), p. 31.
2. Rebekah M. Harleston and Carla J. Stoffle, *Administration of Government Documents Collections* (Littleton, Colo.: Libraries Unlimited, 1974), pp. 36–45.
3. Joe Morehead, *Introduction to United States Public Documents* (Littleton, Colo.: Libraries Unlimited, 1975), pp. 59–65.

143

the most recent *Instructions for Depository Libraries* to determine minimum records required for depository materials. A visit to an established library in the area to examine kinds of records kept is recommended.

RECORD OF HOLDINGS

Most documents librarians will agree that the minimum essential record for a separate collection is a list of holdings. This record can be a shelflist which is generally a combination shelflist and check-in file. A single entry per card is the most flexible method of recording holdings, allowing for interfiling; however, many libraries use the method of placing more than one entry on a card to save considerable card catalog space.[4] (See figure 10.)

Since a majority of government publications fall into the category of series and serials (estimated at about 80 percent), the standard numbered cards (year or numbered) and periodical check-in systems and records may be used. Whether a single shelflist is maintained or whether the periodicals records is separated is a matter of preference. Because of the frequency of checking in periodicals, a separate file is more convenient. In this case, some notation in the shelflist must be made to indicate that HE 3.3:, for example, is a periodical and is checked in elsewhere. Figures 10 to 16 are examples of records and should be regarded as samples only. Recognizing that a standard bibliographic entry is the desirable record, each library may need to adapt records to meet local needs.

In a separate documents collection, the shelflist is generally not used as a public catalog. Therefore, the shelflist is not only a record of holdings but also an information file of some importance. Changes in classification numbers, out-of-print titles, ceased publication notes, and changes in titles are some notations found on shelflist cards, in addition to the usual shelflist notes. The shelflist can also serve as a public catalog if it is not in constant use by staff and if security is not a problem. A public dictionary catalog would of course provide the best access to federal documents, but maintenance of such a catalog is quite costly. Now that access to catalog. Therefore, the shelflist is not only a record of holdings but also an infor-probably offset by the cost of obtaining cards. The cost of obtaining only one card through OCLC is considerably more than having one typed in house. Some libraries use the *Monthly Catalog* as the book catalog, although most libraries cannot devote time to marking holdings and must rely on the shelf list for the holdings record. Depository libraries can rely on the "black dot," which indicates a depository item and therefore one the library is likely to have.

STATISTICS

Statistics should be maintained only if they serve a useful function. (The GPO does not require depository libraries to maintain statistics.) Most libraries require

4. Harleston, *Administration*, p. 37.

Senate   Y 4.B 22/3:
  Committee on Banking and Currency   H 81/32/pt.
  (Hearings) 1035

⌈ 1   Housing act of 1954. 1954. 1124p. 83-2.
⌈ 2   _____ air pollution prevention amendment. 1954.
     pp. 1125-1301. 83-2
⌊ 3   _____ FHA insurance provisions. 1954. pp. 1303-
     2043. 83-2.

⌊ 955 _____ 1955. 627p. 84-1.

⌊ 957 _____ 1957. 1957. 995p. 85-1 (Amendment)

⌊ = bound   Newberry (gift)

Figure 10. More than One Entry per Card

Interior Department   I 19.3:
  Geological Survey Bulletins   nos.
     (Science Library)

ACC. NUMBER	A	B	C	D	E	F	G	H	I	J				
1391-	✓	✓	✓	✓	✓									
1392														
1393														
1394-	✓	✓	✓	✓	✓	✓	✓	✓						
1395-	✓	✓	✓	✓	✓	✓			✓	✓				
1396														
1397-	✓	✓	✓											
1398														
1399														

DEMCO NO. 28-070

Figure 11. Titles with Several Parts

TITLE													FREQUENCY

Government Printing Office FREQUENCY **GP 3.27:**

NOS. PER VOL.	VOLS. PER YEAR	VOLS. BEGIN	TITLE PAGE

Public Documents Highlights

VOLS. BOUND	INDEX

(Sent to all dep. libraries)   DEMCO NO. 28-144

Year	Vol.	Jan.	Feb.	Mar.	Apr.	May	June	July	Aug.	Sept.	Oct.	Nov.	Dec.	T.P.
973						1					2			
974					3	4		5		6				
975					9	10		11		12				
976			14		15	16		17		18		19		
977			20		21	22		23 Supp	24			25		

TITLE	**Energy Department**												FREQUENCY **E 1.11:**

NOS. PER VOL.	VOLS. PER YEAR	VOLS. BEGIN	TITLE PAGE

Energy Abstracts for Policy Analysis

VOLS. BOUND	INDEX

474-A-2   DEMCO NO. 28-144

Year	Vol.	Jan.	Feb.	Mar.	Apr.	May	June	July	Aug.	Sept.	Oct.	Nov.	Dec.	T.P.
977	3	*For earlier see ER 1.9:									*	11	12	Ind.
978	4	1	2											

Figure 12. Two Examples of Serial Records

statistics on holdings, circulation, and some measure of use. Reports of accrediting agencies and agencies of government often request specific counts of government publications. (No standard method of counting government publications exists at the present time.) All statistics are subject to a wide variety of interpretation and figures are not comparable among libraries. Documents librarians have discussed the lack of uniformity in maintaining statistics of government publications and

Forest Service
Research Papers (Pacific N.W. Forest
and Range Experiment Station)(*became dep.)

A 13.78:
PNW-nos.
83-B

101-	THOSE CHECKED ARE AVAILABLE IN LIBRARY								
1	11	21	31	41	51	61	✓ 71	✓ 81	✓ 91
2	12	22	32	42	52	62	72	82	✓ 92
3	13	23	33	43	53	63	✓ 73	✓ 83	✓ 93
4	14	24	34	44	54	64	✓ 74	✓ 84	✓ 94
5	15	25	35	45	55	65	✓ 75	✓ 85	✓ 95
6	16	26	36	46	56	66	✓ 76	86	✓ 96
7	17	27	37	47	57	67	✓ 77	✓ 87	✓ 97
8	18	28	38	48	58	68	✓ 78	✓ 88	✓ 98
9	19	29	39	49	59	69	✓ 79	✱ ✓ 89	✓ 99
10	20	30	✓ 40	50	60	70	✓ 80	✓ 90	✓ 00

80-10-11275

Figure 13. Numbered Series

Maritime Administration
Country:
Domestic oceanborne and Great Lakes
Bureau or Div.
Commerce of United States 233-B
Title
Title: Domestic waterborne trade of the U.S.*

Dept.

C 39.222:

Frequency

LIBRARY HAS THOSE THAT ARE CHECKED

1901	1911	1921	1931	1941	1951	1961 3/63	1971
1902	1912	1922	1932	1942	1952	1962 12/63	1972
1903	1913	1923	1933	1943	1953	1963 3/65	1973
1904	1914	1924	1934	1944	1954	1964	1974
1905	1915	1925	1935	1945	1955	1965 ~72	1975
1906	1916	1926	1936	1946	1956	1966	1976
1907	1917	1927	1937	1947	1957	1967 -74 ✱	1977
1908	1918	1928	1938	1948	1958	1968 -75	1978
1909	1919	1929	1939	1949	1959 ✓ 5/61	1969	1979
1910	1920	1930	1940	1950	1960 ✓ 5/62	1970	1980

Place Pub.   **Date indicates**   Source
Gift; Purchase   **when received in library**
Library Bureau Cat. no. 1163.1   Document record (by year)   KP 1989- ✱

Figure 14. Record by Year

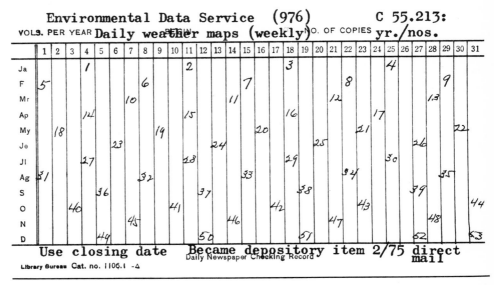

Figure 15. Daily Record Card Used for Weekly Publication

U.S. Census of Housing　　　　　　　　　　　C 3.224/3:
State and small areas, final report (HC(1)970/v.1/pt.
156-A

U.S. *1*	Hawaii *13*	Minn. *25*	Ohio *37*	Wash. *49*
Ala. *2*	Idaho *14*	Miss. *26*	Okla. *38*	W.Va. *50*
Alaska *3*	III. *15*	Mo. *27*	Ore. *39*	Wis. *51*
Ariz. *4*	Ind. *16*	Mont. *28*	Pa. *40*	Wyo. *52*
Ark. *5*	Iowa *17*	Neb. *29*	R.I. *41*	
Calif. *6*	Kan. *18*	Nev. *30*	S.C. *42*	Territories:
Colo. *7*	Ky. *19*	N.H. *31*	S.D. *43*	Canal Zone
Conn. *8*	La. *20*	N.J. *32*	Tenn. *44*	Guam } 54-58
Dela. *9*	Maine *21*	N.M. *33*	Tex. *45*	Samoa
D.C. *10*	Md. *22*	N.Y. *34*	Utah *46*	Virgin Islands
Fla. *11*	Mass. *23*	No.C. *35*	Ver. *47*	P.R. } 53
Ga. *12*	Mich. *24*	No.D. *36*	Va. *48*	

Bound volumes

Figure 16. State Record

asked what items should be counted. Should each piece be counted, since the volume of materials handled gives some indication of staff time required? How should they be counted—by piece, by weight, by item, by linear feet? What should be excluded? The widest variation occurs in the counting of serials; some count only bound volumes, others count each issue. Until some standardization occurs, a statement of policy on what is counted and why should be written to maintain consistency in statistics.

DISPOSITION OF DUPLICATES

One of the major problems of libraries is to dispose of duplicates and other unwanted documents. Depository libraries which are served by regional libraries must follow certain procedures for discarding titles received on deposit but may freely dispose of duplicates and other unwanted publications not received on deposit. (See discussion of exchange lists in the section on regional depository libraries.) Exchanges are most effective at the local level if librarians in the area can be invited personally to look at the materials and select needed titles. Exchange lists have often been a means of picking up that one volume which could not be found through other means. The compilation of these lists is a chore, and the system may not be entirely satisfactory since a deadline date is usually necessary and requests are often filled on a first come, first served basis. (Some regional libraries offer materials on a "something for everyone" basis.) Despite the disadvantages and time involved for the issuing library, an exchange list is a means of promoting interlibrary cooperation and a way by which libraries can obtain documents with little outlay of funds. The receiving library is usually asked to pay the cost of postage. Individual libraries must make their own arrangements for compiling a list of duplicates and for developing a list of potential libraries which may desire the list. A committee of GODORT has established a clearinghouse for exchange lists.

The Universal Serials and Book Exchange welcomes periodicals and serials in any field. It will accept government documents which are, in the judgment of the senders, of value to other libraries. USBE prefers to check title lists but will accept unsorted shipments. If in doubt about the value of materials, write to USBE before you ship. (See earlier note on USBE.)

BINDING

Binding materials not only preserves them but facilitates shelving. All materials of lasting research value, such as annual reports of agencies, selected general publications (those titles used heavily by patrons), serials, periodicals, and hearings and committee prints, should be bound. Circulation records will assist in selecting materials for binding. A policy statement on what materials will be bound on a regular basis will assist a high-level clerical staff member who can be responsible for identifying and processing materials for binding.

Documents Requiring Special Handling

One of the characteristics of government publications which sets them apart from many publications of the commercial book trade is the enormous quantity of material issued in single sheets, preliminary editions, and pamphlets and leaflets and loose-leaf material requiring "change pages" (see "Loose-Leaf Materials"). These materials are important in substance and require special handling.

PRELIMINARY EDITIONS, PREPRINTS

Agencies often issue advanced release of information prior to printing the bound volume. An example is census information issued in a number of preliminary editions. These should be kept until the bound volumes appear. The paper editions can be retained for use as circulating copies, provided the information in the paper copy and the bound edition is similar. Very often the bound editions contain corrections and other material not in the preliminary editions. Preprints (material issued prior to the bound volumes), such as those from the Bureau of Mines *Yearbook,* can be arranged in pamphlet boxes and shelved adjacent to the main work. Preprints can also be kept to serve as circulating copies.

PAMPHLETS AND LEAFLETS

Pamphlets and leaflets are brief treatments of subjects issued as a separate publication, usually in paperbound form. In the absence of slotted shelving which will accommodate small pamphlets in an upright fashion, pamphlet-type material can be placed in pamphlet boxes. Very small leaflets can be placed in pockets mounted on cardboard. In a separate documents collection, having all materials shelved in classification order (rather than placing some materials in vertical files because of their size) is more efficient. Each time material is shelved out of order, records must be noted to indicate location. If the public has access to the stacks, some notation must also be visible on the shelves.

LOOSE-LEAF MATERIALS

To keep handbooks, manuals, and regulations up to date, many series are printed in loose-leaf form. If the pages are of usual standard size, they can be put together with brass brads or placed in a binder. Single, loose sheets can be put together, when appropriate, using a plastic spineback or glueing with a plastic adhesive. Updated pages, often called "change pages," can be stored in vertical files in call-number order until the staff can insert them in the proper publications.

Congressional Publications

A large group of materials requiring special attention and handling are the congressional publications, many of which are shelved out of call-number order because of their bulk and temporary format.

Congressional publications which are issued as separates and reprinted again in the Congressional Set (Serial Set) are issued in four series: Senate reports, House reports, Senate documents, and House documents. These reports can be filed in pamphlet files, arranged by Congress, Senate and House, series, and number. After they appear in the bound edition (Serial Set), they may be discarded or retained as circulating copies.

Before the receipt of the bound volumes of *Statutes-at-Large,* which is the permanent collection of the laws enacted for each session of Congress, the laws are available in two forms that require special handling: bills and resolutions, and slip laws.

BILLS AND RESOLUTIONS

Bills and resolutions are vital government publications and at least one library in a metropolitan or regional area should assume responsibility for them. The resources available in the area, as well as cooperative arrangements, are important factors to consider before selecting this item. The handling problems are enormous because of their sheer bulk. Those who select this category will receive 25,000 to 30,000 bills and resolutions for each Congress. Considering the costs involved in sorting, filing, and providing shelf space, demand should determine whether the library should acquire and service bills and resolutions.

These materials must be filed immediately upon their receipt or their usefulness will be diminished. Recording is not necessary. Arrange them by Congress and bill number as explained in the guidelines below. If shelf space is available (about 16 shelves per Congress), pamphlet boxes will keep the bills in neat order, facilitating retrieval. The Superintendent of Documents requires that they be retained for one year after the close of the Congress. Any policy of retention beyond the required time must be determined by use factor and availability of bills in libraries in the area. *Statutes-at-Large* does not include those bills and resolutions which are not enacted into law; therefore, certain libraries may wish to retain the original bills. Bills and resolutions are available in microfilm from the Library of Congress. They are also available in microfiche format from the Congressional Information Service). If bills are to be retained, an inexpensive method of binding is to use plastic adhesive or the Perma-bind process. The maintenance of these bills requires 10 to 12 hours per week of student or clerical assistance. Clear procedures for handling bills and resolutions should be provided the person who is responsible for the filing. Guidelines for handling bills and resolutions follow.

1. Bills and resolutions are generally received in separate shipments with a shipping list.

2. There are eight categories of bills and resolutions; the House has four and the Senate has a comparable four:

House
  Bills: H.R. 25
  Concurrent Res.: H. Con. Res. 25
  Resolutions: H. Res. 25
  Joint Resolutions: H. J. Res. 25
Senate
  S. 25
  S. Con. Res. 25
  S. Res. 25
  S. J. Res. 25

3. Separate the bills into the eight categories.
4. Arrange each pile numerically, lowest number on top. If bills have identical numbers, arrange by amendment number. If a "star print" (★) is received, discard the original bill. The star print is the corrected version of an original bill.
5. When the shipment containing the shipping list arrives, check off those bill numbers received. Circle missing ones and claim them.
6. File or shelve in area designated.

SLIP LAWS AND OPINIONS

The first official publication of a statute appears in a form known as a "slip law" (GS 4.110:). These may be arranged by Congress and public law number in pamphlet boxes until the bound *Statutes-at-Large* is received. Although these laws can be discarded after the bound volume is received, they are often useful if they are retained for two or three Congresses for use as circulating copies.

Supreme Court decisions (Ju 6.8/b:) also appear in preliminary form "slip opinions," before issuance of the bound volume of *United States Reports*. These can be handled in a similar fashion to the slip laws. Maintaining a temporary index to the "slip opinions" as they are received, listing them alphabetically by name (e.g., *De Funis* v. *Odegaard*) is a way to provide access to these decisions before the bound volume is received. Even though a preliminary print (Ju 6.8/a:) is now available, it does not include the most recent cases.

Weeding

As for all library materials, weeding must be carried out in a judicious manner. All libraries face space problems and a certain amount of weeding is inevitable. Like other materials in the library, a weeding policy should be established. For depository materials, the nearest regional depository library will offer guidance in the disposition of depository items. Many have written guidelines. The substitution of microform with hard copy is a possible solution to the ever increasing need for space.

Weeding policies will differ with the type of library. For example, a research library will require retention of historical materials, whereas a small public library will probably want to maintain a timely collection with emphasis on up-to-date information.

EPILOGUE

The purpose of the foregoing chapters has been to show the complex nature of government publications from their publication to distribution to libraries. The work is designed as a handbook for beginning documents librarians. Sources and aids have been emphasized to assist librarians in giving reference service.

Government publications are essential resources in all types of libraries because of the enormous output of the federal government and the vast arrays of knowledge the publications represent. In content, they cover literature from the very technical to the most popular. Users of government publications are patrons of various types of libraries—academic, public, school, or special—and these users represent students, professionals, business persons, and other citizens. Through a national network of depository libraries, all librarians should be able to provide access to any government publications requested by patrons.

One library educator suggests that a library's major goal should be the "main streaming" of government publications. Computer technology provides us the opportunity to harness the large volume of government publications and the enormous amount of information contained in them. It also offers us many more points of access to information than the traditional card catalog. A challenge for librarians is to find ways of utilizing the potential of applying technology to bibliographical control, to subject access, to shelf maintenance, and to other areas still unexplored.

Machines, however, will not replace librarians, who must continue to make wise choices in the selection of government publications, who must organize them for efficient document delivery, and who must introduce these materials to the library's public, not only to serve immediate needs but also to serve a lifelong learning process.

APPENDIXES

DEPOSITORY LIBRARY PROGRAM

§ 1901. Definition of Government publication

"Government publication" as used in this chapter, means informational matter which is published as an individual document at Government expense, or as required by law.

§ 1902. Availability of Government publications through Superintendent of Documents; lists of publications not ordered from Government Printing Office

Government publications, except those determined by their issuing component to be required for official use only or for strictly administrative or operationa purposes which have no public interest or educational value and publications classified for reasons of national security, shall be made available to depository libraries through the facilities of the Superintendent of Documents for public information. Each component of the Government shall furnish the Superintendent of Documents a list of such publications it issued during the previous month, that were obtained from sources other than the Government Printing Office.

§ 1903. Distribution of publications to depositories; notice to Government components; cost of printing and binding

Upon request of the Superintendent of Documents, components of the Government ordering the printing of publications shall either increase or decrease the number of copies of publications furnished for distribution to designated depository libraries and State libraries so that the number of copies delivered to the Superintendent of Documents is equal to the number of libraries on the list. The number thus delivered may not be restricted by any statutory limitation in force on August 9, 1962. Copies of publications furnished the Superintendent of Documents for distribution to designated depository libraries shall include—

the journal of the Senate and House of Representatives;

all publications, not confidential in character, printed upon the requisition of a congressional committee;

Senate and House public bills and resolutions; and

reports on private bills, concurrent or simple resolutions;

but not so-called cooperative publications which must necessarily be sold in order to be sulf-sustaining.

The Superintendent of Documents shall currently inform the components of

Chapter 19, title 44, *United States Code.*

the Government ordering printing of publications as to the number of copies of their publications required for distribution to depository libraries. The cost of printing and binding those publications distributed to depository libraries obtained elsewhere than from the Government Printing Office, shall be borne by components of the Government responsible for their issuance; those requisitioned from the Government Printing Office shall be charged to appropriations provided the Superintendent of Documents for that purpose.

§ 1904. Classified list of Government publications for selection by depositories

The Superintendent of Documents shall currently issue a classified list of Government publications in suitable form, containing annotations of contents and listed by item identification numbers to facilitate the selection of only those publications needed by depository libraries. The selected publications shall be distributed to depository libraries in accordance with regulations of the Superintendent of Documents, as long as they fulfill the conditions provided by law.

§ 1905. Distribution to depositories; designation of additional libraries; justification; authorization for certain designations

The Government publications selected from lists prepared by the Superintendent of Documents, and when requested from him, shall be distributed to depository libraries specifically designated by law and to libraries designated by Senators, Representatives, and the Resident Commissioner from Puerto Rico, by the Commissioner of the District of Columbia, and by the Governors of Guam, American Samoa, and the Virgin Islands, respectively. Additional libraries within areas served by Representatives or the Resident Commissioner from Puerto Rico may be designated by them to receive Government publications to the extent that the total number of libraries designated by them does not exceed two within each area. Not more than two additional libraries within a State may be designated by each Senator from the State. Before an additional library within a State, congressional district or the Commonwealth of Puerto Rico is designated as a depository for Government publications, the head of that library shall furnish his Senator, Representative, or the Resident Commissioner from Puerto Rico, as the case may be, with justification of the necessity for the additional designation. The justification, which shall also include a certification as to the need for the additional depository library designation, shall be signed by the head of every existing depository library within the congressional district or the Commonwealth of Puerto Rico or by the head of the library authority of the State or the Commonwealth of Puerto Rico, within which the additional depository library is to be located. The justification for additional depository library designations shall be transmitted to the Superintendent of Documents by the Senator, Representative, or the Resident Commissioner from Puerto Rico, as the case may be. The Commissioner of the District of Columbia may designate two depository libraries in the District of Columbia, the Governor of Guam and the Governor of American Samoa may each designate one depository library in Guam and American Samoa, respectively, and the Governor of the Virgin Islands may designate one depository library on the island of Saint Thomas and one on the island of Saint Croix.

§ 1906. Land-grant colleges constituted depositories

Land-grant colleges are constituted depositories to receive Government publications subject to the depository laws.

§ 1907. Libraries of executive departments, service academies, and independent agencies constituted depositories; certifications of need; disposal of unwanted publications

The libraries of the executive departments, of the United States Military Academy, of the United States Naval Academy, of the United States Air Force Academy, of the United States Coast Guard Academy, and of the United States Merchant Marine Academy are designated depositories of Government publications. A depository library within each independent agency may be designated upon certification of need by the head of the independent agency to the Superintendent of Documents. Additional depository libraries within executive departments and independent agencies may be designated to receive Government publications to the extent that the number so designated does not exceed the number of major bureaus or divisions of the departments and independent agencies. These designations may be made only after certification by the head of each executive department or independent agency to the Superintendent of Documents as to the justifiable need for additional depository libraries. Depository libraries within executive departments and independent agencies may dispose of unwanted Government publications after first offering them to the Library of Congress and the Archivist of the United States.

§ 1908. American Antiquarian Society to receive certain publications

One copy of the public journals of the Senate and of the House of Represntatives, and of the documents published under the orders of the Senate and House of Representatives, respectively, shall be transmitted to the Executive of the Commonwealth of Massachusetts for the use and benefit of the American Antiquarian Society of the Commonwealth.

§ 1909. Requirements of depository libraries; reports on conditions; investigations; termination; replacement

Only a library able to provide custody and service for depository materials and located in an area where it can best serve the public need, and within an area not already adequately served by existing depository libraries may be designated by Senators, Representatives, the Resident Commissioner from Puerto Rico, the Commissioner of the District of Columbia, or the Governors of Guam, American Samoa, or the Virgin Islands as a depository of Government publications. The designated depository libraries shall report to the Superintendent of Documents at least every two years concerning their condition.

The Superintendent of Documents shall make firsthand investigation of conditions for which need is indicated and include the results of investigations in his annual report. When he ascertains that the number of books in a depository library is below ten thousand, other than Government publications, or it has ceased to be maintained so as to be accessible to the public, or that the Government publications which have been furnished the library have not been properly maintained, he shall delete the library from the list of depository libraries if the library fails to correct the unsatisfactory conditions within six months. The Representative or the Resident Commissioner from Puerto Rico in whose area the library is located or the Senator who made the designation, or a successor of the Senator, and, in the case of a library in the District of Columbia, the Commissioner of the District of Columbia, and, in the case of a library in Guam, American Samoa, or the Virgin Islands, the Governor, shall be notified and shall then be authorized to designate another library within the area served by him, which shall meet the conditions herein required, but which may not be in excess of the number of depository libraries authorized by law within the State, district, territory, or the Commonwealth of Puerto Rico, as the case may be.

§ 1910. Designations of replacement depositories; limitations on numbers; conditions

The designation of a library to replace a depository library, other than a depository library specifically designated by law, may be made only within the limitations on total numbers specified by section 1905 of this title, and only when the library to be replaced ceases to exist, or when the library voluntarily relinquishes its depository status, or when the Superintendent of Documents determines that it no longer fulfills the conditions provided by law for depository libraries.

§ 1911. Free use of Government publications in depositories; disposal of unwanted publications

Depository libraries shall make Government publications available for the free use of the general public, and may dispose of them after retention for five years under section 1912 of this title, if the depository library is served by a regional depository library. Depository libraries not served by a regional depository library, or that are regional depository libraries themselves, shall retain Government publications permanently in either printed form or in microfacsimile form, except superseded publications or those issued later in bound form which may be discarded as authorized by the Superintendent of Documents.

§ 1912. Regional depositories; designation; functions; disposal of publications

Not more than two depository libraries in each State and the Commonwealth of Puerto Rico may be designated as regional depositories, and shall receive from the Superintendent of Documents copies of all new and revised Government publications authorized for distribution to depository libraries. Designation of regional depository libraries may be made by a Senator or the Resident Commissioner from Puerto Rico within the areas served by them, after approval by the head of the library authority of the State or the Commonwealth of Puerto Rico, as the case may be, who shall first ascertain from the head of the library to be so designated that the library will, in addition to fulfilling the requirements for depository libraries, retain at least one copy of all Government publications either in printed or microfacsimile form (except those authorized to be discarded by the Superintendent of Documents); and within the region served will provide interlibrary loan, reference service, and assistance for depository libraries in the disposal of unwanted Government publications. The agreement to function as a regional depository library shall be transmitted to the Superintendent of Documents by the Senator or the Resident Commissioner from Puerto Rico when the designation is made.

The libraries designated as regional depositories may permit depository libraries, within the areas served by them, to dispose of Government publications which they have retained for five years after first offering them to other depository libraries within their area, then to other libraries.

§ 1913. Appropriations for supplying depository libraries; restriction

Appropriations available for the Office of Superintendent of Documents may not be used to supply depository libraries documents, books, or other printed matter not requested by them, and their requests shall be subject to approval by the Superintendent of Documents.

§ 1914. Implementation of depository library program by Public Printer

The Public Printer, with the approval of the Joint Committee on Printing, as provided by section 103 of this title, may use any measures he considers necessary for the economical and practical implementation of this chapter.

§ 1915. Highest State appellate court libraries as depository libraries

Upon the request of the highest appellate court of a state, the Public Printer is authorized to designate the library of that court as a depository library. The provisions of section 1921 of this title shall not apply to any library so designated. (Added Pub. L. 92–368, August 10, 1972, 82 Stat. 1283.)

§ 1916. Designation of libraries of accredited law schools as depository libraries

Upon the request of any accredited law school, the Public Printer shall designate the library of such law school as a depository library. The Public Printer may not make such designation unless he determines that the library involved meets the requirements of this chapter, other than those requirements of the first undesignated paragraph of section 1909 of this title which relate to the location of such library.

For purposes of this section, the term "accredited law school" means any law school which is accredited by a nationally recognized accrediting agency or association approved by the Commissioner of Education for such purpose or accredited by the highest appellate court of the State in which the law school is located.

SEC. 2. The table of sections for chapter 19 of title 44, United States Code, is amended by adding at the end thereof the following new item:

"1916. Designation of libraries of accredited law schools as depository libraries."

SEC. 3. The amendments made by this Act shall take effect on October 1, 1978. (Added Pub L. 95–261, April 17, 1978, 92 Stat. 199)..

APPENDIX 2

AN EXPLANATION OF THE SUPERINTENDENT OF DOCUMENTS CLASSIFICATION SYSTEM

As currently used in the Library of the Public Documents Department, United States Government Printing Office, and as catalog numbers for the stocks of Government publications sold by the Superintendent of Documents.

Introduction

This system was formed in the Library of the Public Documents Department sometime between 1895 and 1903. The first explanation of it was given in October 1903 by William Leander Post, then in charge of the Library, in the preface to List of Publications of the Agriculture Department 1862-1902, Department List No. 1, issued by the Superintendent of Documents in 1904.

Mr. Post gives credit for the basis of the system (classification by governmental author) to Miss Adelaide R. Hasse, who used this basis in assigning classification numbers to a List of Publications of the U.S. Department of Agriculture from 1841 to June 30, 1895, inclusive. Miss Hasse prepared the list while assistant librarian in the Los Angeles Public Library but it was published by the Department of Agriculture in 1896 as its Library Bulletin No. 9.

Like other classification systems in use for many years, this one has expanded as the Federal Government has grown, and has changed in some details and methods of use, though still retaining the principles upon which it is based.

It has one fundamental weakness—the position in the scheme, of the publications of any Government author (i.e. department, bureau, office, etc.), is determined by the current organizational status of the author. Thus it is at the mercy of any Government reorganization which may be directed by the President, by Congress, or by the head of a department or agency, with the result that the publications of some authors may be located in as many as three different places in the scheme.

Despite this fundamental weakness, it has stood the test of time as a workable arrangement for publications of the United States Government, having been used for over 50 years by the Library of the Public Documents Department (the Division of Public Documents and the Office of the Superintendent of Documents in earlier years) for the collection of public documents which has accumulated as a by-product of the Department's cataloging and publishing functions, and as a catalog system for the stocks of Government publications sold by the Superintendent of Documents.

Foreword

This explanation of the classification system used by the Public Documents Department was prepared to answer frequent inquiries received, and to provide an aid in the training of new personnel in this organization. The original edition was prepared by the late Mr. Joseph A. King; this revised edition was prepared by Norman N. Barbee, Librarian, under the supervision of Mrs. Mae S. Collins, Chief of Library.

It is hoped that this explanation will also provide a helpful guide for depository libraries which use the Superintendent of Documents classification system, as well as for other libraries and persons interested in, or concerned with the catalog numbers assigned to publications by this Department.

Washington, D.C.: Govt. Print. Off., 1973.

PRINCIPLES OF THE SYSTEM

The basis of the classification is the grouping together of the publications of any Government author—the various departments, bureaus, and agencies being considered the authors. In the grouping, the organizational structure of the United States Government is followed, that is, subordinate bureaus and divisions are grouped with the parent organization.

Author Symbols

Each executive department and agency, the Judiciary, Congress, and other major independent establishments are assigned a place in the scheme. The place is determined by the alphabetical designation assigned to each, as "A" for Agriculture Department, "Ju" for Judiciary, and "NS" for National Science Foundation, the designation usually being based on the name of the organization. (See attached Table I for symbols currently in use.)

Subordinate Offices

To set off the subordinate bureaus and offices, numbers are added to the symbols with figure "1" being used for the parent organization and the secretary's or administrator's office. Beginning with the figure "2" the numbers are applied in numerical order to the subordinate bureaus and offices, these having been arranged alphabetically when the system was established, and new subordinate bureaus or offices having been given the next highest number. A period follows the combination of letters and numbers representing the bureau or office. For example:

Agriculture Department (including Secretary's Office)	A 1.
Forest Service	A 13.
Information Office	A 21.
Rural Electrification Administration	A 68.

Series Designations

The second breakdown in the scheme is for the various series of publications issued by a particular bureau or office. A number is assigned to each series and this number is followed by a colon.

In the beginning the following numbers were assigned for the types of publications common to most Government offices:

1: Annual reports
2: General publications (unnumbered publications of a miscellaneous nature)
3: Bulletins
4: Circulars

In setting up classes for new agencies or bureaus, these numbers were reserved for those types of publications. Later, new types common to most offices evolved and the following additional numbers were set aside in the classes of new agencies for particular types of series:

5: Laws (administered by the agency and published by it)
6: Regulations, rules, and instructions
7: Releases
8: Handbooks, manuals, guides

Any additional series issued by an office are given the next highest number in order of issuance—that is, as an office begins publication of a series the next highest number not already assigned to a series is assigned to the new series of the particular office.

Related Series

New series which are closely related to already existing series are not tied-in to the existing series so as to file side by side on the shelf. Originally no provision was made for this except in the case of separates from publications in a series. Tie-in is provided by use of the shilling mark after the number assigned to the existing series, followed by a digit for each related series starting with "2". (The "1" is not generally used in this connection since the existing series is the first.) Separates are distinguished by use of a lower case letter beginning with "a" rather than by numbers.

A theoretical example of these "tie-in" classes is as follows:

    4:      Circulars
    4/a: Separates from Circulars (numbered)
    4/b: Separates from Circulars (unnumbered)
    4/2:   Administrative Circulars
    4/3:   Technical Circulars

Class Stem

Thus by combining the designations for authors and those for the series published by the authors, we obtain the class stems for the various series of publications issued by the United States Government. For example:

    A 1.10:   Agriculture Yearbook
    A 13.1:   Annual Report of Chief of Forest Service
    A 57.38: Soil Survey Reports

Book Numbers

The individual book number follows the colon. For numbered series the original edition of a publication gets simply the number of the book. For example, Department of Agriculture Leaflet 381 would be A 1.35:381. For revisions of numbered publications, the shilling mark and additional figures beginning with 2 are added, as: A 1.35:381/2, A 1.35:381/3, etc.

In the case of annuals, the last three digits of the year are used for the book number, e.g., Annual Report of Secretary of Agriculture, A 1.1:954. For reports or publications covering more than one year, a combination of the dates is used, e.g., Annual Register of the U.S. Naval Academy, 1954-1955 is D 208.107:954-55.

Unnumbered publications (other than continuations) are given a book number based on the principal subject word of the title, using a 2-figure Cutter table. An example is Radioactive Heating of Vehicles Entering the Earth's Atmosphere, NAS 1.2:R 11, "Radioactive" being the key subject word and the Cutter designation being R 11. Another publication, Measurements of Radiation from Flow Fields of Bodies Flying Speeds up to 13.4 Kilometers per Second, issued by the same agency, falling in the same series class (NAS 1.2:), and having the same Cutter number for the principal subject word, is individualized by adding the shilling mark and the figure 2, as NAS 1.2:R 11/2. Subsequent different publications in the same subject group which take the same Cutter designation would be identified as R 11/3, R 11/4, etc.

In assigning book numbers to unnumbered separates or reprints from whole publications, the 3-figure Cutter table is used. This is done for the purpose of providing for finer distinctions in class between publications whose principal subject words begin with the same syllable. The 3-figure table is also sometimes used in regular unnumbered series for the same purpose.

Another use of the 3-figure Cutter table is for non-Government publications which although not officially authored by a particular Government bureau or agency, may have been written by some of its personnel, or may be about it and its work, and it is desirable to have them filed on the shelf with the organization's own publications. The book numbers assigned to the non-Government publications are treated as decimals so as to file with the same subject groups but yet not disturb the sequence of book numbers of publications actually authored by the organization.

Revisions of unnumbered publications are identified by addition of the shilling mark and the last three digits of the year of revision. For example, if the first publication mentioned in the preceding paragraph was revised in 1964, the complete classification would read NAS 1.2:R 11/964. Subsequent revisions in the same year would be identified as 964-2, 964-3, etc.

Periodicals and other continuations are identified by number, or volume and number as the case may be. Volume and number are separated by use of the shilling mark. Some examples are:

    Current Export Bulletin, No. 732, C 42.11/2:732
    Marketing Information Guide, Vol. 17, No. 1, C 41.11:17/1

Unnumbered periodicals and continuations are identified by the year of issuance and order of issuance throughout the year. The last three digits of the year are used, and a number corresponding to the order of issuance within the year is added, the two being separated by the shilling mark. An example is:

    United States Savings Bonds Issued and Redeemed, January 31, 1954, T 63.7:954/1

SPECIAL TREATMENT OF PUBLICATIONS OF CERTAIN AUTHORS

While the foregoing principles and rules govern the classification of the publications and documents of most Government authors, special treatments are employed for those of certain Government agencies. These consist of classes assigned to:

(1) Some series issued by the Interstate Commerce Commission

(2) Boards, Commissions, and Committees established by act of Congress or under authority of act of Congress, not specifically designated in the Executive Branch of the Government nor as completely independent agencies

(3) Congress and its working committees

(4) Multilateral international organizations in which the United States participates

(5) Publications of the President and the Executive Office of the President including Committees and Commissions established by executive order and reporting directly to the President

Interstate Commerce Commission

The classes assigned to publications of this agency were revised in December 1914 to provide better groupings of material than could formerly be given due to the lack of bureau breakdowns within the Commission at that time. Accordingly, those publications of the Commission as a whole, such as annual reports, general publications, bulletins, circulars, etc., continued to follow the regular form of classification, while all others were grouped by subject. This subject grouping took the place of bureau breakdowns and was designated by adding the first three or four letters of the subject word to the main agency designation of IC 1. Thus those publications relating to "accidents" were grouped under IC 1 acci., those relating to "express companies" were under IC 1 exp., and similarly for other subjects. The series designations and individual book numbers were then assigned under each subject grouping as though it were a regular bureau. For example, Accident Bulletin Number 3 is classed as IC 1 acci.3:3. A list of current subject breakdowns is contained in Table II attached.

Boards, Commissions, and Committees

Those agencies established by act of Congress or under authority of act of Congress, not specifically designated in the Executive Branch of the Government nor as completely independent agencies, are grouped under one of the agency symbols assigned to Congressional publications—namely, Y 3. This place in the scheme is reserved for all such agencies. The classification numbers of the publications of these agencies are then literally pushed over to the right so that instead of the series designation following the period, the individual agency designation follows it. This agency designation is the Cutter author number from the 2-figure table for the first main word of the agency name, followed by the colon. Thus the agency designation for Atomic Energy Commission is Y 3.At 7: and that of Selective Service System is Y 3.Se 4:. The shilling mark and numbers are used to distinguish between author designations of agencies having the same or similar first principal word in their names as Y 3.F 31/8: for Federal Deposit Insurance Corp. and Y 3.F 31/13: for Federal Inter-Agency River Basin Committee.

Series designations for publications of these agencies then follow the colon instead of preceding it. These series designations are assigned in the regular way.

Individual book numbers are then added to the series designations with no separation if the individual book numbers begin with letters, and are separated by the shilling mark if they begin with numbers. Thus the Annual Report of the Atomic Energy Commission for the year 1961 is Y 3.At 7:1/961 while the unnumbered AEC Report on Status Centrifuge Technology is classed as Y 3.At 7:2G 21.

Table III attached gives a list of current Boards, commissions, and Committees with their class symbols.

Congress and its Working Committees

The working committees of Congress such as Appropriations, Judiciary, etc., are grouped under one of the agency symbols assigned to Congress—namely, Y 4. As in the case of the Y 3. classifications outlined above, an author designation based on the name of the Committee follows the period and is followed by the colon. Thus the House Committee on Judiciary is Y 4.J 89/1: and the Senate Committee on Judiciary is Y 4.J 89/2:, the shilling mark and the figures 1 and 2 being used to distinguish between the two committees. If other committees were to be appointed having the word "judiciary" as the principal subject word of their name, J 89/3:, J 89/4:, etc., would be used as the author designations. (See Table IV attached for symbols of current committees.)

No regular *numbered* series designations are normally used after the colon for the publications of Congressional Committees since they are for the most part simply unnumbered hearings or committee prints. These are given book numbers by use of the the the two-figure Cutter tables based on the principal subject word of the title of each as for unnumbered publications in the regular classification treatment.

Where series do occur within the publications of a Committee they have been treated in various ways. Some examples follow.

Congressional Directory. This has been given a series designation of "1" following the colon, as Y 4.P93/1:1. Individual book numbers are then marked off by use of the shilling mark following the series designation, as Y 4.P93/1:1/ with the particular issue being designated by Congress and session, as Y 4.P93/1:1/84-1.

Economic Indicators. This monthly periodical issued by the Joint Economic Committee has been assigned a place in the group of publications issued by this Committee by use of the Cutter designation following the colon (instead of the regular numerical series designation), based on the subject word "Economic" as Y 4.Ec7:Ec7. The book numbers for individual issues are then designated by year of issue and number corresponding to the month of issue as 954-1 for January 1954, 954-2 for February 1954, etc. These are added to the series designation of "Ec7" following the colon and separated by the shilling mark, as: June 1954 issue, Y 4.Ec7/954-6.

Serially Numbered Hearings and Committee Prints. Hearings and the committee prints of some Congressional Committees are numbered as serials within each Congress. These are designated by Congress and number (separated by the shilling mark) immediately following the colon, as: House Judiciary Committee Serial 13, 83d Congress would be Y 4.J89/1:83/13, the number of the Congress taking the place of the usual numerical series designation. These are filed behind the hearings and committee prints bearing letter and number Cutter designation—that is, to the right on the shelf.

Congressional Bills, Documents, and Reports. These numbered series of publications issued by Congress are not given a place in the scheme by use of lettered symbols but are simply filed at the end of all other classifications by Congress, session, and individual number with abbreviations being used for the series titles. The order of filing and the manner of designation is as follows: (The examples given were chosen at random.)

Series	*Individual examples*
Senate Bills	91-2:S.528
House Bills	91-2:H.R.15961
Senate Joint Resolutions	91-2:S.J.Res.172
House Joint Resolutions	91-2:H.J.Res.1098
Senate Concurrent Resolutions	91-2:S.Con.Res.70
House Concurrent Resolutions	91-2:H.Con.Res.578
Senate Resolutions	91-2:S.Res.304
House Resolutions	91-2:H.Res.108
Senate Reports	91-2:S.rp.885
House Reports	91-2:H.rp.983
Senate Documents	91-2:S.doc.82
House Documents	91-2:H.doc.342

Other Congressional Publications. Attached as Table V is a list of currently published Congressional series not explained above with notes as to methods of assigning book numbers.

Multilateral International Organizations in which the United States Participates

Many of the publications of these organizations are published simultaneously by the United States and other countries. The United States portions of these organizations may also publish separately, for example, the United States National Commission for UNESCO. Since participation by the United States is in the realm of foreign relations, such publications are classed under the State Department with two main class designations assigned as follows:

S 3. Arbitrations and Mixed Commissions to Settle International Disputes
S 5. International Congresses, Conferences, and Commissions

The individual organizations are then treated as subordinate bureaus or offices, a number being assigned to each as it begins to publish, but following the period rather than preceding it as in regular class construction. Individual book numbers are assigned after the colon, using the 2-figure Cutter table and based on the principal subject word of the title.

If the organization proves to be a prolific publisher, however, issuing several definite series of publications, each is distinquished by adding the shilling mark and digits beginning with 2 to the number assigned to the organization as a bureau designation, as in the case of related series in regular class construction. For example some of the series issued by the U.S. National Commission for UNESCO are classed as follows:

S 5.48/9:   Addresses
S 5.48/10: Maps and posters
S 5.48/11: Executive committee, summary of notice of meetings

Individual book numbers are then assigned in the regular way.

Publications of the President and the Executive Office of the President including Committees and Commissions Established by Executive Order and reporting directly to the President

The agency symbol assigned to the President of the United States is Pr followed by the number corresponding to the ordinal number of succession to the presidency as Pr 37, Richard M. Nixon, 37th president of the United States. Breakdowns under the agency symbol follow normal methods of classification expansion. However, in recent years, presidents have appointed many special committees and commissions to study particular problems and to report their findings directly to the Chief executives. These organizations usually cease to exist after making their report. Since their publications are usually few in number, normal bureau treatment is not practical and special treatment is therefore indicated to prevent establishment of classes which will not be used, and in addition to keep together the publications of all such organizations appointed by one president.

Therefore, beginning with those appointed by President Eisenhower, one series class (Pr --.8:) has been assigned for all such committees and commissions. A Cutter designation using the 2-figure table is then assigned to each based on the principal subject word of its name as Pr 34.8:H81, President's Advisory Committee on Government Housing Policies and Programs. Publications of the committee are distinguished by addition of the shilling mark and Cutter numbers based on the principal subject word of the title as in normal classification.

Beginning with the administration of President Kennedy, the continuing offices assigned to the President, which make up the Executive Office of the President, have been given permanent classes under the symbol PrEx. Thus with a change in administration it will no longer be necessary to change the classes for such offices as Bureau of the Budget, National Security Council, Office of Emergency Planning, etc. These have been given breakdowns as subordinate offices of the Executive Office of the President, the Bureau of the Budget for example, being assigned PrEx2. Series and book numbers are then assigned in the usual manner.

Table I

Department and Agency Symbols Currently in Use

A	Agriculture Department	FR	Federal Reserve System Board of Governors
AA	Action	FT	Federal Trade Commission
AC	Arms Control and Disarmament Agency	FTZ	Foreign Trade Zones Board
C	Commerce Department	GA	General Accounting Office
CC	Federal Communications Commission	GP	Government Printing Office
CR	Civil Rights Commission	GS	General Services Administration
CS	Civil Service Commission	HE	Health, Education, and Welfare Department
CZ	Panama Canal Company and Canal Zone Government	HH	Housing and Urban Development Department (Formerly Housing and Home Finance Agency)
D	Defense Department	I	Interior Department
DC	District of Columbia	IA	United States Information Agency
EP	Environmental Protection Agency	IC	Interstate Commerce Commission
FA	Fine Arts Commission	J	Justice Department
FCA	Farm Credit Administration	Ju	Judiciary (Courts of the United States)
FHL	Federal Home Loan Bank Board	L	Labor Department
FM	Federal Mediation and Conciliation Service	LC	Library of Congress
FMC	Federal Maritime Commission	LR	National Labor Relations Board
FP	Federal Power Commission	NA	National Academy of Sciences

Table I   (con't.)

NAS	National Aeronautics and Space Administration	RnB	Renegotiation Board
NC	National Capital Planning Commission	RR	Railroad Retirement Board
NCU	National Credit Union Administration	S	State Department
NF	National Foundation on the Arts	SBA	Small Business Administration
	and the Humanities	SE	Securities and Exchange Commission
NMB	National Mediation Board	SI	Smithsonian Institution
NS	National Science Foundation	T	Treasury Department
P	United States Postal Service	TC	Tariff Commission
Pr	President of United States	TD	Transportation Department
PrEx	Executive Office of the President	VA	Veterans Administration
RA	National Railroad Adjustment Board	X and Y	Congress

Table II

Current Subject Breakdowns of the Interstate Commerce Commission

Symbol	Publications relating to:	Symbol	Publications relating to:
IC 1 acci.	Accidents	IC 1 mot.	Motor carriers
IC 1 act.	Acts to regulate commerce	IC 1 pip.	Pipe line companies
IC 1 blo.	Block signals	IC 1 rat.	Rates
IC 1 def.	Defense Transport Administration	IC 1 saf.	Safety
IC 1 elec.	Electric Railways	IC 1 sle.	Sleeping car companies
IC 1 exp.	Express companies	IC 1 ste.	Steam roads
IC 1 hou.	Hours of service	IC 1 val.	Valuation of property
IC 1 loc.	Locomotive inspection	IC 1 wat.	Water carriers

Table III

Agency Symbols of Boards, Commissions, and Committees Established by
Act of Congress or under Authority of Act of Congress
(not specifically designated in the Executive Branch of the
Government nor as completely independent agencies.)

Y 3.Ad9/7:	Advisory Commission on Information
Y 3.Ad9/8:	Advisory Commission on Intergovernmental Relations
Y 3.Ad9/9:	United States Advisory Commission on International Educational and Cultural Affairs
Y 3.Al 1 s/4:	Federal Field Committee for Development Planning in Alaska
Y 3.Am3:	American Battle Monuments Commission
Y 3.Am3/6:	American Revolution Bicentennial Commission
Y 3.Ap4/2:	Appalachian Regional Commission
Y 3.At7:	Atomic Energy Commission
Y 3.B61:	Committee on Purchase of Blind-Made Products
Y 3.C49/2:	Civil War Centennial Commission
Y 3.C63/2:	Coastal Plains Regional Commission
Y 3.C66:	Coinage Joint Commission
Y 3.C76:	Construction Industry Collective Bargaining Commission
Y 3.C76/2:	National Commission on Consumer Finance
Y 3.D37/2:	Delaware River Basin Commission

Table III (con't.)

Y 3.Ed8/2:	National Advisory Council on Education of Disadvantaged Children
Y 3.Ed8/3:	National Advisory Council on Education Professions Development
Y 3.Ed8/4:	National Advisory Council on Adult Education
Y 3.Eq2:	Equal Employment Opportunity Commission
Y 3.Ex7/3:	Export-Import Bank of United States
Y 3.F31/8:	Federal Deposit Insurance Corporation
Y 3.F31/13:	Federal Inter-Agency River Basin Committee
Y 3.F31/14:	Federal Inter-Agency Committee on Recreation
Y 3.F31/17:	Federal Radiation Council
Y 3.F76/3:	Foreign Claims Settlement Commission
Y 3.F82:	Four Corners Regional Commission
Y 3.G79/3:	Great Lakes Basin Commission
Y 3.H73:	Permanent Committee for the Oliver Wendell Holmes Devise
Y 3.In2/6:	Indian Claims Commission
Y 3.In2/8:	National Industrial Pollution Control Council
Y 3.In8/6:	Interdepartmental Committee on Children and Youth
Y 3.In8/8:	Inter-Agency Committee on Water Resources
Y 3.In8/13:	Interdepartmental Committee on Nutrition for National Defense
Y 3.In8/15:	Commission on International Rules of Judicial Procedure
Y 3.In8/16:	Interagency Committee on Automatic Data Processing
Y 3.In8/17:	Interdepartmental Committee to Coordinate Federal Urban Area Assistance Programs
Y 3.In8/21:	Interdepartmental Committee on Status of Women
Y 3.J66:	Joint Publications Research Service
Y 3.L58:	Lewis and Clark Trail Commission
Y 3.L61:	National Commission on Libraries and Information Science
Y 3.M33:	Maritime Advisory Committee
Y 3.M33/2:	Marihuana and Drug Abuse Commission
Y 3.M41:	National Commission on Materials Policy
Y 3.M58:	Migratory Bird Conservation Commission
Y 3.M69:	Missouri Basin Inter-Agency Committee
Y 3.M84:	Mortgage Interest Rates Commission
Y 3.N21/16:	National Advisory Council on International Monetary and Financial Problems
Y 3.N21/21:	National Capital Transportation Agency
Y 3.N21/23:	National Visitors Center Study Commission
Y 3.N21/24:	National Water Commission
Y 3.N21/25:	National Commission on Product Safety
Y 3.N21/27:	National Business Council for Consumer Affairs
Y 3.N42/2:	New England Regional Commission
Y 3.N42/3:	New England River Basins Commission
Y 3.Oc 1:	Occupational Safety and Health Review Commission
Y 3.Oc2:	National Advisory Commission on Oceans and Atmosphere
Y 3.Oz 1:	Ozarks Regional Commission
Y 3.P 11/2:	Pacific Southwest Inter-Agency Committee
Y 3.P 11/4:	Pacific Northwest River Basin Commission
Y 3.P96/7:	Public Land Law Review Commission
Y 3.Se4:	Selective Service System
Y 3.Sh6:	Ship Structure Committee
Y 3.Sp2/7:	Cabinet Committee on Opportunities for Spanish Speaking People
Y 3.Su1:	Subversive Activities Control Board
Y 3.T22:	National Commission on Technology, Automation, and Economic Progress
Y 3.T25:	Tennessee Valley Authority
Y 3.Up6:	Upper Great Lakes Regional Commission
Y 3.W29:	Water Resources Council

Table IV

Agency Symbols of Current Congressional Committees
(Temporary select and special committees not included)

Y 4.Ae8:	Aeronautical and Space Sciences (Senate)	Y 4.In8/13:	Interior and Insular Affairs (Senate)
Y 4.Ag4:	Special Committee on Aging (Senate)	Y 4.In8/14:	Interior and Insular Affairs (House)
Y 4.Ag8/1:	Agriculture (House)	Y 4.In8/15:	Internal Security Committee (House)
Y 4.Ag8/2:	Agriculture and Forestry (Senate)	Y 4.J89/1:	Judiciary (House)
Y 4.Ap6/1:	Appropriations (House)	Y 4.J89/2:	Judiciary (Senate)
Y 4.Ap6/2:	Appropriations (Senate)	Y 4.L11/2:	Labor and Public Welfare (Senate)
Y 4.Ar5/2:	Armed Services (House)	Y 4.L61/2:	Joint Committee on the Library
Y 4.Ar5/3:	Armed Services (Senate)	Y 4.M53:	Merchant Marine and Fisheries (House)
Y 4.At7/2:	Joint Committee on Atomic Energy	Y 4.N22/4:	Joint Committee on Navajo-Hopi Indian
Y 4.B22/1:	Banking and Currency (House)		Administration
Y 4.B22/3:	Banking and Currency (Senate)	Y 4.P84/10:	Post Office and Civil Service (House)
Y 4.C73/2:	Commerce (Senate)	Y 4.P84/11:	Post Office and Civil Service (Senate)
Y 4.D36:	Joint Committee on Defense Production	Y 4.P93/1:	Joint Committee on Printing
Y 4.D63/1:	District of Columbia (House)		Public Works (Senate)
Y 4.D63/2:	District of Columbia (Senate)	Y 4.P96/11:	Public Works (House)
Y 4.Ec7:	Joint Economic Committee	Y 4.R24/4:	Joint Committee on Reduction of
Y 4.Ed8/1:	Education and Labor (House)	Y 4.P96/10:	Federal Expenditures
Y 4.F49:	Finance (Senate)	Y 4.R86/1:	Rules (House)
Y 4.F76/1:	Foreign Affairs (House)	Y 4.R86/2:	Rules and Administration (Senate)
Y 4.F76:2:	Foreign Relations (Senate)	Y 4.Sci2:	Science and Astronautics (House)
Y 4.G74/6:	Government Operations (Senate)	Y 4.Sml:	Small Business Select Committee (House)
Y 4.G74/7:	Government Operations (House)	Y 4.Sml/2:	Small Business Select Committee (Senate)
Y 4.H81/3:	House Administration (House)	Y 4.V64/3:	Veterans' Affairs (House)
Y 4.In8/4:	Interstate and Foreign Commerce (House)	Y 4.W36:	Ways and Means (House)
Y 4.In8/11:	Joint Committee on Internal Revenue Taxation		

Table V

Classification of Congressional Publications
(other than bills, documents, and reports)

X.	Congressional Record (bound). Congress and session form the series designation with individual book numbers made up of volume and part. For example: 83d Congress, 2d session, volume 100, part 2, classified X.83/2:100/pt.2.
X/a.	Congressional Record (daily). These are numbered throughout each session with no volume numbers. For example: 83d Congress, 2d session, number 32 is classified X/a.83/2:32.
XJH:	Journal of the House of Representatives. These are simply designated by Congress and session as XJH:83-2.
XJS:	Journal of the Senate. Designated by Congress and session as XJS:83-2.
Y 1.1:	Here are classified joint miscellaneous publications pertaining to both House and Senate, individual book numbers being formed by 2-figure Cutter designations based on the principal subject word of the title. This class may also be used by libraries desiring to file them serially for reports of organizations chartered by Congress such as the Boy Scouts of America, Disabled American Veterans, etc., with dates of the reports being added to the 3-figure Cutter designations for the titles of the organizations. For example, the 1954 report of the Boy Scouts of America would be classified Y 1.1:B691/954.
Y 1.2:	House of Representatives miscellaneous publications. Individual book numbers are assigned in the usual manner for unnumbered publications.

Table V (con't.)

Y 1.2/2:	Calendars of the United States House of Representatives and history of legislation. Book numbers are assigned by Congress, session, and individual number as Y 1.2/2:84-1-13.
Y 1.3:	Senate miscellaneous publications. Individual book numbers are assigned in the usual manner for unnumbered publications. The volumes of the Journal of executive proceedings are given the Cutter designation Ex3 with the volume numbers added as: Y 1.3:Ex3/v.91, pt.2.
Y 1.3/2:	Executive calendar [relating to nominations and treaties]. Book numbers are assigned by date and number as: Y1.3/2:955/1.
Y 1.3/3:	Calendar of business. Book numbers are assigned by Congress and individual number as Y 1.3/3:84-16.
Y 1.Cong.sess:	Senate Executive documents and reports. Congress and session numbers form the series designations for these two series with the individual document letters or report numbers (preceded by the letters "rp") forming the individual book numbers as: Y 1.83/2:A (Senate Executive Document A) and Y 1.83/2:rp.5) (Senate Executive Report 5).
Y2.	This class was originally assigned for Congressional bills and resolutions and may be so used in libraries desiring to keep such material in one group. Classification is completed by use of Congress and session, and individual bill of resolution numbers preceded by the abbreviations S. for Senate bills, H. R. for House bills, S. con. res. for Senate concurrent resolutions, H. res. for House resolutions, etc.
Y 3.	Boards, Commissions, and Committees. (See main text.)
Y 4.	Congressional Committees. (See main text.)
Y 5.	Contested elections. Not used in recent years.
Y 6.	Impeachments. Not used in recent years.
Y 7.1:	Memorial Addresses on life and character of deceased members of Congress. Individual book numbers are assigned by use of the 3-figure Cutter table based on the name of the deceased member.

INSTRUCTIONS TO DEPOSITORY LIBRARIES

SECTION 1.
GENERAL INFORMATION CONCERNING YOUR DEPOSITORY STATUS

Your library is an official depository for U.S. Government publications. It has been designated as such in one of the following ways:

1. By the U.S. Representative who represents your Congressional district or his predecessor.
2. By one of your State's U.S. Senators or his predecessor.
3. By virtue of being a State library or land-grant college library.
4. By special act of Congress.

In accepting the privilege of being a depository library you have agreed to abide fully by the law and regulations governing officially designated depositories.

You are not required to receive all U.S. Government publications which are made available to depositories. You should select **only** those items best suited to the needs of your patrons. You are urged to use your utmost discretion in selecting publications so that there will be no waste of Government funds and so that you can give proper custody to those you do select and make them readily available to your patrons. Keep in mind the depository collection is a **permanent** one. All Government publications supplied to depository libraries under the Depository Program remain the property of the United States Government, and **cannot be disposed** of except as outlined in Section 11 of these instructions. Your regional depository receives everything. Depend upon them for seldom used items.

Government publications received under the depository program should be given the same care and treatment as privately published material, such as books and periodicals. They need not be held together as a special depository collection. If they can circulate as do other books in your collection, so much the better. (Those libraries wishing to keep their depository collection intact may find it convenient to purchase extra copies of Government publications through our Sales Program for use in circulation.) Many Federal Government publications are valuable as reference and bibliographical sources, and this type of material in many instances can profitably be made a part of a reference room collection.

There are also many important periodicals published by the Federal Government. They can form a valuable part of the periodical collection of the library and need not be segregated merely because they are received through depository distribution.

If the practice of the depository library is to keep pamphlet material in vertical files, then similar Government publications may be kept in the same way. However, all material should be kept current. The library should keep a record of this material and put the Superintendent of Documents number on the cover. This facilitates identification of materials from SuDocs citations, as well as assisting both updating and formal discard procedures.

It is necessary to issue many Government publications unbound or in paper covers. Libraries are expected to include these publications in their binding program along with books, periodicals, and other privately published materials. Binders are not furnished for looseleaf material unless the issuing agency includes them as part of its publication.

Depository-collection items which are lost or worn-out, etc., should be subject to the same replacement policy as the library maintains for non-Government materials. The depository should pay for replacement copies, and claims **should not** be filed for this material.

Use of the Superintendent of Documents classification scheme is not mandatory for depository libraries. However, there are many advantages in using this scheme. Librarians have found the SuDocs scheme to be more economical and practical for classifying Federal Government documents. In most instances the stem of the classification is composed of the alphabetical symbols currently being used to identify the issuing agency. The number can be transferred easily and quickly from the Shipping List to the publication by non-professional library employees. This aids in processing the material more rapidly. Most of the bibliographical tools issued by private publishers also use this scheme. Since it is commonly used by many other depository libraries, it provides a

Rev. Nov. 1977. Washington, D.C.: Govt. Print. Off., 1977.

169

specific identification for borrowing, and simplifies compiling or checking duplications lists. These uses save staff time because the SuDoc numbers eliminate the need for bibliographic detail. Any library should carefully weigh the Superintendent of Documents Classification Scheme against other schemes before adopting it. Use G.P.O. Form 3453, "Request for Confirmation of Classification Numbers" when requesting information concerning assignment of Su-Docs classification numbers. (See **Exhibit E** at end of these instructions for sample form.) Direct requests to: Assistant Public Printer, (Superintendent of Documents), Library Division (SLLC), Washington, D.C. 20401.

All shipments should be unpacked and processed as they are received. Failure to do so can result in the loss of your depository status.

Every effort should be made to insure that the depository collection is used and that publications are not merely stored or placed in inaccessible locations.

Publications loaned to other libraries or institutions on an extended loan basis, should be made available for use by the general public upon request. All Government publications supplied under the Depository Program **remain the property of the United States Government.**

SECTION 2.
REGIONAL DEPOSITORIES

Libraries designated to be Regional Depositories must already be designated depositories, and signify their interest to be designated a Regional.

Designation as a Regional Depository requires prior approval by the library authority of the State, the Commonwealth of Puerto Rico, or the Virgin Islands. A U.S. Senator, the Resident Commissioner in the case of Puerto Rico, or the Governor in the case of the Virgin Islands, must make the designation.

In addition to fulfilling the requirements for regular depositories, regional depositories **must receive and retain** at least one copy of **all** Government publications made available to depositories under the Depository Library Program either in printed or microform copy (except those authorized to be discarded by the Superintendent of Documents).

Within the region they serve, designated regional depositories must provide interlibrary loan and reference service to designated depository and non-depository libraries. They must also assist selective non-Federal libraries in the disposal of unwanted Government publications as provided by law.

The Depository Act authorizes Regional Depositories to permit selective non-Federal depository libraries within the area or areas served by them, to dispose of Government publications which have been **retained for at least five years.** However, the Regional Library may refuse to grant permission for disposal of any publication that it feels should be kept by one of its depositories for a longer period of time. Regional depositories in concurrence with the Superintendent of Documents may prepare guidelines and issue any special instructions which they deem necessary for the efficient operation of depositories within their jurisdiction and which will enable the library to better serve the needs of the community where it is situated.

Upon request for permission for disposal of publications, the regional library should ask the depository to prepare a list of the publications, showing the current item number, series title, Superintendent of Documents number, and approximate extent of the holdings to be disposed of. Since, as a Regional Depository you are responsible for interlibrary loan, you may want to check the lists for any publications which may be missing from your own collection.

Selective non-Federal depository libraries should be instructed that disposition of unwanted Government documents should be made in the following prescribed manner. Publications should be first offered to other depository libraries in the State or States, then to some other library or educational institution in the vicinity or area which would be able to make them available to the public and to which requests might be referred. Failing to find such a recipient after reasonable effort, they may be disposed of in any appropriate manner. However, if such disposition should take the form of sale, either as second-hand books or waste paper, the proceeds with a letter of explanation should be sent to the Superintendent of Documents since all depository publications remain the property of the United States Government.

Regional Depositories also have the authority to instruct regular depository libraries regarding the disposal of publications in the event the library decides to relinquish its depository privilege. This disposal should be made in the same afore-mentioned manner, although depository libraries may keep any publications they desire when the depository privilege is terminated.

It is the policy of the Superintendent of Documents to confer with the Regional Depository when a new library in the State or States is designated for depository status. In the official capacity of Regional Depository it is your responsibility to notify the new library of your status and give them any necessary information regarding interlibrary loan, reference, and any other services which you can provide, such as advice on making selections.

A representative from the designated Regional Depository should make periodic visits to the various depository libraries in the State or region in order that they may be familiar with the operations and needs of the depository libraries whom they serve in this capacity.

Regional Depository Libraries have no jurisdiction over depository libraries in the various agencies of the Federal Government within the region they serve. Depository libraries within the various Government agencies are designated by a special provision of the Depository Act and are responsible only to the Superintendent of Documents.

SECTION 3.
CORRESPONDENCE WITH THE ASSISTANT PUBLIC PRINTER (SUPERINTENDENT OF DOCUMENTS)

When writing, always mention that you are a depository library and include your **assigned depository library number** on all correspondence.

To avoid misrouting and insure prompt response, address all letters, claims, amendments of selections, and other correspondence to:

Library Division (SLLA)
Superintendent of Documents
Washington, D.C. 20401

unless self-addressed envelopes or labels are furnished to you. If self-addressed envelopes or labels are provided, **be sure to use them.** These envelopes or labels are usually addressed to a special section or person responsible for a particular phase of the Depository Program.

Use the claim forms **only to request** publications selected but not received. All other matters should be handled in separate correspondence, since notes on the claim forms pertaining to other matters tend to delay the processing of claims. Claim forms should not be used as a means of replacing lost, stolen, or mutilated publications.

Always give the item number from the Classified List, the series title or publication title, the Superintendent of Documents classification number and your depository library number when writing concerning depository publications

SECTION 4.
PERIODIC REPORTS

Under provisions of law all designated depository libraries are required to report to the Superintendent of Documents. Every 2 years the Superintendent sends each depository a questionnaire concerning the use made of the publications furnished as well as conditions under which they are kept. **All designated depository libraries are required to answer the questionnaire fully, and return their copy promptly to the Superintendent of Documents.** Failure to do so can result in the deletion of your library from the list of depository libraries.

Although Federal depositories and Highest State Appellate Court Libraries are designated as depositories by certain other provisions of the depository law, they too are required to report to the Superintendent of Documents regarding their operations and the conditions under which they keep depository publications.

It is not possible for the Superintendent of Documents to personally visit each library. However, he has designated Depository Library Inspectors who have visited over 1,000 libraries in the past two years. His Inspection Program is designed to assist depositories in making Government documents available to the general public. It is also designed to convey to the Superintendent of Documents any matters which require his personal attention.

SECTION 5.
TERMINATION AS A DEPOSITORY LIBRARY

A depository library has the right to relinquish the depository privilege at any time by addressing a letter to the Superintendent of Documents stating that the library no longer wishes to be a depository for U.S. Government publications. If the library is served by a designated Regional Depository the regional library should also be notified of this decision.

The privilege may be terminated by the Superintendent of Documents if the library fails to meet the requirements as set forth in the law or consistently disregards notices and instructions, resulting in unnecessary expense to the Government in administering the program for that particular library.

Upon termination of the depository privilege, either by request or for a cause, the library shall request instructions from the Regional Depository concerning disposition to be made of the depository publications on hand. If the library is not served by a designated

Regional Depository, instructions should be obtained from the Superintendent of Documents.

If the library wishes to keep permanently certain publications which were received under the depository program, it may do so in the following manner. A list of these holdings should be submitted to the Regional Depository and/or the Superintendent of Documents if the depository library is not served by a designated Regional, with an accompanying statement requesting permanent retention. Each request will be reviewed on an individual basis and the depository library will be advised.

SECTION 6.

SELECTION OF PUBLICATIONS BY DEPOSITORY LIBRARIES

The basis for selection is the Classified List of U.S. Government Publications. This list comprises those series or groups of publications having a public interest or educational value which are issued by the various departments and agencies of the U.S. Government. Excluded from the list are publications issued for strictly administrative or operational purposes, those classified for reasons of national security, and so-called cooperative publications.

Cooperative publications are documents which are made available by the issuing agency only for entry into the Monthly Catalog. They are not made available for depository distribution, because the issuing agencies have had to make them self-sustaining in order to continue their publication. Publications such as the National Union Catalog and the Library of Congress Catalog fall within this category.

The Classified List consists of a set of 3- by 5-inch cards, with one card for each series or group of publications available for selection by depository libraries. Each card gives the item number, issuing agency, series title, Superintendent of Documents classification number, information on the series when necessary and space for your assigned depository library number.

Two sets of the Classified List, arranged numerically by item number sequence, are furnished to depository libraries at the time of their acceptance as a depository. One set is to be kept intact for the library's records, and the other to be used in making selections. Selections are made by returning to the Library Division, Superintendent of Documents, one item card for the series desired, properly identified with your assigned depository library number. Depository selections should be returned within 30 days from the time the Classified List is received.

The item number assigned to a series in the Classified List remains the controlling item number for that series regardless of change of title, or transfer, or change in name of the issuing agency. An item number assigned to a series may also govern the distribution of a closely related series of a similar nature (for example a series of numbered manuals and a series of unnumbered manuals with similar content issued by the same agency), in which instance a library selecting this item would also have to take the related series as well. For agencies whose scope and publications issuances are limited, one item number has been established to cover all publications issued. The series name entry on the item card in this case will read "Reports and Publications."

A printed list entitled "List of Classes of U.S. Government Publications Available for Selection by Depository Libraries" which is revised approximately once a year, is furnished to libraries as issued. Libraries should use this list to keep the Classified List up-to-date. This List of Classes should also be consulted when making new selections to determine whether the series is still active.

It is important that selections by a library be centrally controlled within the library and that records be kept accurately in order to avoid misunderstandings. Consideration should be given as to whether the series would meet the needs of your particular area, as well as adequacy of staff available for classifying, cataloging, and shelving the publications and making them readily available for reference.

Libraries are notified when new series are added to the Classified List through announcements in the Daily Depository Shipping List (see Section 7 which follows.)

Material which has not been printed at the Government Printing Office but has been made available for depository distribution is clearly marked "Non-GPO" on the List of Classes and the Daily Depository Shipping List. These publications are subject to the same handling provisions as material printed at the Government Printing Office.

SECTION 7.

SURVEY FOR NEW ITEMS

Notification of new series is made on a special survey which is distributed with the Daily Depository Shipping List.

Two 3- by 5-inch cards are sent to each library for each new item listed, together with a sample copy of the publication whenever possible. If a library desires to receive future copies of publications in the series, one item card properly marked with the assigned depository library number should be returned to the Library Division (SLLA). A self-addressed envelope is provided for the return of the cards and this envelope should be used in order to avoid misrouting in the Public Documents Department. These cards must be returned within the time limit designated on the survey. Returns received after the date indicated on the survey notice cannot be used as the basis for claims for missed publications (libraries outside contiguous United States are excepted).

Cards for items selected should be separated from those items you do not wish to receive. It is recommended that the former be kept in a file by item number. Cards for items not selected should be kept in a separate file so that the library will have a complete record of available items. (See **Exhibit A** at end of these Instructions for sample card.) Survey cards should not be attached to "G.P.O. Form 3454, Amendment of Selections." This form should only be used for material already in the Depository Program.

Regional depositories are not required to return item cards since they automatically receive all material made available under the Depository Program.

When possible a sample copy of the new item is furnished for perusal. If your library selects the new item, the sample copy furnished should be kept as part of the regular depository distribution for the item. If your library does not select the item and the library is served by a designated Regional Depository, the Regional library should be contacted before disposition of the sample copy is made. If the library is not serviced by a Regional Depository, then the sample copy may be discarded.

SECTION 8.
AMENDMENT OF SELECTIONS

Selections can be amended at any time except in certain cases where material has been printed in earlier years and held for later binding. This is particularly true of various decisions issued by the courts and some of the agencies (e.g. Decisions of the Department of Interior). This is also true of the Congressional Serial Set, which may not be bound and distributed until long after being printed, and then only sufficient numbers to supply libraries which had selected the bound volumes prior to the beginning of the Session of Congress which they cover.

Many times we receive only a limited number of copies of a publication from a department or agency for depository distribution. These copies are sent to all designated Regional Depositories, then they are also made available to selective depositories through a "special offer" on a first-come, first-served basis.

Publications cannot be furnished retroactively. New selections will take effect only when new issues in the series selected are ordered printed.

Only series for which item cards have been furnished and made part of the Classified List can be added to a depository's selections.

Selections may be discontinued or added by completing "G.P.O. Form 3454, Amendment of Selections" and sending it to the Library Division (SLLA) with your assigned depository library number. (See **Exhibit D** at the end of these Instructions for sample of G.P.O. Form 3454.)

All selections should be reviewed **once a year** to determine whether the library is receiving material which is not being used and to eliminate wasteful use of taxpayers' money and unnecessary costs to the Federal Government in supplying material which is not needed.

When an item is dropped, the publications received prior to the date that the deletion was requested by the Depository must be retained for the usual five-year period or permanently if there is no Regional in the State.

SECTION 9.
DAILY DEPOSITORY SHIPPING LIST

Since August 1, 1951, the Superintendent of Documents has prepared a Daily Depository Shipping List. The Shipping List serves as an invoice for each shipment and lists all depository publications contained in the package. The List also indicates the item numbers under which the publications were distributed, the titles, and series numbers of the publications, and the Superintendent of Documents classification numbers.

In the event the package does not contain a Shipping List, make a list of at least five items contained in the package, giving complete title and date of publication, and request a copy of the Shipping List for this particular shipment. Should the Shipping List be illegible or mutilated, return it and another copy will be forwarded in its place. Requests for missing, incomplete, or mutilated Shipping Lists should be sent to the **Depository Unit, Library Division, Superintendent of Documents, Washington, D.C. 20402.**

The Shipping Lists and the shipments are numbered in numerical sequence and should be checked to insure that all shipments have been received.

Several shipments are made each day. Upon receipt of a package the indicated item numbers on the list should be checked against the library's selections to determine whether any items previously selected have been omitted from the shipment. Also check against your item cards to avoid claiming series which you have not selected.

Each publication in the shipment should be marked with the word "depository" or some other term, number, or symbol which identifies that publication as having been received through depository distribution. The date of the Shipping List or your processing date should also be on each publication.

Every depository library receives a copy of each Daily Depository Shipping List even though none of the items listed were selected by the library. Certain publications are not listed on the Shipping List, because individual issues are mailed automatically by another section of the Office. These publications are listed in **Appendix B.**

The Shipping List is also used by the Superintendent of Documents as a quick means of informing depository libraries of corrections of previous lists, of issuance of special publications which are available upon individual request, of changes in the List of Classes, of additions to item numbers, and other special announcements pertaining to the Depository Program. (See **Exhibit B** at the end of these instructions for sample Shipping List.)

The separate sheet entitled "List of Price Additions and Class Corrections" which accompanies the Shipping List from time to time may be discarded after corrections or additions have been made.

SECTION 10.

CLAIMS FOR COPIES OF PUBLICATIONS SELECTED BUT NOT RECEIVED AND DUPLICATE SHIPMENTS

All claims for nonreceipt of depository publications must be postmarked **within 15 days** from the date of receipt of the Daily Depository Shipping List on which the publication or publications were listed. Claims for entire missing shipments must also be made **within 15 days** from the date of the subsequent shipment. **No claims will be honored for material which is over 45 days old.**

Publications should be collated when received since claims for defective copies cannot be filled unless they are made promptly.

Claims can be made only for publications actually listed on the Daily Depository Shipping List. The Monthly Catalog cannot be used as a basis for claims. Depository items listed in **Appendix B** which are mailed automatically and thus do not appear on the Shipping List, should be claimed in the same manner as publications which appear on the Shipping List.

Special claim forms are supplied to depository libraries for the **specific purpose of claiming items selected but not received.** These forms should be used in preference to regular letters when making claim for an item or items not received. Do not make notations on the claim form regarding other matters. This tends to delay the processing of claims. Claim forms should not be used as a means of replacing lost, stolen, or mutilated publications.

A separate claim form should be filled out for each separate item. As a rule of thumb, if there are five items or less the library should fill out five separate forms. Selective Depository Libraries claiming complete shipments should obtain a copy of the Daily Depository Shipping List listing the missing documents, encircle the item numbers that were previously selected by that library, attach the list to the form and forward it to the Library Division. Regional Depository Libraries only require submitting a Claim Form with the words "Complete Shipment" and indicate the shipping list number.

In filling out the claim forms **give complete information.** Be sure that the item number, title of publication, and Superintendent of Documents classification number as well as the date and number of the shipment, your depository library number, and complete mailing address are clearly stated. (See **Exhibit C** at the end of these Instructions for sample form.) Send all claim forms to:

> Library Division (SLL)
> Superintendent of Documents
> Washington, DC   20401

Under provisions of law the Superintendent of Documents can provide only one copy of each publication to depository libraries. Duplicate copies of publications can be supplied by this Office only from sales stock which is purchased with an entirely separate appropriation and which is accounted for in a completely different manner. The depository program and the sales program are two entirely separate functions and are in no way interchangeable. When depository publications are ordered, the number of requests on hand when the publication is printed is used as the basis for determining the number of copies to be supplied to depository libraries. For this reason, **requests that come in after the publication has gone to press cannot be honored.** Claims for Congressional Serial Volumes cannot be honored unless the library has selected that particular item prior to the time the individual reports or documents were ordered printed that is prior to the beginning of the Session of Congress which they cover, and not at the time the volumes are bound. A similar situation occurs in the case of other bound publications such as various court decisions and reports in which signatures for certain parts are printed many months prior to the date on which the publication is actually issued. Claims cannot be honored **unless the library has selected the particular item number prior to the time the first signatures were ordered printed.**

Since your library is one of more than one thousand libraries receiving depository shipments, it is possible that you may receive duplicate shipments and/or defective copies occasionally. If your library should receive a duplicate shipment or a defective copy, the Library Division, Superintendent of Documents should be notified immediately in order that our mailing practices can be checked and the necessary corrections can be made. When one library receives a duplicate shipment, some other library has not received a shipment. Notification should be sent to the same address as claims for nonreceipt. Upon notification, a mailing label which requires no postage will be sent to your library in order that you may return the shipment or defective copy to us when appropriate.

The Superintendent of Documents will endeavor to replace defective copies as long as a supply of the publication remains available for distribution, and makes every effort to provide fast and accurate service to depository libraries. However, in distributing many millions of publications to depository libraries each year it is inevitable that mistakes will be made. In all cases where depository libraries have selected publications in advance and have failed to receive them, this Office will endeavor to obtain copies for the library. In some instances, it will be impossible to honor claims because the supply of the publication has become exhausted.

SECTION 11.
DISPOSITION OF DEPOSITORY PUBLICATIONS

All depository libraries **not served** by a designated Regional Depository **must retain permanently** one copy of all Government publications received through depository distribution, except superseded publications or those issued later in bound form or in microcopy form. Government publications received through sources other than the Depository Program may be disposed of in any manner.

Any publication which is a duplicate copy or has been superseded may be discarded.

Those received later in bound form and those for which microform copies have been substituted should be offered first to some other depository library in the State, then to some public library, or educational institution in your vicinity or area which might find use for them. Failing to find such a recipient after reasonable effort, you may dispose of the publications in any appropriate manner, but should such disposition take the form of sale, either as secondhand books or as waste paper, the proceeds with a letter of explanation should be sent to the Library Division, Superintendent of Documents, **as all depository publications remain the property of the United States Government.**

Depository libraries within executive departments and independent agencies may dispose of unwanted publications received under the Depository Program, after first offering them to the Library of Congress and the National Archives.

Depository libraries within the State Appellate Courts may dispose of unwanted Government publications after offering them to the designated Regional Depository Library serving the State. If the State is not served by a designated Regional Depository, publications should be offered to the State Librarian.

Depository libraries which are served by a designated Regional Depository may dispose of any publications which they have retained for at least five years, after obtaining permission and receiving instructions for such disposition from the Regional Depository which has been designated to serve the area. (See Section 2, paragraphs 5, 6, and 7 for additional information.) A list of designated Regional Depositories as of November 1977, with date of designation, can be found in **Appendix A** at the end of these Instructions.

Below are listed some of the types of material which may be disposed of by all libraries:

1. Daily Congressional Record, after bound volumes are received.
2. Slip laws, after bound Statutes at Large are received.
3. House and Senate bills and resolutions, one year after the adjournment of the Congress.
4. Any materials which are cumulated in later issues, such as Supplement to the United States Code, the Code of Laws of the District of Columbia, Digest of Public General Bills, Internal Revenue Bulletin (providing the library has selected the item number for the Cumulative Bulletin), and only after cumulation is received.
5. Any publication upon receipt of a revised edition.
6. Pages from looseleaf publications that are replaced by new pages.
7. Separates, upon receipt of final bound volumes.

8. Senate and House reports and documents, upon receipt of the serial set volumes.
9. Lists and indexes of publications of various agencies, upon receipt of complete new editions (e.g. list of publications of the Bureau of Mines, indexes of Congressional committee hearings issued by the Senate Library, etc.). Small spot lists, such as publication announcements, may be discarded at the end of six months or when they have lost their timeliness.
10. Annual or biennial publications of a statistical nature which merely revise figures or information and bring them up-to-date, such as Index of Specifications and Standards, Light Lists, etc., upon receipt of a new issue. This permission does not apply to annual publications such as annual reports of departments and agencies, each of which covers the activities of the organization for a specific period of time.
11. Material which has an expiring-effect date, such as Civil Service examination announcements. On such material only the latest issues need be kept.
12. Any publication which is superseded by another which is stated to contain similar information.
13. Calendar of the House of Representatives upon receipt of a new issue. However, the Monday issues contain an index while the other issues do not. The final issue of each session of Congress should be kept. All issues of the Senate Calendar must be retained since this publication is not cumulative.
14. Commerce Business Daily within ninety days after receipt.

SECTION 12.

SUBSTITUTION OF MICROCOPIES FOR DEPOSITORY PUBLICATIONS

Permission is granted to **all** designated depositories to substitute microcopies for any holdings of U.S. Government publications, provided the microcopies are properly referenced, can be readily located, and are easily accessible to users. Proper reading equipment must also be available for whichever type of microcopy is substituted for the original.

If the library is served by a designated Regional Depository, your regional library should be notified of this action in order to assist you in the disposal of any unwanted paper copies.

EXHIBIT A

SAMPLE ITEM CARD

```
Item No. 314-A-5

              DEFENSE LOGISTICS AGENCY,
              Defense Department                    SAMPLE


  Defense Administrative Support Center        D 7.6/14:
    Handbooks, DASCH (series)

  Depository Library Name: _____


  _____

    Zip Code:_____

  Survey 77- 274 Depository Library No._____
```

EXHIBIT B(1)

DAILY DEPOSITORY
SHIPPING LIST 10,121

4th Shipment of September 7, 1977

Assistant Public Printer
Superintendent of Documents
Library Division (SLL)
Washington, D.C.   20402

Page 1 of 1 Page

Claims for nonreceipt of publications on this list under item numbers previously selected by a library must be postmarked within fifteen days of receipt of this shipment. (**Instructions to Depository Libraries, Revised November 1977, Page 12.**)

ITEM NUMBER	TITLE	CLASSIFICATION
13–B	Cooperative Marketing Alternatives for Sheep and Lamb Producers, Marketing Research Report No. 1081, August 1977	A 1.82:1081
42–C	The Chicken Broiler Industry: Structures, Practices, and Costs, Agricultural Economic Report No. 381, August 1977	A 1.107:371
147–B	Current Business Reports, Weekly Retail Sales, CB–77–161, August 13, 1977, * on sub	C 3.138/5:77–161
247–E	A Biweekly Cryogenics Current Awareness Service, List No. 631, Aug. 8–19, 1977	C 13.51:631
314–A	Index of Federal Catalog System Publications, DLAH 5025.1, Part 3, July 1977	D 7.6/7:5025.1/pt.3/1977–2
314–A–1	H6–A, B&C, Federal Item Name Directory for Supply Cataloging, July 1977 (Microfiche)	D 7.6/2–2:6/sec.A,B,C/977–3
324	FM 9–45L/CM Field Manual Commander's Manual, MOS 45L Artillery Repairmen, April 5, 1977	D 101.20:9–45L/CM
431–A–27	AC 00–45 A, Aviation Weather Services (A Supplement to Aviation Weather AC 00–6A), Revised 1977, *	TD 4.8/5:00–45A
434–A–9	Strategic Petroleum Reserve, Draft Environmental Impact Statement for Sulphur Mines Salt Dome, DSE 77–6, September 1977	FE 1.21:77–6
437–A–16	National Electric Rate Book, Louisiana, July 1977, *.45¢	FP 1.18:L93/977
437–A–41	National Electric Rate Book, Texas, July 1977, *.45¢	FP 1.18:T31/977
466–A	Educational Resources Information Center, ERIC Resources in Education, Vol. 12, No. 8, August 1977, *$3.60	HE 19.210:12/8
612	The U.S. Fish and Who? S/N 024–010–00435–5,*	I 49.2:F52/10
648	Photogrammetric Recording of Cultural Resources, 1977 S/N 024–005–00684–2,*	I 29.2:P56/3·
768–A–1	Comparative Growth in Manufacturing Productivity and Labor Costs in Selected Industrialized Countries, Bulletin 1958, S/N 029–001–02044–9, *	L 2.3:1958

For sale by the Superintendent of Documents.

Continued on next page

ITEM NUMBER	TITLE	CLASSIFICATION
785–C	Library of Congress Information Bulletin, Vol. 36, No. 34, August 26, 1977	LC 1.18:36/34
856–E	Oil and Gas in Coastal Lands and Waters, April 1977, S/N 040–000–00386–0,*	PrEx 14.2:OI5/3
982–G–14	DOT–FH–11–8592, Guidelines for Designing Travel Surveys for Statewide Transportation Planning, May 1977, Final Report	TD 2.26:11–8593
1062–C–6	For Kids' Sake Think Toy Safety, Adult Discussion Guide (Includes 7 Posters), *$2.40	Y 3.C76/3:8T66

*For sale by the Superintendent of Documents.

EXHIBIT B(2)

DAILY DEPOSITORY
SHIPPING LIST 10,092

Assistant Public Printer
Superintendent of Documents
Library Division (SLL)
Washington, D.C. 20402

4th Shipment of August 26, 1977

Page 1 of 1 Page

Claims for nonreceipt of publications on this list under item numbers previously selected by a library must be postmarked within fifteen days of receipt of this shipment. (**Instructions to Depository Libraries, Revised November 1977, Page 12.**)

ITEM NUMBER	TITLE	CLASSIFICATION

BEING MAILED IN NINE SEPARATE PACKAGES BUT AS PART OF THIS SHIPMENT.

FIRST PACKAGE
152–A–4 — 1974 Census of Agriculture, Vol. 1, Part 14, Indiana, July 1977, S/N 003–024–01327–4* — C 3.31/4:974/v.1/pt.14

SECOND PACKAGE
152–A–9 — 1974 Census of Agriculture, Vol. 1, Part 15, Iowa, July 1977, S/N 003–024–01328–2* — C 3.31/4:974/v.1/pt.15

THIRD PACKAGE
152–A–12 — 1974 Census of Agriculture, Vol. 1, Part 27, Nebraska, July 1977, S/N 003–024–01340–1* — C 3.31/4:974/v.1/pt.27

FOURTH PACKAGE
445 — Asian American Reference Data Directory, 1977 — HE 1.2:As 4

FIFTH PACKAGE
795 — Catalog of Copyright Entries: Third Series, Vol. 29, Part 5, No. 2, Section 1, Music, Index, July-December 1975* on sub — LC 3.6/5:v.29/pt.5/no.2/sec.1

SIXTH PACKAGE
795 — Catalog of Copyright Entries: Third Series, Vol. 29, Part 5, No. 2, Section 2, Music, Current and Renewal Registrations, July-December 1975* on sub — LC 3.6/5:v.29/pt.5/no.2/sec.2

SEVENTH PACKAGE
927 — Customs Bulletin, Vol. 10, January-December S/N 048–000–00293–5* — T 1.11/4:10

EIGHTH PACKAGE
1059–A–1 — Minorities and Women in State and Local Government, Vol. 5, State Statistical Summary, Michigan-New Mexico, 1975, 1977, S/N 052–015–00045–6,* — Y 3.Eq2:2 St. 2/975v.5

NINTH PACKAGE
1059–A–1 — Minorities and Women in State and Local Government, Vol. 6, State Statistical Summary, New York-South Carolina, 1975, 1977, S/N 052–015–00046–4* — Y 3.Eq2:2 St. 2/975/v.6

*For Sale by the Superintendent of Documents.

DAILY DEPOSITORY
SHIPPING LIST 10,123

Assistant Public Printer
Superintendent of Documents
Library Division (SLL)
Washington, D.C. 20402

2d Shipment of September 8, 1977

Page 1 of 1 Page

Claims for nonreceipt of publications on this list under item numbers previously selected by a library must be postmarked within fifteen days of receipt of this shipment. (**Instructions to Depository Libraries, Revised November 1977, Page 12.**)

ITEM NUMBER	TITLE

1006   *95/1: House Bill Numbers:* 2753; 2889; 3350 (H. rp. 588, pt. 1); 3813 (H. rp. 581); 5027 (S. rp. 390) (an act) (star print); 5258; 6831 (1 amdt. no. 813); 6964; 7132 (H. rp. 567); 7185; 7424; 7474; 7738 (3 amdts. nos. 821 to 823); 7764; 7797 (an act); 7797 (10 amdts. nos. 772, 775, 780, 783, 786, 794, 799, 802, 817, 818); 8175 (H. rp. 585); 8465; 8471; 8493; 8512; 8529; 8638 (H. rp. 587); 8673; 8696, 8697; 8698 (H. rp. 580); 8701 (H. rp. 586); 8706; 8714 to 8723; 8726; 8732, 8733; 8737; 8739, 8740; 8744 to 8746; 8748; 8754 to 8757; 8763; 8765, 8766; 8768; 8770, 8771; 8773; 8775, 8776; 8783; 8785; 8790 to 8796; 8799; 8805, 8806; 8813; 8817 to 8819; 8823; 8826, 8827; 8830; 8832 to 8835; 8839, 8840; 8842; 8845; 8847, 8848; 8854; 8856, 8857; 8863; 8865, 8866; 8869; 8871; 8873; 8876, 8877; 8879 to 8881; 8885; 8887, 8888; 8891, 8892; 8897; 8899; 8901; 8905, 8906. 8908; 8910; 8913 to 8915; 8917 to 8919; 8921 to 8924.

95/1: House Resolution Numbers: 608 (H. rp. 555); 724 (H. rp. 578); 731 (H. rp. 558); 736; 739; 742; 744 to 746.

95/1: Senate Bill Numbers: 262 (S. rp. 396); 270 (1 amdt. no. 762); 457 (1 amdt. no. 815); 896 (an act); 897; 897 (1 amdt. no. 745); 926 (58 amdts nos. 605, 609, 619, 620, 622, 623, 625, 629, 631, 648, 650, 654, 656 to 661, 664, 672 to 674, 677 to 682, 684, 686 to 688, 690, 693, 699, 701 to 703, 707 to 709, 718, 719, 721 to 723, 725, 727, 728, 731 to 733, 738 to 743); 977 (2 amdts. nos. 638, 824); 1614 (an act); 1617 (an act); 1682 (1 amdt. no. 811); 1731 (S. rp. 400); 1866 (S. rp. 389); 1904, 1905; 1907, 1908; 1914, 1972; 1978; 1981; 1984; 1997; 2000; 2004; 2006; 2008; 2012; 2015; 2030; 2037; 2043; 2053.

95/1: Senate Resolution Numbers: 228 (S. rp. 394); 229 (S. rp. 397); 232; 233; 235 (S. rp. 398); 238; 239 (S. rp. 387); 242; 243 (S. rp. 395); 244; 246; 250 to 254; 256.

95/1: Senate Joint Resolution Number: 78.

95/1: Senate Concurrent Resolution Number: 43 (S. rp. 399).

EXHIBIT C

UNITED STATES GOVERNMENT PRINTING OFFICE

CLAIM FOR DEPOSITORY PUBLICATIONS SELECTED BUT NOT RECEIVED

All claims for nonreceipt of depository publications must be postmarked within 15 days from the date of receipt of the Daily Depository Shipping List on which they appear. Only one item may be requested on each claim form. When filing a claim for an entire shipment, circle the items on the Daily Depository Shipping List to which you are entitled, and attach it to your completed claim form.

A false statement on this application is punishable by law (U.S. Code, Title 18, Section 287).

Mail claims to: Assistant Public Printer
(Superintendent of Documents)
Library Division (SLL)
Washington, DC 20401

I certify that this depository library did not receive the following item listed on Daily Depository Shipping List No. _____, dated _____. This item number was previously selected by the depository. The Daily Depository Shipping List on which this publication was listed was received on _____ .

Item Number...

Title ....

....

Classification ....

Signature of librarian authorized to make claim ....

Depository Library No. .... Date ....

☐ *Check here if Regional Library.*

SAMPLE COPY

All checked items should be completed when making claim for publications selected but not received.

PLEASE **PRINT OR TYPE** ADDRESS ON LABEL BELOW INCLUDING **YOUR ZIP CODE**

GPO Form 3451

U.S. GOVERNMENT PRINTING OFFICE
ASSISTANT PUBLIC PRINTER
(SUPERINTENDENT OF DOCUMENTS)
WASHINGTON, D.C. 20401

OFFICIAL BUSINESS

Penalty For Private Use
$300

✓ **Depository Library No.** ....

✓ Name ....

✓ Street address ....

✓ City and State... ZIP Code ....

POSTAGE AND FEES PAID
U.S. GOVERNMENT PRINTING OFFICE
377
SPECIAL FOURTH-CLASS RATE
BOOK

INFORMATION FOR LIBRARIANS

This single item claim form is designed to allow faster, more efficient processing of Depository Library claims. Enter all requested information and mail the form to the address indicated. After your claim has been processed, the form will be returned for your records.

The following symbols will be used to explain how your claim was handled.

RED CHECK . . . . . Requested publications are enclosed.

A . . . . Your list of selections has been amended as requested. Publications printed prior to selection of an item cannot be furnished.

B . . . . Claims for depository publications selected but not received **must be postmarked within 15 days** of the date of receipt of the Daily Depository Shipping List on which the publications appear. Claims must be submitted on the special claim form or they cannot be honored. (INSTRUCTIONS TO DEPOSITORY LIBRARIES, Revised November 1977, page 12.)

D . . . . A new copy has been mailed to replace your defective copy. Do not return the defective publication unless a return mailing label is enclosed.

E . . . . All sources of the requested publication are exhausted.

F . . . . Additional blank claim forms are enclosed. Please retain them for future use.

NS . . . . Your claim cannot be honored. The item number in the Classified List, under which the publication was printed, was not selected by your library prior to the time the publication was ordered printed. If you wish publications under this item number to be mailed in the future, please furnish this Office one item card (or typewritten facsimile) marked with your correct Library Number, and your selections will be amended.

S . . . . Prices are given for publications available from our sales stock. Publications not available from us may be available from the issuing Government agency.

X abd * . . . . For Office Use Only.

Assistant Public Printer
(Superintendent of Documents)

EXHIBIT D

UNITED STATES GOVERNMENT PRINTING OFFICE

AMENDMENT OF SELECTIONS

Depository Library No. _____   Date _____

The item number(s) listed below have been reviewed and we wish to add to our selections or discontinue the material listed under the following Item number(s) (Please list all amendments of selections in numerical sequence):

ADDITIONS	DELETIONS

Signature of Librarian authorized to amend selections on behalf of depository:

_____

Mail amendments of selections to: **Assistant Public Printer**
                                    (Superintendent of Documents)
                                    Library Division (SLLA)
                                    Washington, D.C.   20401

GPO Form 3454
(1–76)

UNITED STATES GOVERNMENT PRINTING OFFICE

REQUEST FOR CONFIRMATION OF CLASSIFICATION NUMBERS

Depository Library No. _____   Date _____

It is requested that the classification number _____ listed on

Daily Depository Shipping List No. _____, dated _____, be confirmed.

Title: _____
_____

Details of request: _____
_____
_____
_____

☐　　Class correct as listed on Shipping List.

REMARKS: _____
_____
_____
_____

Mail requests to: **Assistant Public Printer**
(Superintendent of Documents)
Library Division (SLLC)
Washington, D.C.　20401

GPC Form 3453
(1–76)

APPENDIX A

DESIGNATED REGIONAL DEPOSITORY LIBRARIES WITH DATE OF DESIGNATION AS OF NOVEMBER 1977

ALABAMA (DR 8B)—Auburn University at Montgomery Library (Montgomery) (June 6, 1976)

(DR 12)—University of Alabama Library (University) (May 10, 1965)

ARIZONA (DR 22)—Department of Library & Archives (Phoenix) (Jan. 22, 1964)

(DR 23)—University of Arizona Library (Tucson) (Jan. 17, 1964)

CALIFORNIA (DR 40)—California State Library (Sacramento) (Oct. 3, 1962)

COLORADO (DR 69)—University of Colorado Libraries (Boulder) (Apr. 1, 1963)

(DR 71)—Denver Public Library (Denver) (Apr. 1, 1963)

CONNECTICUT (DR 75)—Connecticut State Library (Hartford) (Sept. 26, 1962)

FLORIDA (DR 103)—University of Florida Libraries (Gainesville) (Jan. 24, 1963)

GEORGIA (DR 114)—University of Georgia Libraries (Athens) (Jan. 17, 1977)

HAWAII (DR 129)—University of Hawaii Library (Honolulu) (Jan. 5, 1977)

IDAHO (DR 135)—University of Idaho Library (Moscow) (Aug. 6, 1963)

ILLINOIS (DR 140)—Illinois State Library (Springfield) (Mar. 8, 1963)

INDIANA (DR 170)—Indiana State Library (Indianapolis) (July 30, 1963)

IOWA (DR 189A)—University of Iowa Library (Iowa City) (July 25, 1963)

KANSAS (DR 199)—University of Kansas Library (Lawrence) (Aug. 16, 1976)

KENTUCKY (DR 208)—University of Kentucky, Margaret I. King Library (Lexington) (Feb. 14, 1967)

LOUISIANA (DR 222)—Louisiana State University Library (Baton Rouge) (Feb. 26, 1964)

(DR 230)—Louisiana Polytechnic Institute, Prescott Memorial Library (Ruston) (Feb. 25, 1964)

MAINE, NEW HAMPSHIRE, AND VERMONT (DR 235)—University of Maine Library (Orono) (Dec. 3, 1963)

MARYLAND (DR 242)—University of Maryland, McKeldin Library (College Park) (June 29, 1965)

MASSACHUSETTS (DR 268A)—Boston Public Library (Boston) (June 16, 1971)

MICHIGAN (DR 273)—Michigan State Library (Lansing) (Jan. 31, 1964)

(DR 275)—Detroit Public Library (Detroit) (Apr. 22, 1964)

MINNESOTA (DR 295)—University of Minnesota, Walter Library (Minneapolis) (May 2, 1963)

MISSISSIPPI (DR 312)—University of Mississippi Library (University) (Dec. 15, 1976)

MONTANA (DR 341)—University of Montana Library (Missoula) (Jan. 6, 1965)

NEBRASKA (DR 346A)—Nebraska Publications Clearinghouse (Lincoln) (July 8, 1974)

(DR 345)—University of Nebraska (Lincoln) (October 26, 1977)

NEVADA (DR 353)—University of Nevada Library (Reno) (Mar. 5, 1963)

NEW JERSEY (DR 376)—Newark Public Library (Newark) (Oct. 31, 1963)

NEW MEXICO (DR 383)—University of New Mexico, Zimmerman Library (Albuquerque) (Dec. 28, 1967) (DR 386)—New Mexico State Library (Sante Fe) (Oct. 9, 1962)

NEW YORK (DR 387)—New York State Library (Albany) (Nov. 14, 1963)

NORTH CAROLINA (DR 447)—University of North Carolina Library (Chapel Hill) (Aug. 20, 1963)

NORTH DAKOTA (DR 455)—North Dakota State University Library (Fargo) (Mar. 3, 1969)

(DR 456)—University of North Dakota, Chester Fritz Library (Grand Forks) (Mar. 3, 1969)

OHIO (DR 460)—Ohio State Library (Columbus) (Sept. 25, 1962)

OKLAHOMA (DR 487)—Oklahoma State Library (Oklahoma City) (Dec. 18, 1962)

OREGON (DR 506A)—Portland State University Library (Portland) (Mar. 7, 1972)

PENNSYLVANIA (DR 508)—Pennsylvania State Library (Harrisburg) (Aug. 13, 1968)

TEXAS (DR 591)—Texas State Library (Austin) (Feb. 21, 1963)

(DR 614)—Texas Technological University Library (Lubbock) (Feb. 21, 1963)

UTAH (DR 618)—Utah State University Library (Logan) (May 9, 1963)

VIRGINIA (DR 640)—University of Virginia, Alderman Library (Charlottesville) (Aug. 1, 1969)

WASHINGTON (DR 642)—Washington State Library (Olympia) (May 10, 1965)

WEST VIRGINIA (DR 653)—West Virginia University Library (Morgantown) (Jan. 28, 1964)

WISCONSIN (DR 668)—State Historical Society Library (Madison) (Oct. 9, 1962)

(DR 670)—Milwaukee Public Library (Milwaukee) (Apr. 9, 1963)

WYOMING (DR 677)—Wyoming State Library (Cheyenne) (Aug. 7, 1974)

PUBLICATIONS MAILED AUTOMATICALLY AND NOT LISTED ON THE SHIPPING LIST

Average Monthly Weather Outlook
Business Service Checklist
Calendar of Business, Senate of United States
Calendars of United States House of Representatives and History of Legislation
Commerce America
Commerce Business Daily
Daily Congressional Record
Daily Weather Maps Weekly Series
Daily Statement of the Treasury
Federal Register
HUD Newsletter
Internal Revenue Bulletins
Official Gazette (Patents)
SEC Docket
Weekly Compilation of Presidential Documents

GUIDELINES FOR THE DEPOSITORY LIBRARY SYSTEM

1. OBJECTIVES OF THE DEPOSITORY LIBRARY SYSTEM.

1-1 The purpose of depository libraries is to make U.S. Government publications easily accessible to the general public and to insure their continued availability in the future.

1-2 The purpose shall be achieved by a system of cooperation wherein depository libraries will receive free Federal public documents in return for making them accessible to the general public in their areas.

1-3 The guidelines are to be considered a recommended level of conduct by all depositories unless otherwise specified by statute or regulations thereunder.

2. SUPERINTENDENT OF DOCUMENTS, U.S. GOVERNMENT PRINTING OFFICE.

2-1 Obtain new Federal publications and forward free of expense to depository libraries without delay in accordance with Chapter 19, Title 44 U.S.C.

2-2 Provide all issues of series in the <u>List of Classes of United States Government Publications Available for Selection by Depository Libraries</u>, including those issues not printed at the Government Printing Office.

2-3 Actively gather and distribute in paper or microformat all Federal publications of public interest or educational value not printed at the Government Printing Office which are within the scope of 44 U.S.C. 1902.

2-4 Provide samples and/or annotations for new titles offered to depositories, and return cards for selection purposes.

2-5 Subdivide item numbers as necessary to insure that libraries need receive only wanted documents.

2-6 Supply shipping lists containing item numbers, titles of documents, classification numbers, information on classification changes, corrections to previous lists, and price information (if available) for sales publications.

2-7 Supply forms for claiming items selected but missing from the shipment, damaged or incomplete.

Washington, D.C.: Govt. Print. Off., 1977.

2-8   Offer choice of format: paper, microform or other; however, the
Government Printing Office, in consultation with depository libraries,
should have the option of providing only one format when the nature
of the material warrants it.

2-9   Provide a timely and comprehensive system of catalogs, bibliographies
and indexes to Federal publications.

2-10 Provide a standard classification system for Federal documents and
related aids such as lists of subject headings.

2-11 Provide assistance to libraries on problems of using the Sudocs system
of classification.

2-12 Cooperate with the National Archives that the Archives may acquire
and preserve a comprehensive collection of Federal publications.

2-13 Issue instructions for the selection, claiming, retention, and
withdrawal of depository documents and other activities related to
depository libraries.

2-14 Allocate funds for the evaluation of depository libraries through
questionnaires, surveys, and inspections at intervals considered
necessary by the Superintendent of Documents, to insure compliance
with the depository law.

2-15 After advance notice to the library concerned, investigate conditions
in depository libraries by personal visits.

2-16 Provide written notice to a library about unsatisfactory conditions,
and if not corrected within six months, consider deletion of the
library from the list of depositories.

2-17 Announce new policies and changes on a regular basis to all
depositories.

2-18 Cooperate with publication projects which contribute to use of
Federal documents.

2-19 Consult at regular intervals with the Depository Library Council to
the Public Printer on matters related to depository libraries,
including the development of standards and bibliographic aids, changes
in the Sudocs classification system and the selection of materials
for micropublication.

2-20 Collect, compile, analyze and publish pertinent statistics on a
regular basis.

2-21 Provide sufficient copies to fill claims for publications missing
from depository shipments.

3.   DESIGNATION OF NEW DEPOSITORY LIBRARIES.

3-1   There may be up to two depositories in each Congressional district
to be designated by Representatives, not more than two others within
the state designated by Senators, and other depository libraries
specifically provided for in Chapter 19, Title 44 U.S.C.

3-2   The library shall be open to the general public for the free use of depository publications, as provided in Chapter 19, Title 44 U.S.C.

3-3   The library shall have the interest, resources and ability to provide custody of the documents and public service.

3-4   The library should possess at least 15,000 titles other than government publications.

3-5   The library should be prepared to keep its documents collections open the same hours as other major parts of the library, when the library is open for full range of services.

3-6   When a new vacancy occurs through redistricting or by the resignation or deletion of an existing depository, this fact should be made known by the Superintendent of Documents to the state library authority, the regional depository, if any, and the state professional associations.

3-7   Eligible libraries shall apply to the state library authority for evaluation and recommendation, with notice of the application to the regional depository, if any. The library should be prepared to offer statistics on the size and character of its collection, population served, budget, and if an academic library, the size of the student body, and need for research materials.

3-8   The evaluation should relate to community interests and indicate staff, space and budget to be allocated to the collection and the number, scope and character of the items to be selected. The state library authority after consulting with other libraries, the regional depository, if any, and representatives from the professional associations, will make a recommendation to the Senator or Representative based on location in relation to other depositories, the need for an additional depository and the ability of the library to provide custody and service.

3-9   Libraries of independent agencies and additional libraries in executive departments may be designated depositories upon certification of need according to the provisions of 44 U.S.C. 1907.

4.   DEPOSITORY COLLECTIONS.

4-1   Each depository library should maintain a basic collection available for immediate use consisting of all titles in Appendix A (attached).

4-2   Each library should acquire and maintain the basic catalogs, guides and indexes, retrospective and current, considered essential to the reference use of the collection. This should include selected non-governmental reference tools.

-3   Each depository should select frequently used and potentially useful materials appropriate to the objectives of the library.

-4   Each depository should select materials responsive to the needs of the users in the Congressional district it serves.

-5   Selection of at least 25% of the available Item Numbers on the Classified List is suggested as the minimum number necessary to undertake the role of depository library. A prospective depository intending to select fewer than 25% should provide additional justification for its designation as a depository.

4-6   Depository libraries should coordinate selections with other depositories in the district to insure adequate coverage within the area.

5.   ORGANIZATION OF THE DEPOSITORY COLLECTION.

5-1   The library should check all daily shipping lists to insure that items selected are received, and if not, promptly claimed.

5-2   Each publication in the shipment should be marked to distinguish it from publications received from other sources. Each publication should be marked with the date of the shipping list or the date of receipt.

5-3   The library should record its depository accessions.

5-4   The minimum record for a depository library should show the library's holdings and the call numbers or locations where they may be found.

5-5   A method of classification should be adopted for precise identification and location of materials requested by library users.

5-6   The method of classification adopted shall be optional with the library; however, it is suggested that libraries which integrate their documents should maintain a shelf list by Sudocs number showing disposition of the publication.

5-7   Whenever possible documents should be available for public use within 10 days after receipt; they should be retrievable even if cataloging information is not yet available.

5-8   The library should maintain statistics of the collection needed for the Biennial Survey.

5-9   The library will retain one set of item cards, both items selected and not selected.

6.   MAINTENANCE OF THE DEPOSITORY COLLECTION.

6-1   Collections should be maintained in as good physical condition as other library materials, including binding when desirable.

6-2   Lost materials should be replaced if possible.

6-3   Unneeded publications should be made available to other libraries in accordance with Chapter 19, Title 44 U.S.C.

6-4   Libraries served by a regional depository may withdraw publications retained for a period of at least five years after securing permission from the regional library for disposal in accordance with the provision of 44 U.S.C. 1912.

6-5   Depository libraries within executive departments and independent agencies may dispose of unwanted Government publications after first offering them to the Library of Congress and the Archivist of the United States, in accordance with the provisions of 44 U.S.C. 1907.

6-6   The provisions of 44 U.S.C. 1911, disposal of unwanted publications, do not apply to libraries of the highest appellate courts of the states   (see 44 U.S.C. 1915).

6-7   Superseded material should be withdrawn according to <u>Instructions to Depository Libraries</u> (latest edition).

6-8   Depository publications should be protected from unlawful removal as are other parts of the library's collections.

7.   STAFFING.

7-1   One person should be designated by the library to coordinate activities and to act as liaison with the Superintendent of Documents in all matters relating to depository libraries.

7-2   This person should be responsible for
  a)   selection, receipt and claiming of depository distributions
  b)   replies to correspondence and surveys from the Superintendent of Documents
  c)   interpreting the depository program to the administrative level of the library
  d)   performance and/or supervision of stated aspects of service, or in an integrated collection, a knowledge of persons to whom responsibilities are delegated, such as:

    (1)   organization for use
    (2)   maintainance of records of the collection
    (3)   physical maintenance of the collection
    (4)   establishment of withdrawal procedures
    (5)   maintainance of reader services
    (6)   promotion of use of collection
    (7)   preparation of budgets
    (8)   submission of reports.

7-3   The liaison person should be a professionally qualified librarian.

7-4   The liaison person should be directly responsibile to the administrative level of the library.

7-5   Additional professional staff should be added depending on the size and scope of the library and the methods of organization of the collection.

7-6   Professional staff should be assisted by support staff. A suggested proportion is 1 professional to 3 support staff.

7-7   Librarians and such support staff as indicated by their responsibilities should keep up to date on new developments through participation in professional societies, attendance at document workshops, and professional reading.

8.   SPACE STANDARDS.

8-1   Space for depository operations should be of the same quality as other
      areas of the library. It should be attractive, comfortable and have
      acceptable levels of lighting, temperature, ventilation and noise
      control. It should be functional, flexible and expandable.

8-2   The space should contain well planned areas for services provided,
      reference, circulation, loan and other public service activities as
      well as adequate space for the processing of new materials and
      housing of the collection.

8-3   It should include private work areas for staff members and the
      administrator.

8-4   All parts of the collection should be readily accessible, preferably
      open shelf, but in all circumstances, should be located so that
      materials may be retrieved in a reasonable period of time.

8-5   If documents are maintained in a separate division of the library,
      the space provided should be conveniently located to encourage use
      of the materials.

8-6   The library should abide by the recommended standards for access by
      handicapped users.

8-7   Tables and/or carrels should be provided for in-library use of
      documents.

8-8   Microform readers and reader/printers for the principal types of
      microforms should be provided.

8-9   Microform storage should be located convenient to the documents
      area.

9.   SERVICE TO THE GENERAL PUBLIC.

9-1   Libraries shall make depository publications available for the free
      use of the general public. Highest appellate court libraries of the
      states are exempt from the provisions of 44 U.S.C. 1911 (see 44 U.S.C.
      1915).

9-2   In each depository library, there should be recognized focal points
      for inquiries about government publications. At this point it should
      be possible to find:

      a) resources in the collection, including specific titles
      b) location of wanted publications in the library
      c) answers to reference questions or a referral to a source or
          place where answers can be found
      d) guidance on the use of the collection, including the principal
          available reference sources, catalogs, abstracts, indexes and
          other aids
      e) availability of additional resources in the region
      f) assistance in borrowing documents from a regional or other
          libraries
      g) user privileges for other libraries, educational agencies,

culturally deprived, disadvantaged, handicapped, retired users and the community at large.

9-3   The library should have the option of establishing its own circulation policies for use of depository materials outside the library.

9-4   The library should provide facilities for using materials within the library, including copying facilities and equipment for reading microforms.

9-5   The library should publicize the depository collection through displays and announcements of significant new titles.

9-6   The library should provide to all users reference assistance with regard to depository publications.

10.   COOPERATION WITH THE GOVERNMENT PRINTING OFFICE.

10-1   Depository library staff should familiarize themselves with the depository instructions and abide by their conditions.

10-2   Claims should be submitted within stated time limits.

10-3   Depository library staff should use correct address when corresponding with the Government Printing Office.

10-4   Questionnaires and surveys submitted by the Superintendent of Documents to depository libraries should be completed and returned promptly.

11.   INTERLIBRARY COOPERATION.

11-1   All depository libraries should be considered as part of a network of libraries consisting of selective, regional, and national.

11-2   Selective depositories should cooperate in building up the collections of the regional depositories.

11-3   Selective depositories should cooperate with the regional depositories in the redistribution of documents not needed in their own organizations.

11-4   All depository libraries should cooperate in reporting to the Superintendent of Documents new Federal documents not listed in the Monthly Catalog.

11-5   All depository libraries should cooperate in the development of tools for the identification and location of documents in other libraries.

11-6   Depository libraries borrowing documents from other libraries should verify bibliographic information as completely as possible.

11-7   All depository libraries should provide material on interlibrary loan at least for the regional depository.

11-8   All depository libraries should have a policy of providing photocopies of depository materials to other libraries no less liberal than for other library materials.

12.   REGIONAL DEPOSITORIES.

12-1   Eligibility to become a regional depository library:

a)   There may not be more than two regional depositories in one
state.   A regional library may serve two or more states, or
regional status may be shared by more than one library.
b)   A regional library must be an existing depository.
c)   A regional depository should be conveniently located to serve
the largest number of libraries possible.
d)   The library selected for regional status should have an adequate
retrospective collection, space, personnel and a continuing basis
of financial support sufficient to fulfill the obligations of a
regional depository.
e)   The selection of a regional depository should be agreed upon by
the state library authority and a majority of depository libraries
within the region.
f)   Designation of the regional must be made by one of the U. S.
Senators of the state.

12-2   Responsibilities of regional libraries include:

a)   receiving and maintaining permanently all depository publications
in either printed or microform as provided in the depository
instructions
b)   attempting to complete their retrospective collections of major
serials, annuals and other research materials by means of gift,
exchange or purchase, including microforms
c)   screening all lists of documents withdrawn from selective
depositories to insure their future availability in the region
d)   acquiring additional copies where necessary
e)   assisting selective depositories with reference questions,
interlibrary loans and photocopies
f)   granting permission to selective depositories to dispose of
unwanted documents according to the Instructions to Depository
Libraries (latest edition)
g)   providing guidelines to selective depositories for preparing
disposal lists of unwanted documents
h)   contributing to the effectiveness of the depository network
through workshops, training sessions and consultive services
within their region.

12-3   The regional depository may authorize the transfer of depository
material within the state between depositories to insure maximum
use.   Transfer of material is not to be regarded as disposal.

12-4   The initial receiving depository library remains responsible and
accountable for the documents during the period required by law.

Appendix A

Budget of the United States Government
Catalog of Federal Domestic Assistance
Census Bureau Catalog
Census of Housing (for State of Depository only)

Census of Population (for State of Depository only)
Code of Federal Regulations
Congressional Directory
Congressional District Data Book
Congressional Record
County-City Data Book
Federal Register
Historical Statistics of the United States
Monthly Catalog
Numerical Lists and Schedule of Volumes
Publications Reference File
Slip Laws (Public)
Statistical Abstract
Statutes at Large
Subject Bibliographies (S.B. Series)
Supreme Court Reports
United States Code
United States Government Manual
Weekly Compilation of Presidential Documents

BYLAWS

of the

DEPOSITORY LIBRARY COUNCIL TO THE PUBLIC PRINTER

as amended October 18, 1977

ARTICLE I –   Name. The name of this organization shall be the Depository
                 Library Council to the Public Printer.

ARTICLE II –   Purpose. The purpose of the Depository Library Council to
                 the Public Printer shall be to advise the Public Printer and
                 the Assistant Public Printer (Superintendent of Documents) on
                 matters dealing with the Depository Library Program,
                 specifically:

                 a. Needs of depository libraries relative to Government
                     publications.

                 b. Cataloging and indexing of documents.

                 c. Shipping and handling publications.

                 d. Availability of publications to patrons and the public.

                 e. General administration of the program.

ARTICLE III –   <u>Membership</u>.

   Section 1 – General Membership. The Membership of the Depository Library Council shall consist of not more than 15 members of the Library community appointed by the Public Printer. The Public Printer and the Assistant Public Printer (Superintendent of Documents) are ex-officio members.

   Section 2 – Membership Makeup. At least five of the members of the Council shall be persons who work full time with Government documents in a depository library.

   Section 3 – Term of Office. The members shall serve three years; five retiring each year and five entering each year, and members may be reappointed for a second term. Terms shall begin October 1.

   Section 4 – Vacancies. Vacancies on the Council will be filled by the Public Printer after consideration of recommendations from library associations, Council members and other librarians.

   Section 5 – Alternates. A member of the Council may designate a non-voting alternate to serve as an observer in his absence.

ARTICLE IV –   <u>Officers of the Council</u>.

   Section 1 – Officers. The Officers of the Council shall be a Chairman, a Chairman-elect and a Secretary. The terms of office shall begin October 1.

   Section 2 – Selection of Officers. The Chairman-elect shall be nominated by the Council during its spring meeting and confirmed by the Public Printer no later than July 1. The Chairman-elect shall be selected from

the members of Council who are in the first year of
their term on the Council, shall serve as vice-chairman
for the year beginning October 1 following selection,
and shall automatically become Chairman for the
second year following selection. If, for any reason,
the Chairman-elect shall not be able to complete
the term for which confirmed, the Council shall
nominate at its next regular meeting a person to
complete that term.

The Secretary shall be appointed by the Chairman-
elect for a term to coincide with the Chairman-elect's
tenure as Chairman. The Secretary shall be eligible
for reappointment.

ARTICLE V -   Duties of the Officers.

Section 1 - Chairman. The Chairman shall preside over meetings
of the Council. He will have the duty of organizing
the Council. He shall appoint such committees as
necessary to carry out the duties of the Council.
He shall serve as direct liaison between the Council
and the Public Printer.

Section 2 - Chairman-elect. The Chairman-elect shall be
responsible for the agenda for the fall meeting.
The Chairman-elect shall perform all acts and
duties ordinarily required of the Chairman in the
absence of the Chairman. Should the Chairman and
the Chairman-elect be absent from any meeting, the
Council shall select from the members present a
person to act as Chairman for that particular meeting.

Section 3 - The Secretary. The Secretary shall arrange for

preparation of records of meetings and proceedings.
The Secretary shall further handle all official
correspondence of the Council and each notice of
meetings and keep all other records of the Council.

ARTICLE VI – Meetings.

Section 1 – Regular meetings. The Council shall meet twice a
year, in the spring and in the fall, at times and
locations designated by the Public Printer.

Section 2 – Additional meetings. The Chairman may call additional
meetings upon the written request of the Public
Printer or a written request of eight or more members
of the Council.

Section 3 – Notice of meetings. Notice of meetings shall be
mailed to the membership at least 30 days before
the date of each meeting, and notice will be published
in the Federal Register.

Section 4 – Open meetings. Meetings of the Council will be
open to the public.
Archives Records Service. This report will be
listed in the Monthly Catalog and will be available
for purchase.

ARTICLE VIII – Rules of Order. The rules contained in the latest edition of
Robert's Rules of Order shall govern the meetings of the
Council in all cases to which they can be applied and are not
inconsistent with the charter or special rules of the Public
Printer.

ARTICLE IX – Amendments. These bylaws may be amended by majority vote of the
Council at a duly constituted meeting.

ARTICLE VII -   Reports.

        Section 1 - Reports of meetings. The secretary will prepare a report of each meeting for the signature of the Chairman and the Public Printer. A synopsis of the action taken by the Council at the meeting will be included.

        Section 2 - Annual reports. The Chairman shall present to the Public Printer an annual written report of the activities of the Council. Such reports shall be published and disseminated to the Council as soon as approved by the Public Printer. A copy of such approved Annual Report shall be forwarded to all Depository Libraries and be filed with the National

APPENDIX 5

LIST OF PRESIDENTS OF THE UNITED STATES AND SESSIONS OF CONGRESS

This table is a quick reference guide to Presidents of the United States and to sessions of Congress. The Superintendent of Documents designation assigned to publications of Presidents is *Pr*. Each President has his own number. Sessions of Congress are usually cited by Congress and session, 95–2.

PRESIDENTS

1. George Washington (Apr. 30, 1789–Mar. 3, 1793; Mar. 4, 1793–Mar. 3, 1797)
2. John Adams (Mar. 4, 1797–Mar. 3, 1801)
3. Thomas Jefferson (Mar. 4, 1801–Mar. 3, 1805; Mar. 4, 1805–Mar. 3, 1809)
4. James Madison (Mar. 4, 1809–Mar. 3, 1813; Mar. 4, 1813–Mar. 3, 1817)
5. James Monroe (Mar. 4, 1817–Mar. 3, 1821; Mar. 4, 1821–Mar. 3, 1825)
6. John Quincy Adams (Mar. 4, 1825–Mar. 3, 1829)
7. Andrew Jackson (Mar. 4, 1829–Mar. 3, 1833; Mar. 4, 1833–Mar. 3, 1837)
8. Martin Van Buren (Mar. 4, 1837–Mar. 3, 1841)
9. William Henry Harrison (Mar. 4, 1841–Apr. 4, 1841)
10. John Tyler (Apr. 6, 1841–Mar. 3, 1845)
11. James Knox Polk (Mar. 4, 1845–Mar. 3, 1849)
12. Zachary Taylor (Mar. 4, 1849–July 9, 1850)
13. Millard Fillmore (July 10, 1850–Mar. 3, 1853)
14. Franklin Pierce (Mar. 4, 1853–Mar. 3, 1857)
15. James Buchanan (Mar. 4, 1857–Mar. 3, 1861)
16. Abraham Lincoln (Mar. 4, 1861–Mar. 3, 1865; Mar. 4, 1865–Apr. 15, 1865)
17. Andrew Johnson (Apr. 15, 1865–Mar. 3, 1869)
18. Ulysses Simpson Grant (Mar. 4, 1869–Mar. 3, 1873; Mar. 4, 1873–Mar. 3, 1877)
19. Rutherford Birchard Hayes (Mar. 4, 1877–Mar. 3, 1881)
20. James Abram Garfield (Mar. 4, 1881–Sept. 19, 1881)
21. Chester A. Arthur (Sept. 20, 1881–Mar. 3, 1885)
22. Grover Cleveland (Mar. 4, 1885–Mar. 3, 1889)
23. Benjamin Harrison (Mar. 4, 1889–Mar. 3, 1893)
Pr 24. not used; see Pr. 22. Grover Cleveland (Mar. 4, 1893–Mar. 3, 1897)
25. William McKinley (Mar. 4, 1897–Mar. 3, 1901; Mar. 4, 1901–Sept. 14, 1901)
26. Theodore Roosevelt (Sept. 14, 1901–Mar. 3, 1905; Mar. 4, 1905–Mar. 3, 1909)
27. William H. Taft (Mar. 4, 1909–Mar. 3, 1913)

Sources: *Biographical Directory of the American Congress, 1774–1971*. 92d Cong., 1st Sess. Senate document 92-8. Serial 12938 (Washington, D.C.: Govt. Print. Off., 1971).

Congressional Quarterly Almanac, vols. 28–33. Washington, D.C.: Congressional Quarterly, 1972–77.

28. Woodrow Wilson (Mar. 4, 1913–Mar. 3, 1917; Mar. 4, 1917–Mar. 3, 1921)
29. Warren G. Harding (Mar. 4, 1921–Aug. 2, 1923)
30. Calvin Coolidge (Aug. 3, 1923–Mar. 3, 1925; Mar. 4, 1925–Mar. 3, 1929)
31. Herbert Hoover (Mar. 4, 1929–Mar. 3, 1933)
32. Franklin D. Roosevelt (Mar. 4, 1933–Jan. 20, 1937; Jan. 20, 1937–Jan. 20, 1941; Jan. 20, 1941–Jan. 20, 1945; Jan. 20, 1945–Apr. 12, 1945)
33. Harry S. Truman (Apr. 12, 1945–Jan. 20, 1949; Jan. 20, 1949–Jan. 20, 1953)
34. Dwight D. Eisenhower (Jan. 20, 1953–Jan. 20, 1957; Jan. 20, 1957–Jan. 20, 1961)
35. John F. Kennedy (Jan. 20, 1961–Nov. 22, 1963)
36. Lyndon B. Johnson (Nov. 22, 1963–Jan. 20, 1965; Jan. 20, 1965–Jan. 20, 1969)
37. Richard M. Nixon (Jan. 20, 1969–Jan. 20, 1973; Jan. 20, 1973–Aug. 9, 1974)
38. Gerald R. Ford (Aug. 9, 1974–Jan. 20, 1977)
39. Jimmy Carter (Jan. 20, 1977–   )

SESSIONS OF CONGRESS

1   1—Mar. 4–Sept. 29, 1789
    2—Jan. 4–Aug. 12, 1790
    3—Dec. 6, 1790–Mar. 3, 1791
2   1—Oct. 24, 1791–May 8, 1792
    2—Nov. 5, 1792–Mar. 2, 1793
    Spec.—Mar. 4, 1791
3   1—Dec. 2, 1793–June 9, 1794
    2—Nov. 3, 1794–Mar. 3, 1795
    Spec.—Mar. 4, 1793
4   1—Dec. 7, 1795–June 1, 1796
    2—Dec. 5, 1796–Mar. 3, 1797
    Spec.—June 8–26, 1795
5   1—May 15–July 10, 1797
    2—Nov. 13, 1797–July 16, 1798
    3—Dec. 3, 1798–Mar. 3, 1799
    Spec.—Mar. 4, 1797; July 17–19, 1798
6   1—Dec. 2, 1799–May 14, 1800
    2—Nov. 17, 1800–Mar. 3, 1801
7   1—Dec. 7, 1801–May 3, 1802
    2—Dec. 6, 1802–Mar. 3, 1803
    Spec.—Mar. 4–5, 1801
8   1—Oct. 17, 1803–Mar. 27, 1804
    2—Nov. 5, 1804–Mar. 3, 1805
9   1—Dec. 2, 1805–Apr. 21, 1806
    2—Dec. 1, 1806–Mar. 3, 1807
    Spec.—Mar. 4, 1805

10   1—Oct. 26, 1807–Apr. 25, 1808
     2—Nov. 7, 1808–Mar. 3, 1809
11   1—May 22–June 28, 1809
     2—Nov. 27, 1809–May 1, 1810
     3—Dec. 3, 1810–Mar. 3, 1811
     Spec.—Mar. 4–7, 1809
12   1—Nov. 4, 1811–July 6, 1812
     2—Nov. 2, 1812–Mar. 3, 1813
13   1—May 24–Aug. 2, 1813
     2—Dec. 6, 1813–Apr. 18, 1814
     3—Sept. 19, 1814–Mar. 3, 1815
14   1—Dec. 4, 1815–Apr. 30, 1816
     2—Dec. 2, 1816–Mar. 3, 1817
15   1—Dec. 1, 1817–Apr. 20, 1818
     2—Nov. 16, 1818–Mar. 3, 1819
     Spec.—Mar. 4–6, 1817
16   1—Dec. 6, 1819–May 15, 1820
     2—Nov. 13, 1820–Mar. 3, 1821
17   1—Dec. 3, 1821–May 8, 1822
     2—Dec. 2, 1822–Mar. 3, 1823
18   1—Dec. 1, 1823–May 27, 1824
     2—Dec. 6, 1824–Mar. 3, 1825
19   1—Dec. 5, 1825–May 22, 1826
     2—Dec. 4, 1826–Mar. 3, 1827
     Spec.—Mar. 4–9, 1825
20   1—Dec. 3, 1827–May 26, 1828
     2—Dec. 1, 1828–Mar. 3, 1829

Pursuant to the twentieth amendment to the Constitution, regular sessions of Congress begin on January 3 of each year unless Congress, by law, designates a different day.

Spec. = Special sessions of the Senate.

21 1—Dec. 7, 1829–May 31, 1830
    2—Dec. 6, 1830–Mar. 3, 1831
    Spec.—Mar. 4–17, 1829
22 1—Dec. 5, 1831–July 16, 1832
    2—Dec. 3, 1832–Mar. 2, 1833
23 1—Dec. 2, 1833–June 30, 1834
    2—Dec. 1, 1834–Mar. 3, 1835
24 1—Dec. 7, 1835–July 4, 1836
    2—Dec. 5, 1836–Mar. 3, 1837
25 1—Sept. 4–Oct. 16, 1837
    2—Dec. 4, 1837–July 9, 1838
    3—Dec. 3, 1838–Mar. 3, 1839
    Spec.—Mar. 4–10, 1837
26 1—Dec. 2, 1839–July 21, 1840
    2—Dec. 7, 1840–Mar. 3, 1841
27 1—May 31–Sept. 13, 1841
    2—Dec. 6, 1841–Aug. 31, 1842
    3—Dec. 5, 1842–Mar. 3, 1843
    Spec.—Mar. 4–15, 1841
28 1—Dec. 4, 1843–June 17, 1844
    2—Dec. 2, 1844–Mar. 3, 1845
29 1—Dec. 1, 1845–Aug. 10, 1846
    2—Dec. 7, 1846–Mar. 3, 1847
    Spec.—Mar. 4–20, 1845
30 1—Dec. 6, 1847–Aug. 14, 1848
    2—Dec. 4, 1848–Mar. 3, 1849
31 1—Dec. 3, 1849–Sept. 30, 1850
    2—Dec. 2, 1850–Mar. 3, 1851
    Spec.—Mar. 5–23, 1849
32 1—Dec. 1, 1851–Aug. 31, 1852
    2—Dec. 6, 1852–Mar. 3, 1853
    Spec.—Mar. 4–13, 1851
33 1—Dec. 5, 1853–Aug. 7, 1854
    2—Dec. 4, 1854–Mar. 3, 1855
    Spec.—Mar. 4–Apr. 11, 1853
34 1—Dec. 3, 1855–Aug. 18, 1856
    2—Aug. 21–30, 1856
    3—Dec. 1, 1856–Mar. 3, 1857
35 1—Dec. 7, 1857–June 14, 1858
    2—Dec. 6, 1858–Mar. 3, 1859
    Spec.—Mar. 4–14, 1857; June 15–16,
    1858
36 1—Dec. 5, 1859–June 25, 1860
    2—Dec. 3, 1860–Mar. 3, 1861
    Spec.—Mar. 4–10, 1859; June 26–28,
    1860
37 1—July 4–Aug. 6, 1861
    2—Dec. 2, 1861–July 17, 1862

    3—Dec. 1, 1862–Mar. 3, 1863
    Spec.—Mar. 4–28, 1861
38 1—Dec. 7, 1863–July 4, 1864
    2—Dec. 5, 1864–Mar. 3, 1865
    Spec.—Mar. 4–14, 1863
39 1—Dec. 4, 1865–July 28, 1866
    2—Dec. 3, 1866–Mar. 3, 1867
    Spec.—Mar. 4–11, 1865
40 1—Mar. 4–30, July 3–20, Nov. 21–
    Dec. 1, 1867
    2—Dec. 2, 1867–July 27, 1868; Sept.
    21, Oct. 16, and Nov. 10, 1868
    3—Dec. 7, 1868–Mar. 3, 1869
    Spec.—Apr. 1–20, 1867
41 1—Mar. 4–Apr. 10, 1869
    2—Dec. 6, 1869–July 15, 1870
    3—Dec. 5, 1870–Mar. 3, 1871
    Spec.—Apr. 12–22, 1869
42 1—Mar. 4–Apr. 20, 1871
    2—Dec. 4, 1871–June 10, 1872
    3—Dec. 2, 1872–Mar. 3, 1873
    Spec.—May 10–27, 1871
43 1—Dec. 1, 1873–June 23, 1874
    2—Dec. 7, 1874–Mar. 3, 1875
    Spec.—Mar. 4–26, 1873
44 1—Dec. 6, 1875–Aug. 15, 1876
    2—Dec. 4, 1876–Mar. 3, 1877
    Spec.—Mar. 5–24, 1875
45 1—Oct. 15–Dec. 3, 1877
    2—Dec. 3, 1877–June 20, 1878
    3—Dec. 2, 1878–Mar. 3, 1879
    Spec.—Mar. 5–17, 1877
46 1—Mar. 18–July 1, 1879
    2—Dec. 1, 1879–June 16, 1880
    3—Dec. 6, 1880–Mar. 3, 1881
47 1—Dec. 5, 1881–Aug. 8, 1882
    2—Dec. 4, 1882–Mar. 3, 1883
    Spec.—Mar. 4–May 20, 1881; Oct.
    10–29, 1881
48 1—Dec. 3, 1883–July 7, 1884
    2—Dec. 1, 1884–Mar. 3, 1885
49 1—Dec. 7, 1885–Aug. 5, 1886
    2—Dec. 6, 1886–Mar. 3, 1887
    Spec.—Mar. 4–Apr. 2, 1885
50 1—Dec. 5, 1887–Oct. 20, 1888
    2—Dec. 3, 1888–Mar. 3, 1889

51 1—Dec. 2, 1889–Oct. 1, 1890
    2—Dec. 1, 1890–Mar. 2, 1891
    Spec.—Mar. 4–Apr. 2, 1889
52 1—Dec. 7, 1891–Aug. 5, 1892
    2—Dec. 5, 1892–Mar. 3, 1893
53 1—Aug. 7–Nov. 3, 1893
    2—Dec. 4, 1893–Aug. 28, 1894
    3—Dec. 3, 1894–Mar. 3, 1895
    Spec.—Mar. 4–Apr. 15, 1893
54 1—Dec. 2, 1895–June 11, 1896
    2—Dec. 7, 1896–Mar. 3, 1897
55 1—Mar. 15–July 24, 1897
    2—Dec. 6, 1897–July 8, 1898
    3—Dec. 5, 1898–Mar. 3, 1899
    Spec.—Mar. 4–10, 1897
56 1—Dec. 4, 1899–June 7, 1900
    2—Dec. 3, 1900–Mar. 3, 1901
57 1—Dec. 2, 1901–July 1, 1902
    2—Dec. 1, 1902–Mar. 3, 1903
    Spec.—Mar. 4–9, 1901
58 1—Nov. 9–Dec. 7, 1903
    2—Dec. 7, 1903–Apr. 28, 1904
    3—Dec. 5, 1904–Mar. 3, 1905
    Spec.—Mar. 5–19, 1903
59 1—Dec. 4, 1905–June 30, 1906
    2—Dec. 3, 1906–Mar. 3, 1907
    Spec.—Mar. 4–18, 1905
60 1—Dec. 2, 1907–May 30, 1908
    2—Dec. 7, 1908–Mar. 3, 1909
61 1—Mar. 15–Aug. 5, 1909
    2—Dec. 6, 1909–June 25, 1910
    3—Dec. 5, 1910–Mar. 3, 1911
    Spec.—Mar. 4–6, 1909
62 1—Apr. 4–Aug. 22, 1911
    2—Dec. 4, 1911–Aug. 26, 1912
    3—Dec. 2, 1912–Mar. 3, 1913
63 1—Apr. 7–Dec. 1, 1913
    2—Dec. 1, 1913–Oct. 24, 1914
    3—Dec. 7, 1914–Mar. 3, 1915
    Spec.—Mar. 4–17, 1913
64 1—Dec. 6, 1915–Sept. 8, 1916
    2—Dec. 4, 1916–Mar. 3, 1917
65 1—Apr. 2–Oct. 6, 1917
    2—Dec. 3, 1917–Nov. 21, 1918
    3—Dec. 2, 1918–Mar. 3, 1919
    Spec.—Mar. 5–16, 1917
66 1—May 19–Nov. 19, 1919
    2—Dec. 1, 1919–June 5, 1920
    3—Dec. 6, 1920–Mar. 3, 1921

67 1—Apr. 11–Nov. 23, 1921
    2—Dec. 5, 1921–Sept. 22, 1922
    3—Nov. 20–Dec. 4, 1922
    4—Dec. 4, 1922–Mar. 3, 1923
    Spec.—Mar. 4–15, 1921
68 1—Dec. 3, 1923–June 7, 1924
    2—Dec. 1, 1924–Mar. 3, 1925
69 1—Dec. 7, 1925–July 3, 1926; Nov. 10, 1926
    2—Dec. 6, 1926–Mar. 3, 1927
    Spec.—Mar. 4–18, 1925
70 1—Dec. 5, 1927–May 29, 1928
    2—Dec. 3, 1928–Mar. 3, 1929
71 1—Apr. 15–Nov. 22, 1929
    2—Dec. 2, 1929–July 3, 1930
    3—Dec. 1, 1930–Mar. 3, 1931
    Spec.—Mar. 4–5, 1929; July 7–21, 1930
72 1—Dec. 7, 1931–July 16, 1932
    2—Dec. 5, 1932–Mar. 3, 1933
73 1—Mar. 9–June 15, 1933
    2—Jan. 3–June 18, 1934
    Spec.—Mar. 4–6, 1933
74 1—Jan. 3–Aug. 26, 1935
    2—Jan. 3–June 20, 1936
75 1—Jan. 5–Aug. 21, 1937
    2—Nov. 15–Dec. 21, 1937
    3—Jan. 3–June 16, 1938
76 1—Jan. 3–Aug. 5, 1939
    2—Sept. 21–Nov. 3, 1939
    3—Jan. 3, 1940–Jan. 3, 1941
77 1—Jan. 3, 1941–Jan. 2, 1942
    2—Jan. 5–Dec. 16, 1942
78 1—Jan. 6–Dec. 21, 1943
    2—Jan. 10–Dec. 19, 1944
79 1—Jan. 3–Dec. 21, 1945
    2—Jan. 14–Aug. 2, 1946
80 1—Jan. 3–Dec. 19, 1947
    2—Jan. 6–Dec. 31, 1948
81 1—Jan. 3–Oct. 19, 1949
    2—Jan. 3, 1950–Jan. 2, 1951
82 1—Jan. 3–Oct. 20, 1951
    2—Jan. 8–July 7, 1952
83 1—Jan. 3–Aug. 3, 1953
    2—Jan. 6–Dec. 2, 1954
84 1—Jan. 5–Aug. 2, 1955
    2—Jan. 3–July 27, 1956
85 1—Jan. 3–Aug. 30, 1957
    2—Jan. 7–Aug. 24, 1958

86 1—Jan. 7–Sept. 15, 1959
  2—Jan. 6–Sept. 1, 1960
87 1—Jan. 3–Sept. 26, 1961
  2—Jan. 10–Oct. 13, 1962
88 1—Jan. 9–Dec. 30, 1963
  2—Jan. 7–Oct. 3, 1964
89 1—Jan. 4–Oct. 23, 1965
  2—Jan. 10–Oct. 22, 1966
90 1—Jan. 10–Dec. 15, 1967
  2—Jan. 15–Oct. 14, 1968
91 1—Jan. 3–Dec. 23, 1969
  2—Jan. 19, 1970–Jan. 2, 1971

92 1—Jan. 21–Dec. 17, 1971
  2—Jan. 18–Oct. 18, 1972
93 1—Jan. 3–Dec. 22, 1973
  2—Jan. 21–Dec. 20, 1974
94 1—Jan. 14–Dec. 19, 1975
  2—Jan. 19–Oct. 1, 1976
95 1—Jan. 4–Dec. 15, 1977
  2—Jan. 19–Oct. 15, 1978
96. 1—Jan. 15, 1979–

INDEX

Designed by Vladimir Reichl
Composed by Modern Typographers in Times Roman,
Printed on 50# Warren's Olde Style, a pH neutral stock, by
Chicago Press Corporation, and
Bound by Zonne Bookbinders